JONES, David A. (David Arthur). History of criminology: a philosophical perspective. Greenwood, 1986. 243p ill (Contributions in criminology and penology, 10) bibl index 85-17724. 35.00 ISBN 0-313-23647-X. HV 6021. CIP

Jones has written a valuable analysis of the criminological enterprise. More than a history of "schools of thought," the work is organized around philosophical paradigms that dominated periods of change in criminological theory, crime detection, and the treatment of offenders. This linkage of paradigm and practice offers a unique perspective for examining the roots of criminological thought in Europe and North America. Jones's approach provides an overview of important developments in both disciplines. His treatment of these pivotal points compares the work of major proponents in each discipline from 1764 to the present. The author's discussions are easy to follow and draw out related developments from other disciplines, such as art, history, and theology. Jones does a better job in tackling the early theories of crime and their philosophical antecedents than more recent developments in areas such as European critical theory, the interactionist school, and ethnomethodology. His final chapter on existentialism, however, is quite informative. A worthwhile addition to any library with even a peripheral interest in criminology. Upper-division undergraduates and above.— *J. Lynxwiler, University of Alabama in Birmingham*

History
of
Criminology

Recent Titles in Contributions in Criminology and Penology

HISTORY OF CRIMINOLOGY
A PHILOSOPHICAL PERSPECTIVE

DAVID A. JONES

CONTRIBUTIONS IN CRIMINOLOGY AND PENOLOGY, NUMBER 10

GREENWOOD PRESS

NEW YORK
WESTPORT, CONNECTICUT
LONDON

Library of Congress Cataloging-in-Publication Data

Jones, David Arthur, 1946–
  History of criminology.

  (Contributions in criminology and penology,
ISSN 0732-4464 ; no. 10)
  Bibliography: p.
  Includes index.
  1. Crime and criminals—History. I. Title.
II. Series.
HV6021.J66   1986   364′.9   85-17724
ISBN 0-313-23647-X (lib. bdg. : alk. paper)

Library of Congress Catalog Card Number: 85-17724
ISBN: 0-313-23647-X
ISSN: 0732-4464

First published in 1986

Greenwood Press, Inc.
88 Post Road West
Westport, Connecticut 06881

Printed in the United States of America

The paper used in this book complies with the
Permanent Paper Standard issued by the National
Information Standards Organization (Z39.48-1984).

10 9 8 7 6 5 4 3 2 1

OCLC

To Stanley F. Little and Laura T. Little

Contents

List of Illustrations

The illustrations are reprinted with permission from *Crime and the Man* by Earnest Albert Hooton
© 1939.

History
of
Criminology

1

Connections in the History and Philosophy of Criminology

"Compared to war, all other forms of human endeavor shrink to insignificance. God, how I love it!"[1] United States Army General George S. Patton, Jr., made this remark during World War II. One may advance a reasoned argument why, compared with crime, all forms of human endeavor other than war shrink to insignificance, also. Indeed, one could say that crime is a form of warfare, perhaps even a substitute for warfare during peacetime. Patton declared further: "Men have always loved to fight. If they didn't love to fight, they wouldn't be men."[2] Is this true? If it is true, even partly, does this mean that men are born to crime? What about women? Is crime a part of the intrinsic nature of human beings, or some of them? Of animals generally? Of all or most living things in one way or another? This we cannot say for sure because we do not know.

"Twentieth century criminology is a product of the theories of the eighteenth and nineteenth centuries. An historical evaluation of criminology is of no value unless we relate it to the things which criminologists are doing today."[3] This is the reminder made in 1959 by Clarence Ray Jeffery, and the admonition holds true today. Yet, eighteenth-century criminology emerged as an enlightened reaction against the barbaric punishments meted out during that era largely in the name of religion, and nineteenth-century criminology evolved as thinkers of the time reexamined the idealism of the eighteenth century only to find that it did not cope with the cruel reality of crime. To a substantial extent, the preoccupation of science during the nineteenth century turned back the intellectually forward-yearning drive of the eighteenth century.

So always does time alternatively produce progress and regression. But, out of regression, greater progress is spawned, and the scientific method pioneered in the eighteenth and nineteenth centuries reached fruition during the twentieth century. Our century has witnessed a greater enlightenment than anyone could have dreamed about during the eighteenth century, and this is clearly visible in criminology as well as in other natural and behavioral sciences. During the twentieth century, we have probed the human mind, finding hard evidence of how it affects what we do with our bodies and how we live our lives. During this century, moreover, we have invented technologies that permit us to record and to analyze events that take place as people interact in groups. The contribution of radio waves has not peaked, and that of the silicon chip has barely begun. We might be on the threshold of starting to understand crime, but that is all. In criminology, if we are lucky, the balance of the twentieth century may bring about a new enlightenment or fulfill the goals of the first one.

More than any other discipline except the fine arts, criminology has produced an evident linkage of ideas from one century to another and, in addition, from one generation to the following one even within the same century. Pioneers in criminology have drawn upon thoughts of their contemporaries in forming their own theories in much the same way as the painters Degas, Monet, and Renoir formed their impressionist style by studying the techniques of their mentor, Manet. As in the field of computer technology, the state of the art in criminology changes rapidly, but each change is linked both to the one that preceded it and to the one that will follow it. The "new" critical criminology embodies the same concern and thought process in the 1970s and 1980s that marked its recognized origin in 1764, just as the microchips that permit pocket computers contain refinements of the same technology that empowered the Univac computers of the 1950s. Neither microchips nor critical criminology will remain new for long, but some aspects of each field will seem new at any given moment.

Jeffery has observed also that criminology involves three problem areas: (1) detecting the lawbreaker; (2) the custody and treatment of the offender; and (3) explaining crime and criminal behavior: "The problems associated with the detection, treatment, and explanation of crime and criminals are mutually interrelated, and there is a great deal of overlapping of fields."[4] The linkage of ideas in criminology crosses the boundaries of these three problem areas. Thus, if Cesare Lombroso's lifelong search for physical characteristics common at birth to all criminals proved fruitless in explaining criminal behavior, it proved invaluable in generating forensic investigatory techniques used today to detect evidence of crime and to apprehend suspected criminals.

THE ORIGIN OF MODERN CRIMINOLOGY

Criminology has become an independent academic discipline in the twentieth century, in large measure on account of the efforts of a small number of people who may be deemed "pioneers" in this field.[5] The connection of ideas in criminology over time and also within approximately the same epoch but across the different problem areas has not been charted closely enough or memorialized sufficiently. Criminology owes to some artists, natural scientists, and philosophers who never devoted any detailed attention themselves to the study of crime at least as much as, and perhaps more than, it owes to those few persons who have been targeted as being pioneers in criminology. Recognition of the linkage between criminology, on the one hand, and, on the other hand, art, the natural sciences, and philosophy has been neglected. This void is one reason why criminology has met with delay in being accepted as an autonomous discipline by the full range of academicians, particularly in the United States.

Most scholars agree that modern criminology came into being in 1764 with the publication at Livorno, Italy, of the *Trattato dei délitti è elle pèna*,[6] written by Cesare Bonesana, the Italian Marchese di Beccaria. The book was republished at London in 1767 under the English title, *Essay on Crimes and Punishment*,[7] and its author received wide acclaim immediately as "Beccaria." There is significance that this book was published when it was and that it received the reception that it did. Beccaria commenced to write his *Essay* in March 1763 and completed it the following January. The previous March, in 1762, an elderly man named Jean Calas had been sentenced to death in Toulouse, France, convicted of having killed his own son. Calas was a Huguenot, or French protestant, whom the royal prosecutor alleged had killed his son because the son converted to Roman Catholicism. In fact, the son committed suicide, as the French philosopher Voltaire documented subsequently in his 1763 *Traité sur la tolérance* (Treatise on Tolerance). In Voltaire's famous letter to a friend, Jean d'Alembert, dated November 28, 1762, Voltaire condemned court-approved torture for the purpose of persecuting religious dissidents and closed that letter with a phrase that would become a watchword of the French Revolution: "*Écrasez-l'infâme*" (Stamp out the infamous thing). Ultimately, Voltaire succeeded in obtaining a posthumous reversal of Calas' conviction and in focusing worldwide attention upon the practices of torture in French prisons.

During the years before and during the time when Beccaria authored his *Essay*, he was fascinated by the tenets of other French encyclopédists, and particularly by Montesquieu's *De l' Esprit des lois* (The Spirit of Laws), published in 1748. Without the influence of the encyclopédist movement, and especially without Montesquieu's thoughts as a background, the young Beccaria is unlikely to have written his *Essay*, and it is even less likely that this *Essay* would have gained notoriety. A hundred Beccarias could have lived and died and written the same essay or a better one. Beccaria's popular success stemmed from what he wrote when and where he wrote it: he wrote on a stage set by Montesquieu and for an audience amplified by Voltaire. He wrote what his readership wanted to read. They adored what he wrote.

Classical Realism

Montesquieu, Voltaire, and Beccaria were idealists, and the ideal they shared was a system of justice for the criminal offender that would stand in contrast to the realism dominated by religion that had motivated the enforcement of the laws in most of Europe until the end of the eighteenth century. The social philosophy prevalent in Europe until the eighteenth century has become known as classical realism and encompassed the thoughts of both secular and theological writers. Among the secular philosophers were Plato and Aristotle from the golden age of Greece, and Marcus Tullius Cicero from the Roman Republic.

During the Middle Ages, however, realist principles that had begun without religious overtones became infatuated with the guilt orientations of medieval Christian monks and priests, such as St. Augustine, St. Anselm, and St. Thomas Aquinas. The early realist thinkers from Greece and Rome viewed the state as deriving its authority from its citizenry, and its power to punish wrongdoers from its need to protect the collective welfare of its population. This theme begins in Plato's *Republic* and is carried across through Aristotle's *Politics* and his *Nicomachean Ethics* to the three political works of Cicero: *De Republica* (On the Republic), *De Officiis* (On Duty), and *De Legibus* (On Laws). The realist theologians, on the other hand, viewed the state as deriving its authority from God as interpreted by the Roman Catholic Church, and they saw the state's power to punish wrongdoers as inherent in the majesty of the state's absolute monarch who ruled by Divine Right. This theme begins in St. Augustine's *City of God*, and it is carried forward in later theological treatises such as St. Anselm's *Proslogion* and St. Thomas Aquinas' *Summa Theologica* containing his famous passage, "On the Essence of Law."

Classical Idealism

Montesquieu, Voltaire, Beccaria, and other idealists of the mid-eighteenth century looked back to Plato, Aristotle, and Cicero for guidance away from what they witnessed as abuse of power by the state in the name of religion. In effect, they looked back longingly upon a "classical" age and dreamed that they might revive the same. The emergence of what became known as the "classical" school of criminology accompanied a period of intellectual and artistic romanticism that yearned for, and eventually found, classical revival. What is of immense importance to be understood, because it has been overlooked in recent years, is the fact that the "classical" school of criminology, embodying the liberal principles of Montesquieu, Voltaire, and Beccaria, follows the thought pattern of idealism, not of realism, despite the paradox that both share as a modifier the word "classical."

Sir Leon Radzinowicz has observed incisively:

The first modern penal ideology was forged during that memorable turning point in human affairs, the eighteenth century, . . . in Europe . . . when Europe was the centre of the world. Its precursors were French philosophers at a time when France was the centre of Europe. Negatively, it was part of the revolt against many ancient abuses, [but] positively it was part of a new view of man in relation to himself and to society. Powerful as was the immediate impact, the more far-reaching efforts permeated criminal law and its enforcement throughout the nineteenth century and beyond.[8]

From the revolutionary fires that erupted at the end of the eighteenth century, then, was criminology inaugurated as a field of inquiry separate unto itself. The egalitarian fervor that pervaded Europe and America at the close of the eighteenth century inspired people to speak out against injustice. As they did so, and looked about them, conflicting viewpoints began to spill out, and debate arose concerning why people commit crimes; how best to detect, deter, and prevent criminal activity; and how both effectively and efficiently to impose sanctions against those convicted of criminal acts. To be sure, idealism appeared at first to reflect the specious chatter of the aristocracy, albeit the rebellious aristocracy. Beccaria was an aristocrat. Virtually all of the eighteenth-century philosophers were the descendants of upper-class parents, for no one else could do more than dream about escaping from the daily drudgeries necessary to sustain their existence. This changed with the utilitarian movement and the turn of the nineteenth century.

The Industrial Revolution and Utilitarianism

The social change for which the leaders of the eighteenth century-revolutions had clamored started to become a reality early in the nineteenth century. What made the difference was new technology far more than changing social sentiments, although, possibly, both mechanical and social ideas stemmed from a common source in the Enlightenment. Various inventors had toyed with using steam as energy to power machinery from the early part of the eighteenth century, but the kinetic use of steam power awaited the nineteenth century and followed the "mechanical revolution." Ordinarily, at the time, steam was generated from coal furnaces, but, once perfected, steam engines could produce more coal and, consequently, more steam exponentially, in a similar though more primitive fashion as a breeder-reactor of today generates more nuclear energy. English coal mines flooded in winter, curbing mining operations seasonally. The steam engine pumped the coal mines and provided via locomotives the capability of transporting large quantities of coal across longer distances. In this way, coal fueled the steam engines at the factories, and the engines turned machinery used to fashion products. The ability to transport large amounts of coal permitted conversion of some coal into coke, and coke could be used to smelt iron ore into lighter and stronger steel. Steel was useful in constructing prisons containing tall tiers of cells where hundreds of prisoners could live for protracted periods of time.

England became industrialized within a generation, and industrialization followed swiftly on the European continent and in the New World. As factories appeared, towns grew and prospered into cities. People migrated from rural to urban locations, encountering bandits along the way and perilous housing conditions at their destinations. Crime flourished during the industrial revolution, as new opportunities for pilfering emerged. The lone traveler was a sitting duck for highwaymen against whom, unarmed, he was defenseless. Busy trading ports, such as London, became centers of crime where offenders plying different criminal trades could rip off imported commodities sequentially. The need arose for efficient policing.

As man learned to maximize industrial production through a minimum of physical effort on his own part, he began to adapt this principle to his social interactions, also, and the utilitarian mission evolved. Led primarily by English lawyer Jeremy Bentham for the first three decades of the nineteenth century, utilitarians directed their concerns toward the prevention of crime by policing of the streets and by carefully planned programs designed to put convicted criminal offenders to work at hard labor in prisons.

What the Benthamite utilitarians misapprehended was that the criminal population adapted to the utilitarian demand for efficiency, also. Jeremy Bentham and others such as Sir John Fielding and Sir Edwin Chadwick succeeded at implementing a system of efficient policing, first in London, later elsewhere across England. Police were organized in major cities of Europe and the United States during the first quarter of the nineteenth century. The amazing discovery, however, was that systematic policing disperses crime away from heavily patrolled areas and into locations that lie beyond the watchful eye of the policemen. As a community hires more police, the police identify more crime, and more people become targeted as criminals falling within the arms of the law.

Similarly, Benthamite utilitarians endeavored to construct numerous fortress-style prisons where convicted offenders could be housed and made to do hard work while paying for their own upkeep and, hopefully, turning over a profit. The utilitarians found instead that, to break even, a prison has to have a constantly increasing population; as a prison population increases, the need arises for the size and capacity of the prison itself to expand; as it does so, a larger segment of the population must be sent to prison to occupy the space already created. An endless circle of events ensues at considerable expense to the state and, predictably, without completely eliminating crime or reforming offenders. Utilitarians ignored the obvious reality that the lure of criminal opportunities entices an endless steam of would-be offenders ready, willing, and able to step in and take the place of the ex-offenders once they have been targeted and imprisoned.

Positivism and the Scientific Method

The burgeoning costs of both policing the cities and maintaining prisons caught up with most states during the second half of the nineteenth century. For the first time since the Englightenment, really, it became evident that no state could afford the luxury of imprisoning everyone whom those empowered to imprison disliked. The offenders who would be likely to recidivate, or repeat, serious crimes had to be distinguished from those who would not. The scientific method approached its zenith in western Europe at that time and inspired the growth of empirical research to try to identify what traits, if any, observable in any given person, could predict with reasonable certainty whether the person would engage in serious criminal behavior during his lifetime. Positivism emerged as a philosophy in criminology, therefore, and the search began for "the criminal man," led principally by an Italian army physician named Cesare Lombroso. Stephen Schafer observed poignantly that the appearance of positivist criminology "symbolized clearly that the era of faith was over and the scientific age had begun."[9]

For some reason, Lombroso's search for and self-declared "discovery" of "the criminal man" became immensely popular at the end of

the nineteenth century. The reason for his popularity has been speculated:

It may be that the history of the born criminal offered a convenient rationali-
zation of the failure of preventive effort and an escape from the implications of
the dangerous doctrine that crime is an essential product of our social organization.[10]

Sir Leon Radzinowicz has offered a similar but slightly different reason
for Lombroso's popularity:

It served the interests and relieved the conscience of those at the top to look
upon the dangerous classes as an independent category, detached from the prevailing social conditions. They were portrayed as a race apart, morally depraved and vicious, living by violating the fundamental law of orderly society,
which was that a man should maintain himself by honest, steady work.[11]

For whatever reason, the positivist movement in criminology took root,
and Lombroso did not disappoint his readership. The first edition of his
L'Uomo delinquente contained 252 pages; the second, appearing in 1878,
required 740 pages. By the fourth edition, in 1889, two volumes were
needed for all 1,241 pages. By the fifth edition, in 1896–97, all 1,903
pages could fit barely into three volumes. George Vold has noted:

Thus, 252 pages may have sufficed for an exposition of his original doctrine of
evolutionary atavism as the explanation of crime, but 20 years later he needed
over 1900 pages to include all the items and elements that appeared to be related to crime causation, running all the way from climate, rainfall, the price
of grain, sex and marriage customs, criminal laws, and banking practices to
national tariff policies, structure of government, church organization, and the
state of religious belief.[12]

People of the late nineteenth and early twentieth centuries seem to have
wanted to find some easy way to distinguish the criminal from themselves, perhaps as a means of attenuating their own misconduct well
hidden in the closet, or of attesting to their personal outward conformity
during the height of the Victorian age when conformity was in flower.
Lombroso tried to give his readers what they wanted, using simple explanations undocumented by rigorous analysis but appearing to have the
imprimatur (official sanction) of the scientific method. His field of study
was called anthropometry, which means the study and technique of human body measurement for use in anthropological classification and
comparison.

The search went on to find the principal causes of criminal behavior, led by Lombroso and his followers, the most important of whom were Enrico Ferri and Raffaele Garofalo. Ferri drafted a revised penal code for Italy in 1921 which the Chamber of Deputies rejected as being too radical. It offers excellent insight into the jurisprudence of the positivists. Garofalo focused away from law and onto what he called the psychic anomaly,[13] or instincts, toward behavior which he concluded could be inherited or learned from early experiences during infancy. While Lombroso studied physiological traits of the body, Garofalo concentrated on psychological attributes of the mind, a subject popularized by Sigmund Freud in the first four decades of the twentieth century. In 1913, Charles Buckman Goring published his study, *The English Convict*,[14] within which he used rigorous statistical analysis to invalidate most of Lombroso's work.

True to Darwin's theory of physical evolution, only the fittest ideas have survived scientific testing, and Lombroso's version of positivism failed to adapt to intellectual evolution. Nevertheless, positivist criminology has not disappeared entirely. A recent study of innate infant behavior[15] has implications on the role heredity may play in criminology, as does another study of the defective brain.[16] A number of researchers have investigated the relationship, if any, between chromosomal abnormality (e.g., the "XYY Syndrome") and unusual propensity toward violence.[17] Although Lombroso's conclusions have been discredited as having been drawn prematurely, the search for "the criminal man" continues.[18]

Physiological studies popularized by Lombroso have yielded some serendipity. Late in the nineteenth century, concern arose over how to identify known criminal offenders. A French policeman named Alphonse Bertillon devised an anthropometric method of classifying offenders by numerous bodily measurements, but it proved ineffective. In 1880, a Scottish physician working in Japan conceived the notion that skin designs left at crime scenes could be traced to offenders by making careful notation of the circles and ridges.[19] During the twentieth century, methods have been devised for classifying blood, hair, saliva, semen, skin, and other bodily residue, all of which derive from Lombroso's popularization of anthropometry.

Naturalism and Psychological Dysfunction

Throughout much of the nineteenth century, beginning well before positivism became popular, varieties of naturalism emerged in the thoughts of early criminologists. From the phrenology of both Gall and Spurzheim[20] to the constitutional psychiatry of William H. Sheldon[21] with Sigmund

Freud's adaptation of Friedrich von Schelling's *Naturphilosophie*[22] in between, criminality has been studied as the product of both physical and emotional illness. Against an illness model, in contrast to the prevailing early nineteenth century view that crime stemmed from moral wickedness, emerged what became known as the asylum, constructed to care for and try to cure the mentally ill. From Jean Etienne Dominique Esquirol's early asylum, the Salpetriere, to the modern mental hospitals such as New York's Mattawan or Maryland's Patuxant Institution, most states in Amercia have built "state hospitals" to house the criminally insane separately from other prisoners, or to appear at least to do so.[23]

So also, in the middle of the nineteenth century, did many jurisdictions come to excuse criminal behavior without punishing the same where the offender knew not the difference between what is right and wrong. Insanity emerged as a defense to criminal responsibility, beginning with the decision by England's House of Lords in the 1843 case against Daniel M'Naghten.[24] Other types of insanity defenses evolved during the twentieth century, also, and remained absolute barriers to convicting the insane of crimes, at least until 1985 when New Hampshire began to consider legislation aimed at eliminating insanity altogether as a criminal defense.

Pragmatism and Social Interaction

Some nineteenth century criminologists viewed social experience as impacting criminality. For instance, Edward Livingston wrote in the 1830s:

The bridewell of a large city is the place in which those representatives of human nature, in its most degraded shape, are assembled; brought into close contact, so that no art of fraud, no means of depredation, no shift to avoid detection, known to one, may be hid from the other; . . . Here, he who can "commit the oldest crime in the newest sort of way," is hailed as a genius . . . and having no interest to secure the exclusive use of the discovery, he freely imparts it to his less instructed companions.[25]

In this passage alone, as well as several others, Livingston anticipated twentieth century social ecologists such as Burgess, McKenzie and Park[26] plus twentieth century interactionists such as Sutherland[27] and his progeny. Yet, despite Livingston's prescience a century earlier, the value of the social learning experience in molding the child as a delinquent or right-thinking person did not become understood until pragmatism attained popularity in twentieth-century America, largely as a result of the impact the "Chicago School of Sociology" exerted upon American criminologists, the makers of American public policy since 1933, and the American public itself.

Although Livingston and other nineteenth century penologists recognized the likely impact the rise of cities would exert on the way people would behave in the future, actually they were unable to study cities in any detail because cities had not developed fully and plentifully in America very far in advance of this century. By the turn of this century, however, America had produced large cities several in number, and these continued to swell through the two world wars, functioning as valuable laboratories for a theoretical criminologist and practical training grounds within which to plan and execute applied experiments such as Clifford Shaw's Chicago Area Project from 1932 until 1957.

Early pragmatist criminologists, such as the ecologists Park, Burgess and McKenzie, attempted to reason how people could come to live harmoniously by achieving a social balance much as fish do in a balanced aquarium. Early interactionists, such as Edwin H. Sutherland, examined social imbalance in their efforts to identify why people, or at least why some people, fail to discover social balance. Subculturalists, such as Edward M. Lemert, explained social balance in relative terms, cautioning that, although subcultures may clash with each other and the overall culture of a society, members who are part of a given subculture may live harmoniously therein. The year 1938 produced Shaw's *Brothers in Crime*, portraying similarity between delinquents and non-delinquents in most respects, as well as the manuscript for Sutherland's theory of differential association[28] and Robert K. Merton's famous paper, "Social Structure and Anomie."[29] One could argue that, by 1938, pragmatist criminology had peaked and the world awaited something new. Twenty years later analytic criminology arrived in the form of conflict theory.

Analytic Criminology

The year 1958 witnessed publication of two classic works on conflict theory in criminology: Ralf Dahrendorf's article entitled, "Out of Utopia"[30] and George B. Vold's book, *Theoretical Criminology*. Dahrendorf contrasted dominant social classes from subjects who are dominated by others, all the while rejecting Karl Marx. In Vold, political corruption became the primary example of conflict theory adumbrating criminality. Both Dahrendorf and Vold reflect inescapably segments of Thorsten Sellin's book, *Culture, Conflict and Crime*, published relatively uneventfully during that momentous year for criminology, 1938. From Dahrendorf and Vold have emerged most aspects of the "new criminology" both with and without references to Karl Marx. From Richard Quinney's book, *The Social Reality of Crime*, in 1970, to *The New Criminology*[31] in 1973; and from Quinney's 1977 book, *Class, State, and Crime*, onward, we have seen how, arguably, some definitions of crime may have been inspired politically, all of which remind us, as the Mad Hatter warned long ago in *Alice in Wonderland*, that the law is the law because those in power say it is, for better or for worse.

Existential Criminology

Existentialism has yet to make its mark in criminology. How could it have? Criminology is among the youngest of the scientific disciplines. Except for some works by Fyodor Dostoevsky[32] and Franz Kafka,[33] crime as an existential experience remains to be developed in the future. Yet, existentialism is discernible in the roots of crime, particularly if one views crime as an example of a "will to power."[34] If, as Friedrich Nietzsche contended, "there are no moral phenomena at all, but only a moral interpretation of phenomena," then crime can be understood only in the context of knowledge that goes beyond right and wrong. But what *is* this knowledge that transcends conventional morality, or, possibly, any morality at all? Does this knowledge amount to nihilism? These questions are unanswerable presently, until existential criminology develops further.

What is answerable is the question: How can criminology be understood? The answer to this question is simple and evident as one reads the chapters of this book. New schools of criminology emerge constantly and, undoubtedly, will continue to do so. New notions about the nature and etiology of crime, as about methods and strategies for social intervention, emerge out of older schools of thought on the same subject. The idealism of Beccaria and the utilitarianism of Bentham remain with us, even as does the positivism of Lombroso, but they merge into the changing language of the "new" criminology, whatever that is at a given time, be it analytic or existential or something else far beyond either. The history of criminology reflects the philosophy of the times—of any time in history, including our own time. The philosophy of criminology can vary and does, but all philosophies of criminology are influenced by the history of criminology. The history and philosophy of criminology interface.

NOTES

1. *The War Lover,* Review of Ladislas Farago, ORDEAL AND TRIUMPH (1964) 84 TIME 112 (October 30, 1964).
   2. *Id.*

3. C. Jeffery, *The Historical Development of Criminology*, 50 J. CRIM. L., CRIM. & POL. SCI. 1 (1959), reprinted in H. Mannheim, ed., PIONEERS IN CRIMINOLOGY 458 (ed. 1972).

4. *Id*. Mannheim at 459.

5. See H. Mannheim, PIONEERS IN CRIMINOLOGY (1960 and 1972).

6. Dutch Marxist criminologist Willem Bonger argued that "criminology" as a term was used first in 1879 by French anthropologist P. Topinard, penology having been the widely used term before then. See H. Mannheim, ed., PIONEERS IN CRIMINOLOGY 1 (2d ed., 1960).

7. The first American edition (New York, 1809) was translated by Stephen Gould. A more recent edition (Indianapolis, 1963) was translated by Henry Paolucci.

8. L. Radzinowicz, IDEOLOGY AND CRIME 1 (1966).

9. S. Schafer, THEORIES IN CRIMINOLOGY 123 (1969).

10. See A. Lindesmith and Y. Levin, *The Lombrosian Myth in Criminology*, 42 AM. J. SOC. 653-71 (1937).

11. *Supra*, note 8 at 38-39.

12. G. Vold, THEORETICAL CRIMINOLOGY 37 (Bernard ed., 1979). Lombroso's last work, CRIME, ITS CAUSES AND REMEDIES, published in 1911, two years after his death, Vold said "was specially prepared by Lombroso for the American reader as a summary of his life work." *Id*.

13. R. Garofalo, CRIMINOLOGY 79 (1914).

14. C. Goring, THE ENGLISH CONVICT: A STATISTICAL STUDY.

15. See E. Wilson, ON HUMAN NATURE (1978).

16. See V. Mark and F. Ervin, VIOLENCE AND THE BRAIN (1970).

17. See P. Moody, GENETICS OF MAN (1967).

18. For a thorough review of the genetic causes of criminal behavior, see L. Taylor, BORN TO CRIME (1983), and Y. Rennie, THE SEARCH FOR CRIMINAL MAN (1978).

19. Faulds, *On the Skin Furrows of the Hand*, 22 NATURE 605 (1880). The first textbook on fingerprinting appeared at the height of positivist criminology, in 1892, written by Sir Francis Galton. F. Galton, FINGERPRINTS (1892; reprinted 1965).

20. F. Gall and J. Spurzheim, ANATOMIE ET PHYSIOLOGIE DU SYSTEME NERVEUSE (1819).

21. W. Sheldon, VARIETIES OF DELINQUENT YOUTH: AN INTRODUCTION TO CONSTITUTIONAL PSYCHIATRY (1949).

22. S. Freud and J. Breuer, STUDIES IN HYSTERIA (1895) and S. Freud, THE PSYCHOPATHOLOGY OF EVERYDAY LIFE (1904).

23. See D. Rothman, THE DISCOVERY OF THE ASYLUM: SOCIAL ORDER AND DISORDER IN THE NEW REPUBLIC (1971).

24. 10 Cl. & F. 200, 8 Eng. Rep. 718 (1843).

25. E. Livingston, THE COMPLETE WORKS OF EDWARD LIVINGSTON ON CRIMINAL JURISPRUDENCE 538 (1873; reprinted 1968). See also R. Owen, A NEW VIEW OF SOCIETY (1813).

26. R. Park, E. Burgess, and R. McKenzie, THE CITY: THE ECOLOGI-CAL APPROACH TO THE STUDY OF THE HUMAN COMMUNITY (1925).

27. E. Sutherland, PRINCIPLES OF CRIMINOLOGY 4-9 (4th ed., 1947).

28. *Id.* (1st ed., 1939).

29. 3 AM. SOC. REV. 672-82.

30. R. Dahrendorf, *Out of Utopia: Toward a Reorientation of Sociological Analysis*, 64 AM. J. SOC. 115-27 (1958).

31. I. Taylor, P. Walton, and J. Young, THE NEW CRIMINOLOGY (1973).

32. F. Dostoevsky, CRIME AND PUNISHMENT (1866–67) and THE BROTHERS KARAMAZOV (1879–80).

33. F. Kafka, THE TRIAL (1925).

34. F. Nietzsche, BEYOND GOOD AND EVIL 108 (W. Kaufmann, tr., 1966).

2

Realism before the Enlightenment

The predominant social philosophy before the Enlightenment of the eighteenth-century Western world was classical realism, which originated during the "golden" age of Greece and was expanded during the Middle Ages by Christian monks and priests. Aristotle followed Pythagoras (c. 530 B.C.) in expressing the need to comprehend an ordered "cosmos" or physical universe. Aristotle identified an additional need of human nature to search for happiness through moral virtues such as courage and temperance, as well as intellectual virtues such as art, prudence, and wisdom. Greek philosophers before and after Aristotle taught that man needs society in order to realize fully his capacity. Without the external support from society, man in isolation remains incapable of becoming a rational animal, Aristotle warned. For this reason, the Greek philosophers held that the state, if properly ordered according to just principles, is organic in that its purpose is to serve the common good of its population. This theme dominates Aristotle's *Politics* and *Nicomachean Ethics*. It has been carried forth by Romans such as Cicero and into the Middle Ages by John of Salisbury (1120–80) and Marsilius of Padua (1275–1343).

Along the way, beginning at least with publication of St. Augustine's *City of God* after the Visigoths sacked Rome in the year 410, emerged the dual theme within "classical" realism that man requires also the Grace of God to reach perfection. From Pope Gelasius (492–96) came the notion that a Christian belongs to two societies—one natural and temporal, resembling Aristotle's city-state; the other supernatural but eternal, and made possible by the additional Christian virtues of faith, hope, and charity. This theme was carried forth by St. Anselm (1033–1109) in his *Monologion* and *Proslogion* and by St. Thomas Aquinas (1226–74) in *Summa Theologica*.

REALISM IN THE MIDDLE AGES

Viewed either in the light of, or without, Christianity, realism as a philosophy contemplates a well-ordered "cosmos" or universe that it dissembles into rational subparts. Aristotle argued that everything has four "causes" for its own existence: (1) the material cause, or substance such as wood or metal of which it is made; (2) the efficient cause, or energy that molds it into shape; (3) the formal cause, or label that characterizes its class and nature; and (4) the final cause, reflecting its ultimate purpose and reason for existence. Similarly, St. Thomas Aquinas argued that there are four "levels" of law: (1) divine law directs a person's inner effort to achieve salvation; (2) eternal law is imprinted on all creatures, and from it they derive their inclinations; (3) natural law prescribes what is good and prohibits what is wrong universally; and (4) human laws are framed by men as part of their effort within society to achieve the degree of peace and order necessary if they are to strive for perfection.

Not surprisingly, therefore, realists have been a prescriptive lot. Christian realists have argued invariably that the state's power to govern its subjects, including its power to punish them for criminal wrongdoing, is derived from God. Consider the following passage from St. Augustine's *City of God*:

The peace of mortal man with immortal God, is an orderly obedience unto His eternal law, performed in faith. Peace of man in man, is a mutual concord: peace of a family, an orderly rule and subjection amongst the parts thereof: peace of a city, an orderly command, and obedience amongst the citizens: peace of God's City a most orderly coherence in God, and fruition of God: peace of all things, is a well disposed order. For order, is a good disposition of discrepant parts, each in the fittest place, and therefore the miserable (as they are miserable), are out of order wanting that peaceable and unperturbed state which order exacts. But because their own merits have incurred this misery, therefore even herein they are imposed in a certain set order howsoever. Being not conjoined with the blessed, but severed from them by the law of order, and being exposed to miseries, yet these are adapted unto the places wherein they are resident. . . . The devil abode not in the truth, yet escaped he not the sentence of the truth: for he transgressed the peaceful law of order, yet could not avoid the powerful hand of the Orderer.[1]

John of Salisbury spoke in the same vein some seven centuries after St. Augustine, writing "What Is Meant by a Prince":

[A]ll power is from the Lord God, and has been with Him always, and is from everlasting. The power which the prince has is therefore from God, for the power of God is never lost, nor severed from Him, but He merely exercises it through a subordinate hand, making all things teach His mercy or justice. "Who, therefore, resists the ruling power, resists the ordinance of God," in whose hand is the authority of conferring that power, and when He so desires, of withdrawing it again, or diminishing it. For it is not the ruler's own act when his will is turned to cruelty against his subjects, but it is rather the dispensation of God for His good pleasure to punish or chasten them.[2]

Even when realist legal philosophy has been secular it has been snobbish, as is evident from the following passage written a century later by Marsilius of Padua:

[I]t can pertain to any citizen to discover the law taken materially and . . . as the science of civil justice and benefit. Such inquiry, however, can be carried on more appropriately and be completed better by those men who are able to have leisure, who are older and experienced in practical affairs, and who are called "prudent men," than by the mechanics who must bend all their efforts to acquiring the necessities of life.[3]

The church-dominated realist legal philosophy that was the most influential during the Middle Ages across western Europe left considerably less doubt as to whose privilege it would be to interpret laws. Witness the following passage from Dante Alighieri (1265–1361):

[T]he authority of Empire has not its source in the Chief Pontiff. . . . [I]f the authority does not depend on the Vicar of God, we conclude that it depends on God Himself. . . .

Wherefore a twofold directive was necessary to man, in accordance with the twofold end; the Supreme Pontiff to lead the human race to life eternal by means of revelation, and the Emperor to guide it to temporal felicity by means of philosophic instruction. . . . The order of the world follows the order inherent in the revolution of the heavens. To attain this order, it is necessary that instruction productive of liberality and peace should be applied by the guardian of the realm, in due place and time, as dispensed by Him who is the ever present Watcher of the whole order of the heavens. And He alone fordained this order, that by it in His providence He might link together all things, each in its own place. . . .

It is established, then, that the authority of temporal Monarchy descends without mediation from the fountain of universal authority. And this fountain, one in its purity of source, flows into multifarious channels out of the abundance of its excellence. . . .

[That] the authority of the Monarch derived from God immediately . . . must not be restricted to mean that the Roman Prince shall not be subject in some degree to the Roman Pontiff, for felicity that is mortal is ordered in a measure after felicity that is immortal. Wherefore let Caesar honor Peter as a first-born son should honor his father, so that, refulgent with the light of paternal grace, he may illuminate with greater radiance the earthly sphere over which he has been set by Him who alone is Ruler of all things spiritual and temporal.[4]

By the fourteenth century, therefore, classical realism embodied an intellectual truce between the Roman Catholic Church and European monarchies. The interface between church and state during the period between the fourteenth and nineteenth centuries holds the clue to understanding the methods and purposes of punishing people for criminal behavior throughout Europe.

The Power of the Kings

Realist philosophy of the European Middle Ages presumed that the power exercised by rulers of states was ordained by God. Thus, the "classical" realists subscribed invariably to the theory of the Divine Right of Kings. Assuming, as they were willing to do, that a monarch inherited his authority directly from God, then it followed naturally that his source of power could not be questioned by his subjects, nor could they question his abuse of that power. What was more, any attack upon the throne became also an assault upon the church and upon God, subjecting the offender to being charged with heresy as well as treason.

A notion that the community was responsible for what individuals living within it did or failed to do pervaded Europe during the Middle Ages before the Enlightenment. Scandinavian, German, and French traditions reinforced this view, well rooted in England under its native Celtic heritage even before the Norman invasion of 1066. In England, every freeman over twelve years of age had to belong to a tything, a small paramilitary group headed by a tything-man whose responsibility it was to ensure payment of local debts to the monarch and other lords, such as fines or taxes. (People paid a "tythe," or ten percent of their annual earnings, to the crown, usually in the form of crops harvested.) Members of a tything took a frank pledge promising to produce for punishment anyone over fourteen years of age who perpetrated a crime in their town or village and to hold harmless their monarch for the loss of his interest in their property occasioned by crime. A monarch was deemed to own all property used by his subjects, and so their loss he viewed as being his own loss, also. Every one hundred tythings were organized into a larger unit known as the hundred, headed by a hundredman who reported to the shire reeve or king's representative in each county. A shire reeve, later known as a sheriff, could muster together a *posse com-*

itatus or band of citizens drawn from the tythings in times of danger or necessity, such as to form a hue and cry to search for a fugitive criminal offender. Saxon laws exacted fines called fightwitt, grithbryce, and frithbrec. To avoid the double burden of losing their property to thieves and being made to pay for its value to the crown, Saxon citizens banded together into voluntary associations known as frithguilds for mutual protection against theft and insurance in case the monarch imposed a fine or a forfeiture of property.

Under early Saxon laws, an offender convicted of a crime could escape death by indemnifying the victim of his crime, either in property or services. Thus, the killer of a married man could live if he served the victim's widow! After the Norman invasion of England by William the Conqueror in 1066, the punishment for most offenses became death accompanied by forfeiture to the crown of all property the offender possessed at the time. An offender who escaped death was likely to have his body mutilated. The entire family of anyone convicted of a serious crime, such as a felony, was left destitute as the king seized what little property they had enjoyed. Monarchs and nobles became richer as more ordinary people were convicted of crimes. Therefore, rulers and the landed gentry who wielded legislative power found it lucrative to create additional crimes exponentially, to support the burgeoning costs of maintaining a feudal empire.

Courts emerged at every feudal level—in the villages, at feudal manors, at county seats, and at the king's center of national government. Initially, the monarch presided personally over his national courts, as did his vassals over courts within their territorial jurisdictions. The highest court in England during the Middle Ages was the Court of the King's Bench. Gradually, monarchs and nobles delegated authority to convene courts to judges who served as their representatives, often as political cronies. Norman judges who dispensed justice in England after 1066 decided the fate of native Anglo-Saxon subjects, but seldom fairly.

The Origin of Trials

European monarchies devised ways of identifying whom they might accuse of crimes and how these people would be convicted. Procedures to be followed in criminal cases were pronounced in royal enactments known in England as assizes. In the Assize of Clarendon, 1166, came the inquisitorial system known as the grand jury:

[Chapter I] First the aforesaid King Henry established by the councel of all his barons for the maintenance of peace and justice, that inquiry shall be made in every county and in every hundred by the twelve most lawful men of the hundred and by the four most lawful men of every vill, upon oath that they shall speak the truth, whether in their hundred or vill there by any man who is accused or believed to be a robber, murderer, thief, or a receiver of robbers, murderers, or thieves since the King's accession. And this the justices and sheriffs shall enquire before themselves.

[Chapter II] And he who shall be found, by the oath of the aforesaid, accused or believed to be a robber, murderer, thief, or a receiver of such since the King's accession shall be taken and put to the ordeal of water and made to swear that he was no robber, murderer, thief, or receiver of such up to the value of five shillings, as far as he knows, since the King's accession.

[Chapter IV] And when a robber, murderer, thief, or receiver of such is captured as a result of the oath, the sheriff shall send to the nearest justice (if there are no justices shortly visiting the county wherein he was captured) by an intelligent man saying that he has captured so many men. And the justices shall reply telling the sheriff where the prisoners are to be brought before them. And the sheriff shall bring them before the justices together with two lawful men from the hundred and the vill where they were captured to bring the record of the county and the hundred as to why they were captured; and there they shall make their law before the justices.

[Chapter XII] And if anyone is captured in possession of stolen or robbed goods and is of bad repute and can produce no testimony of public purchase nor a warrantor of title he shall not make his law. And if the goods were not publicly acquired he shall go to the water because they were found in his possession.

[Chapter XIV] The lord King also wishes that those who make their law and clear themselves shall, nevertheless, forswear the King's land if they are of bad renown and publicly and evilly reputed by the testimony of many lawful men(.)

Thus, England created a system of trial predicated upon superstition rather than reason. Early trials were by "wager of law," ordeal, or battle.

Trial by wager of law was, in effect, a trial of the reputation of an accused person among residents of the community where he lived. He had to find a number of lawabiding persons, usually twelve of them, who would take a solemn oath that they believed him when, under oath himself, he swore to his innocence. They became his compurgators who attested to the character of the person accused rather than to the facts of the controversy. An accused who was unsuccessful in mustering the required number of compurgators was said not to have "made his law," and, consequently, he was found guilty.

One accused of a crime in medieval England had the option of going to trial by ordeal, and this became his major option if the court denied him trial by wager of law. Trial by ordeal rested upon a religious assumption of the day that God would not permit a man who swore his innocence to perish, unless he lied. A freeman went to trial by hot water, as a rule, while an unfree person (serf) went to trial by cold water. Trial by any ordeal accompanied a mass, customarily celebrated by a priest. First, the accused took an oath swearing to his innocence. Next, in the case of trial by hot iron and hot water, he grasped a hot iron and carried it a distance of nine feet or reached into a bowl of hot water and retrieved a stone. Thereafter, his hand was bandaged for three nights. When the bandages were removed, the accused was declared innocent if his wounds were not infected, otherwise guilty.

In the case of trial by cold water, the accused was bound in a squatting position with his hands tied by rope under his knees. The rope extended above his head, where a knot was tied at the distance of the length of his hair. The accused was immersed into a body of water without a splash. He was declared innocent if he sank down to the knot in the rope, otherwise guilty. Clergy who were accused of crimes were tried by another form of ordeal, known as the cursed morsel. The accused swallowed some food in which a feather was concealed. He was declared innocent if he failed to choke, otherwise guilty. Most absurd of all, two cases were reported in 1202 where the accused was offered the opportunity either to carry the hot iron himself or to have his accuser do the same. Both times, the accused elected the latter procedure![5]

In trial by battle, the accused fought his accuser to the death and, if alive at the conclusion of the battle, was hanged if defeated. Trial by battle was the means of resolving purely private accusations. Where the crown prosecuted a criminal case, this form of trial was unavailable. On the eve of the American Revolution, the colonial Massachusetts legislature abolished trial by battle as a method of appealing a murder accusation, an act that is said to have annoyed the English, who valued the heritage of this method of trial,[6] which they no longer used.

Eventually, trial by jury replaced trials by wager of law, ordeal, and battle in England. By the middle of the thirteenth century, an Englishman could "put himself upon his country" for trial, meaning that he could elect to stand trial before a jury of twelve men, almost always prominent in the community, whose verdict had to be unanimous.[7] A person found standing over a corpse wielding in his hands a bloody knife was conclusively presumed guilty and could not stand trial, however, as was a person within whose house someone else was found murdered, unless the occupant possessed wounds documenting that he had defended the deceased against someone else's attack.[8] Even an entire jury could be put on trial for perjury in front of another and even larger jury of twenty-four persons, where the crown contended they had returned a verdict that was demonstrably false, usually by acquitting the accused. If the second jury found the first jurors guilty, they were attainted and punished as follows:

All of the first jury shall be committed to the King's prison, their goods shall be confiscated, their possessions seized into the King's hands, their habitations and houses shall be pulled down, their woodland shall be felled, their meadows shall be plowed up and they themselves forever thenceforward be esteemed in the eye of the law infamous.[9]

Obstinate jurors who disagreed with the majority could receive similar opprobrium and sanctions, unless they "confessed" their error and made the majority verdict unanimous. In 1554, for instance, Sir Nicholas Throckmorton stood trial charged with high treason and accused of trying to depose Queen Mary. He addressed his jury as follows:

The trial of our whole controversy, the trial of my innocency, the trial of my life, lands, and goods, and the destruction of my posterity for ever, doth rest on your good judgments.[10]

Lord Chief Justice Bromley retorted with a threat:

Remember yourselves better. Have you considered substantially the whole evidence as it was declared and recited? The matter doth touch the Queen's highness and yourselves also;—take good heed what you do.[11]

When the jury acquitted Throckmorton anyway, the prosecutor rose and demanded:

And it please you, my lords, forasmuch as it seemeth these men of the jury, which have strangely acquitted the prisoner of his treasons whereof he was indicted, will forthwith depart the court, I pray you for the Queen that they and every of them may be bound in a recognizance of £ 500 a-piece to answer to such matters as they shall be charged with in the Queen's behalf, whensoever they shall be charged or called.[12]

All were taken to the Star Chamber, where four "confessed" they had "offended in not considering the truth of the matter."[13]

The good citizen of the European Middle Ages did what he was told to do by those who wielded more power in the church or state than he did. Most subjects possessed no power at all and tried to obey the laws handed down by church and secular officials both. Religious and social dissidents entered the grasp of the criminal justice system rapidly and were eliminated by torture and execution. Unfortunately, ordinary people might wander quite innocently into the grasp of the same system that unjustly would affix its tentacles to their bodies. The fact is that whenever a humble subject was pointed out as having done something wrong, no matter how trivial, he was expected to admit guilt and beg for God's mercy by becoming a supplicant of the church and crown. Those who went along with the system as it then existed met their doom nevertheless, but perhaps more speedily than those who resisted. Those who displayed the tenacity of resistance met with an unspeakable fate.

The Use of Torture

The paramount objective of the criminal justice system prevalent throughout Europe at this time was to exact from a person suspected of criminal behavior an admission of guilt. A slightly less important objective was to elicit from anyone who admitted his own guilt the names of others who may have participated with him in a forbidden activity. In either situation, the method used was torture, and its purported justification was the state's need to protect the community from any further wrath from an angry God. An aim of considerably lesser importance was to restore to the accused offender and his cohorts the hope of personal salvation through repentence.

The torture used in France before and throughout most of the eighteenth century was typical of most countries on the European continent. Pursuant to the French Ordinance of 1670, whenever the monarchy came to suspect a person of complicity in any criminal offense, the slightest amount of inculpatory evidence created a ''half-proof'' and was sufficient to constitute an indice or legal presumption of guilt. Thereupon, the accused became subjected to inquisition, a process whereby a judge submitted written questions which the accused would be required to answer under oath while enduring physical pain known as torture. Torture was divided first into two stages, ''preparatory'' (*question preparatoire*) and ''preliminary'' (*question prealable*): the former designed to elicit from the accused a confession of his own personal guilt; the latter intended to exact from one who had admitted his guilt already the name of each accomplice, if any, who may have participated with him in the crime. At any time, the judge enjoyed the prerogative of terminating ''ordinary'' torture and proceeding to increase the severity of the pain via ''extraordinary'' torture. Ultimately, the person who ''confessed'' to having committed a crime would be put to death. Torture would be protracted for as long as possible until each detail of the crime could be described by the accused to the judge.

In 1757, one Damiens stabbed King Louis XV, for which the French judges resolved to impose the most gruesome "preliminary" tortures imaginable on the pretext of discovering his co-conspirators, even though it was well known the man was insane and had acted alone. At seven o'clock in the morning of his execution day, Damiens was led to the torture chamber, where his legs were placed in "boots" that were squeezed gradually as wedges were inserted. A total of eight wedges were inserted, each at fifteen-minute intervals, until the attending physicians warned that an additional wedge could provoke an "accident" (Damiens' premature death). Thereupon, Damiens was removed to the place where he would be executed, the front steps of the Paris city hall, filled with spectators who were kept in order by French and Swiss guards stationed along all nearby avenues. The condemned man was placed on a scaffold, where a rope was tied to each arm and leg. Then, Damiens' hand was burned with a brazier containing burning sulphur, after which red-hot tongs were used to pinch his arms, thighs, and chest. Molten lead and boiling oil were poured onto his open wounds several times, and after each time the prisoner screamed in agony. Next, four huge horses were whipped by attendants as they pulled the ropes around Damiens' bleeding wounds for an hour. Only after some of the tendons were cut did two legs and one arm separate from Damiens' torso. He remained alive and breathing until the second arm was cut from his body. All parts of Damiens' body were hurled into a nearby fire for burning.[14] The spectacle accomplished little more than to instill in the minds of the citizenry the awesome power of the monarchy.

England used a different method of torture, and used it more sparingly, than did the countries on the European continent. Indeed, an accused offender who had not been convicted of a crime could avoid torture before conviction altogether if he "put himself upon his country" and consented to be tried before a jury of his peers. When one accused of a criminal offense refused trial by jury, the crown could force him to submit to *peine forte et dure*, commonly known as "pressing." Under this form of torture, the accused was placed in solitary confinement, naked, stretched out on his back underneath a heavy weight. Sometimes he would be starved right from the beginning. Frequently, the initial weight would be as much as, or more than, he could withstand. In 1658, a Major Strangeways died in about ten minutes of pressing after several people stood atop the weights to hasten his death; but, in 1726, someone named Burnworth spent one and three-quarters hours beneath four hundred weight of iron only to change his mind, demand a jury trial, be convicted and hanged.[15] Commonly, the accused would be given a piece of bread on the first day, three mouthfuls of stagnant water on the second, with this procedure being repeated alternatively until he "confessed" or died. On occasion, the accused was literally flattened to death by application of progressively heavier weights.

Many accused offenders preferred being pressed to death instead of being tried by jury because, unless they broke and admitted wrongdoing, they could die without being convicted of any crime.[16] In this way, the crown was unable to confiscate from the accused's family his land holdings or movable property. Such seizures, known as escheat, were part of the punishment typically meted out in addition to death upon one's being convicted in England of treason or any felony. A few pressings took place in seventeenth-century New England, and this torture was not abolished in England until 1772.[17]

Torture was employed even in England during the actual execution of criminal offenders after they possessed no more information to share with their torturers. For instance, a person convicted of treason in England was subject to being disemboweled while alive, so that the entrails could be burned before the offender died. A traitor could be quartered while alive, also, meaning that arms and legs could be severed from the living torso. Under English common law, it was treason for a woman to plot the death of her husband, or of a servant to plot the death of his master, in addition to a subject plotting the death of his monarch. During the seventeenth and eighteenth centuries, however, executioners were allowed to exercise discretion,[18] and often they delayed disemboweling condemned women until the accused stopped breathing.

Continental countries burned heretics at the stake and broke some religious dissidents on the wheel. Nobles were beheaded, customarily, and common thieves tended to be hanged. In England, most criminals who were executed were hanged, but they suffocated slowly after being strung up, in contrast to the modern way of dropping the condemned from the air whereupon the weight of his body (frequently in chains) should break the neck and cause death instantly. Torture was utilized in noncapital punishments before the Enlightenment, also, in England and elsewhere across Europe. Virtually all countries used flogging. England used branding until 1779.[19] Continental countries slit or pierced the offender's tongue, cut off his nose, burned or cut off the offender's hand, or performed similar mutilations throughout most if not all of the eighteenth century.[20] A lighter punishment of the day consisted of the offender's head and limbs being locked into a pillory, where citizens could observe the offender in disgrace and, if they chose, hurl stones or other missiles at him.[21]

THE CHINESE COUNTERPART

Realist criminology does not appear to have differed much in China from Europe during the many years when East and West followed a similar philosophy of dealing with crime. A good example of the Chinese realist philosophy of criminology can be gained from examining the *Code* of the T'ang dynasty (A.D. 619–906), known formally as the *Ku T'ang-lü shu-yi*. Known popularly as the T'ang Code, it is associated with Ch'ang-sun Wu-chi, who died in A.D. 659 and who was the brother-in-law of the Emperor T'ai-tsung (A.D. 627-649).[22] Although Ch'ang-sun Wu-chi wrote the preface to the Code, therein he acknowledged that the Code had been predicated upon the *Fa ching*, or *Cannon of Laws*, which had been expounded by Shang Yang, prime minister of Ch'in circa 350 B.C.E., and which became known popularly as the Ch'in Code.[23]

Under the T'ang Code, ten particularly reprehensible crimes became known as "The Ten Abominations," or *shih-o*, which included:

1. Plotting rebellion (*mou-fan*)
2. Plotting great sedition (*mou ta-ni*)
3. Plotting treason (*mou-p'an*)
4. Contumacy (*o-ni*)
5. Depravity (*pu-tao*)
6. Great irreverence (*ta pu-ching*)
7. Lack of filial piety (*pu-hsiao*)
8. Discord (*pu-mu*)
9. Unrighteousness (*pu-yi*)
10. Incest (*nei-luan*)

Plotting rebellion consisted of plotting to endanger the state or its ruler, whereas plotting great sedition meant plotting to destroy ancestral temples, tombs or palaces of the reigning monarchy, such as in protest to its authority. Plotting treason consisted of plotting to betray the nation to its enemies. These first two abominations were punished by decapitation of the offender as well as any of his accessories and accomplices in addition to each one's male ancestors and male descendants over age fifteen. Female ancestors and female descendants, plus male descendants under age fifteen, were enslaved by the state. All property belonging to any of these persons was confiscated by the state. Paternal uncles and nephews would be exiled for life, but without confiscation of their property.[24] For plotting treason, deemed a less serious offense, fewer relatives were punished. Wives and sons were exiled for life, as were parents, also, if the plotters gathered more than one hundred follow-ers.[25] Property forfeiture practices and "corruption of the blood" prac-tices in Imperial China differed only slightly, therefore, from those in practice in England for treasons and related offenses against the reigning powers.

The fourth abomination, contumacy, could result from various con-duct pertaining to familial disloyalty, such as (a) beating or plotting to kill (but without actually killing) the offender's parents or paternal grandparents; (b) actually killing one's paternal uncles or their wives; his older siblings; his maternal grandparents; or (c) a wife's actual kill-ing of her husband, of her husband's parents, or of her husband's pater-nal grandparents. Contumacy was punished by decapitation of the of-fender(s) and life exile of his subordinate collateral relatives.

The fifth abomination, depravity, occurred when an offender killed three members of a single household, provided that none of the three victims had committed a capital crime; or, when the offender dismem-bered the victim. In this sense, depravity parallels some aspects of may-hem under English common law. Once again, the penalty of decapita-tion was imposed for depravity. The punishment was death by strangulation where the offender killed but one or two members of a household, or where one or more of the victims had been convicted of a capital offense. The distinction between China's two forms of capital punishment, decapitation and strangulation, is significant to oriental phi-losophy in that decapitation severs the body into two parts. The Chinese tenets of filial piety held that the body should remain in a single part because it comes from one's parents.[26] Another form of depravity oc-curred when the offender engaged in a form of sorcery by making poi-son or supervising others in its making. Such poison was known as *ku*, and its making may be viewed as a Chinese counterpart to witchcraft in England, for which the death penalty was imposed by hanging or burn-ing. *Ku* depravity was usually punished in China by strangulation rather than decapitation.[27]

Among the remaining five abominations, great irreverence took place when religious objects were stolen, such as from ancestral temples, or when objects being transported to or from the emperor were stolen or obstructed. Thus, great irreverence could occur when a servant failed to prepare properly the emperor's food or medicine. In a sense, perhaps, this crime is a precursor of strict criminal liability in the United States for "regulatory" offenses.[28] Lack of filial piety encompassed such seemingly disparate conduct as cursing one's parents or grandparents or acting contemptuously in court. In addition, this offense could be per-petrated by a son who jeopardized supporting (or refused to support) his living ancestors by maintaining a separate household from them or buying household goods separate from these ancestors. Discord occurred when one plotted to kill relatives or to sell them into slavery, except, of course, that plotting to do this to one's paternal ancestors constituted the higher crime of contumacy. Unrighteousness consisted of killing a teacher from whom a student received his education, killing a magistrate, or killing a supervisor. Incest in China occurred when sexual intercourse took place between relatives who were within the fourth degree of mourning, or with the concubines of persons within such degrees of mourning. Strangulation, rather than decapitation, was the punishment for these last five abominations.

Ordinarily, The Ten Abominations were not subject to commutation, known as The Eight Deliberations, or *pa-yi*. However, the emperor alone could approve the death penalty, and, consequently, if he refused to do so, it could not be carried out.[29] As to offenses besides the Abominations, The Eight Deliberations were considered in mitigating punishment. They included:

1. Deliberation for relatives of the emperor
2. Deliberation for old retainers of the emperor
3. Deliberation for the morally worthy
4. Deliberation for ability
5. Deliberation for achievement
6. Deliberation for high position
7. Deliberation for diligence
8. Deliberation for guests of the state[30]

Thus, official privilege in China as in England and France played a significant role in fixing actual punishment for criminal behavior. In addition, punishment could be mitigated by redemption through the payment of copper[31] or through the exchange of social rank for a lower rank instead of other punishment.

NOTES

1. XV, 13. Translated by John Healey (1893).
2. IV, 1. John Dickinson, tr., THE STATESMAN'S BOOK OF JOHN OF SALISBURY (1927), quoting *Romans*, XIII, 2.
3. XII, 2. Marsilius of Padua, THE DEFENDER OF PEACE (Alan Gewirth, tr., 1956).
4. Dante Alighieri, *De Monarchia* III, 16. (Aurelia Henry, tr., 1904).

5. See T. Plucknett, A CONCISE HISTORY OF THE COMMON LAW 115 (1956), citing Lady Stenton, 22 LINCOLNSHIRE ASSIZE ROLL nos. 595, 843.

6. *Id.* at 117-18, citing 17 PARLIAMENTARY HISTORY 1291.

7. W. Forsyth, HISTORY OF TRIAL BY JURY 206-9 (1852). Jurors had to

possess an annual income of ten pounds issuing from lands of freehold, copyhold, or customary tenure, or of ancient demesne, in fee simple, free tail, or for the life of himself or some other person; or of twenty pounds from leasehold property, the term being twenty-one years or longer . . . ; or he must be a householder, rated and assessed to the relief of the poor on a value of not less than £20 . . . ; or he must occupy a house containing not less than fifteen windows.

Id. at 208, n. 2, citing Stat. Geo. IV, c. 50.

8. *Id.* at 203. One accused of murder by secret poisoning had to be tried by combat (battle) because the crown possessed no evidence to offer before a jury. *Id.* at 202.

9. *Supra*, note 5 at 131.

10. *Supra*, note 7 at 393.

11. *Id.*

12. *Id.* at 394.

13. *Supra*, note 5 at 133, quoting Crompton, AUTHORITIE ET JURISDICTION DES COURTS f. 32b. The other eight were remanded to prison indefinitely. Two were fined £2,000 each and the rest £200 each. *Supra*, note 7 at 394.

14. See Voltaire, OEUVRES 98-99 (Moland, ed., 1885).

15. See L. Pike, A HISTORY OF CRIME IN ENGLAND 194-95, 283 (1968).

16. See W. Blackstone, COMMENTARIES ON THE LAWS OF ENGLAND 324-28 (1769).

17. See Stephen, A HISTORY OF THE CRIMINAL LAW OF ENGLAND 298 (1849).

18. *Id.* at 477.

19. *Id.* 463, 490.

20. K. Bar, A HISTORY OF CONTINENTAL CRIMINAL LAW 273 (1968).

21. *Id.* at 248.

22. See W. Johnson, THE T'ANG CODE 5 (1979).

23. *Id.* at 7.

24. *Id.* at 18. Exile would be for a distance of 3,000 *li*.

25. *Id.* at 19. An exception was when the offender was a foreigner. There, only the offender himself was executed, and by strangulation. The foreign offender's family went unpunished. Moreover, even the Chinese offender was strangled unless the treasonous conduct had already begun. *Id.* at 65, note 107.

26. *Id.* at 60, note 4.

27. *Id.* at 20. All those who possessed real estate or personal property in

common with the offender convicted of making *ku* poison were exiled for life to a distance of 3,000 *li*. *Id*.

28. See *Morisette v. United States*, 342 U.S. 246 (1952).

29. *Id*. at 88. Examples of amnesty discussed in the *Rites of Chou*: (a) youth and weakness, where the offender is under the age of ten; (b) age and senility, where the offender is over the age of eighty; and (c) feeblemindedness. *Id*. at 171-71.

30. *Id*., Chapter 2, *passim*.

31. *Id*. at 171. One hundred *chin* in copper was required to redeem a sentence of exile for life to a distance of 3,000 *li*. For plotting rebellion, however, the offender could not be redeemed, but his relatives could be by paying this sum in copper. *Id*. One reason why the Chinese governments meeted out such severe penalties was to reduce private revenge by relatives of the victim. See T. Ch'u, *Law and Society in Traditional China* 81 (1961). Another reason was to maintain the social order through moral education of the population, referred to by Ch'u as "the confucianization of law" in his distinction between law and *li*. *Id*. at 267. Ch'u quoted Han Fei tzŭ: "Heavy punishment is what people dislike. Therefore the sage displays that which they fear in order to keep them from depravity, and puts forth what they dislike in order to prevent them from doing evil so that the nation will be peaceful, and that disturbance and disorder will not arise." *Id*. at 266.

3

Idealism from the Eighteenth Century

Idealism in criminology stems from the encyclopédist movement that swept France and then the rest of Europe in the two decades between 1751 and 1772, just as does idealism in art, architecture, music, philosophy, and the natural sciences. During these two decades, some seventy artists, scientists, and scholars collaborated with the French writers Denis Diderot and Chevalier de Jaucourt who edited the *Encyclopédie*, to prepare this repertoire of new ideas that, together, have become known as the Enlightenment. The *Encyclopédie* contained articles by Boucher D'Argis on jurisprudence, Jacques François Blondel on architecture, Louis Daubenton on natural history, André Deslandes on navigation, Antoine Louis on medicine, Jean Jacques Rousseau on music, and Diderot himself on painting. The first seven volumes were published at the rate of one per year until, by 1759, French censors suppressed them. Diderot published the last ten volumes without official authorization in 1756–66.

One original purpose of publishing the *Encyclopédie* was to explain to the literate population the mechanics of the new technologies that recently had been invented. In the wake of censorship, however, the volumes exploited the political reality of Europe in the two generations prior to the French Revolution and inquired why absolutist governments repressed freedom, particularly of religion, by means of torture ordered or sanctioned by courts of law. Many contributors to the *Encyclopédie* drew upon thoughts written by Montesquieu, who died in 1755 just as, about half of the encyclopedist articles appeared in print. These articles relied upon Montesquieu's *Lettres Persanes* (Persian Letters) of 1721, a satire of the French monarchy and royalist society of that epoch; and upon his *De l'Esprit des Lois* (The Spirit of Laws) of 1748 that advocated the separation of the legislative, executive, and judicial branches of government to achieve a check and balance of power. In *The Federalist* No. 47, James Madison acknowledged Montesquieu as being at least the functional author of the separation of powers principle so important to the constitutional organization of both the Federal and state governments in the United States of America.[1]

The combined force of the encyclopédists contributed to the French Revolution, the United States Constitution, and the "classical" school of criminology fashioned in part by Cesare Bonesana, the Italian Marchese di Beccaria, with publication in his *Trattato dei délitti è elle pèna* in Italy during 1764, and of its translation as *Essay on Crimes and Punishment* in London during 1767. In his *Essay*, Beccaria paid tribute to Montesquieu expressly, noting that while Montesquieu paid but brief attention to the deplorable state of the administration of criminal justice throughout eighteenth-century Europe, nevertheless Montesquieu inspired many of Beccaria's own ideas.[2] How many of Beccaria's ideas were induced by Montesquieu, or by anyone else for that matter, cannot be measured with certainty, as Sir Leon Radzinowicz has concluded:

It is hard to generalize from the theories of philosophers so diverse as Rousseau and Voltaire, Montesquieu and Diderot. . . . But a few leading ideas emerge beyond dispute. All were affected by the growing scientific approach. All turned to reason and common sense as weapons against the old order. All revolted against the unquestioned acceptance of tradition and authority. All found easy targets in the inefficiency, corruption and sheer chaos of existing institutions. All protested against the pervading superstition and cruelty.[3]

FROM REALISM TO IDEALISM

In his *Essay on Crimes and Punishment*, consisting of forty-two short sections, Beccaria covers six major areas of thought, as the English barrister Coleman Phillipson has observed:

1. Measure of crimes and punishment.
2. Certainty of punishment with no right of pardon.
3. Nature and division of crimes and relative punishments.
4. Consideration of certain punishments.
5. Criminal procedure, including secret accusations and torture.
6. Prevention of crimes.[4]

Each of these six areas of thought reflects an important tenet of both the "classical" school of criminology and of eighteenth-century idealism in general, from which Beccaria's ideas emerged.

Beccaria declared that the true measure of crimes is the injury done to society and not the offender's mental disposition, known as intent, on which turned punishments for most crimes under the English common law. Nor should crimes be measured by the rank or social position of the victim, or by religious doctrine if the conduct does not endanger the public security, in contrast to the practice under the civil law of France and most other continental European countries of the time. These were objectives under the English common law. The law must be certain and invariable, Beccaria warned, and it should not depend upon the capriciousness or temperament of a particular judge. For this reason, he urged, the law should be definite and fixed, free from obscurity, publicized in the vernacular language, and not subject to judicial interpretation. Only in this fashion, Beccaria thought, could the population depend on the law to be uniform from case to case.

Punishment has to be certain and prompt, Beccaria declared, because the more speedily the penalty follows the crime, the more closely the punishment is connected with the wrongful conduct of the offender. Moreover, the criminal offender should be spared suspense and have his guilt or innocence resolved without delay. The objective of punishment should not be simply to inflict pain on the offender or to undo a crime already perpetrated, Beccaria reasoned, relying upon Plato[5] and Seneca.[6] Instead, the purpose of punishment should be to prevent a wrongdoer from repeating his offense and to deter other potential criminals from committing similar offenses. For this reason, Beccaria opposed the transportation of criminal offenders to the then-remote areas of the world such as Australia and New Zealand, because there they would not be visible to the public and, consequently, would exert no deterrent impact. However, Beccaria felt that punishments as well as the methods of inflicting them should be selected in proportion to the severity of the offense alone, disregarding the intent or motive of the offender. On balance, the punishment inflicted upon an offender's body should be the least amount necessary to achieve the greatest impression on that offender's mind and on the minds of other persons. Thus, the disadvantage of punishment should exceed the advantage of the crime for which the punishment is inflicted, but just barely so. Any greater amount of punishment, Beccaria declared, would be superfluous, useless, and tyrannical. The value of punishment rests in its inevitability more than in its violence, Beccaria thought.

In the eighteenth century, as now, the victim of a crime was free to elect whether to bring a civil action at law against his offender to seek money damages as reparation for the private harm done to him. With this, Beccaria had no quarrel. However, in the eighteenth century, unlike today, the victim of a minor crime enjoyed the prerogative of par-

don, and he could unilaterally release his offender from punishment for
the crime. Although Beccaria found this practice to be humane and merciful, he argued against it because he deemed it contrary to public policy. The right of punishment rests with the community at large through
the power of the state, Beccaria reckoned, and over this collective right
an individual should possess no control. When people perceive that a
crime may be pardoned, Beccaria worried, then they are encouraged to
hope for impunity, and, if punished anyway, they will come to feel that
their punishment is capricious. Instead, Beccaria insisted, the law should
be inexorable. If punishments are moderate and applied both expedi-
tiously and regularly, Beccaria felt there should be no need for mercy.
Clemency is the virtue of the legislator, not of those whose duty it is to
enforce the laws, according to Beccaria. Clearly, he viewed the judicial
role as being one of law enforcement as opposed to legislation.

Beccaria discerned three classes of crimes: (1) acts affecting the security of the state or of its sovereign, such as treason; (2) acts injuring
the life, property, or honor of an individual citizen; and (3) acts contrary
to the positive or negative obligations which bind all people to the public weal. Every citizen should be free to do whatever he pleases provided what he does is not forbidden by law, Beccaria asserted, because
it is this sort of freedom that produces vigorous souls and enlightened
minds.

Injuries to the victim's person should be punished by corporal penalties, Beccaria reflected, just as injuries to the victim's honor should be
punished by the offender's disgrace. Theft should be punished by means
of a fine, Beccaria concluded, because one who enriches himself at another's expense should suffer at his own expense. However, Beccaria
recognized that, frequently, impoverished people steal, and their despair
would be aggravated by fines. Therefore, Beccaria recommended that
thieves provide compensation to society through temporary servitude.
When a thief uses violence in the commission of his crime, Beccaria
said that he should receive both corporal and servile punishment. The
smuggler should lose not only the contraband but also everything else
found in his possession. Thus, Beccaria suggested forfeiture of property
as a punishment for smuggling.

In the first edition of his *Essay*, Beccaria contended that a bankrupt
person ought to be kept guarded in pledge of his debts or else employed
as a slave to labor for his creditors. Subsequently, Beccaria wrote that
he was ashamed of advocating such penalties and that in doing so he
offended the rights of humanity.[7] He came to distinguish between the
innocent and the fraudulent insolvent debtor. He found it barbarous to
throw the innocent bankrupt in prison when, instead, he should be per-

mitted to satisfy his creditors while working at liberty. As to fraudulent insolvent debtors, however, Beccaria would treat them as he would counterfeiters, by imprisonment. Beccaria proposed that society strive to avoid bankruptcies, such as by requiring contracts to be registered, and by establishing a public bank with funds from taxes levied on prosperous commercial transactions and using this bank to relieve the debts of unfortunate but deserving citizens.

Effective use of the police should prevent the third class of crimes, Beccaria foresaw. Crimes such as adultery, infanticide, and pederasty (sexuality between adults and children), being so difficult to prove, call for preventive measures rather than indiscriminate punishment, Beccaria urged, and suicide should not be punished at all but left to God.

Contrary to virtually all of the encyclopedists, including Diderot, Montesquieu, Rousseau, and Voltaire, Beccaria opposed capital punishment as a penalty for most crimes. In fact, Beccaria found the death penalty justifiable only under two circumstances: when the offender's existence threatens a dangerous revolution against a popular government; and when taking the offender's life is the only way possible to deter others from committing crimes similar to his. Phillipson noted that Beccaria was "the first noteworthy writer to contest the very legitimacy of the death penalty." [8] Beccaria witnessed the spectacle of capital punishment as making martyrs out of those who were executed, principally because onlookers tend to feel compassion for anyone who is killed. However, Beccaria advanced two major arguments in opposition to the death penalty: (1) it is unjust because, in most instances, it is unnecessary; and (2) it is not the most efficacious deterrent to crime. Beccaria regarded penal servitude as being a deterrent much greater than capital punishment, because it can be stretched out over a longer period of time and because it is more painful to those who watch or hear about it than it is for those who receive it.

On the other hand, Beccaria favored banishment from the locality, although he distinguished this from the popular European practice of transporting offenders to faraway places. Beccaria viewed banishment as an appropriate penalty for persons who disturbed the public peace. Also, he saw it as a proper punishment even for atrocious offenders whose guilt was probable but not certain, because it would give a convict time to establish his innocence, an opportunity foreclosed by death.

Beccaria condemned secret accusations, known as *lettres de cachet*, because he admonished that secrecy is the strongest shield of tyranny. In the absence of prima facie evidence pointing to the guilt of someone accused of a crime, Beccaria argued that the accused should not be kept in pretrial confinement. He thought that an accused should have some opportunity to challenge the selection of his judges or jurors and that if an accused offender was of a different social rank from his alleged victim, then half of the jury selected to decide his fate should be comprised of persons of his own rank and the other half of persons of the victim's rank.

A great deal of Beccaria's attention focused on the quantity and quality of proof that should be necessary to support a criminal conviction. He insisted that all proof should be set forth in public and that each verdict should be pronounced in open court. He thought that a jury should be selected by lot and that their verdict should be supported by proof to a moral certainty. The defendant should be allowed an amount of time fixed by law within which to discover the evidence against him and prepare his defense. Beccaria maintained steadfastly that a person accused of a crime should be permitted to offer evidence like any other witness, and he opposed the tradition of the times whereby a person accused of a crime became "civilly dead" and, therefore, prohibited from testifying.

Beccaria warned that the value of testimony is dependent upon the credibility of the witness offering it. The more marked the hostility or the closer the friendship of a witness to the accused, the less reliable his testimony becomes. What is more, Beccaria took exception to an assumption of the times whereupon the more serious the crime alleged, the more credible each witness became. On the contrary, Beccaria retorted that the more serious the crime, the less credible a witness' testimony should be. He was skeptical of the practice, still used today, of promising impunity to an accomplice if he would turn "king's evidence" (now state's evidence) and testify against a codefendant, because of the opportunity for treachery.

Torture, Beccaria stated incisively, is a certain method for the acquittal of robust villains and for the condemnation of innocent but feeble men. He found torture barbarous, useless, wrong, and more harmful to the innocent who have nothing to gain from it than to the guilty who seek to shield themselves from punishment.

It is better to prevent than to punish crimes, Beccaria declared at the end of his *Essay*. Many crimes are more preventable than they are discoverable. Beccaria felt that laws prescribing criminal penalties lacked justice unless their provisions maximized prevention of the conduct they would punish. Crime prevention can be accentuated also by magistrates who seek to preserve rather than to corrupt the laws, Beccaria noted, and he suggested that where a greater rather than a lesser number of people serve as magistrates, the less likely it is that they will be corrupt. Beccaria offered additional suggestions for preventing crime, including improvement of education generally and a system of prizes offered to reward virtue.

The Spread of Beccaria's Influence

The influence of Beccaria extended to the other major reformists of eighteenth-century Europe and America and, through them, to the new ideas in government which they created. Voltaire added his *Commentary* to the French edition of Beccaria's *Essay* and recommended it to his friends, many of whom held high office. Among Voltaire's admirers were Pope Clement XIV, Emperor Josef II of Austria, Emperor Frederick the Great of Prussia, Empress Catherine II of Russia, King Gustavus III of Sweden, King Christian VII of Denmark, and King Stanislas of Poland. Thomas Jefferson's *Commonplace Book* (1776) contains twenty-six extracts from Beccaria's *Essay*, most quoted in the original Italian.[9] When John Adams rose in Boston to deliver his famous speech in defense of Corporal William Wemms and five other British soldiers accused of murder in the event that became known as the Boston Massacre, whom he defended successfully, his opening words were:

May it please your honors, and you, gentlemen of the jury: I am for the prisoners at the bar, and shall apologize for it only in the words of the marquis Beccaria: If I can but be the instrument of preserving one life; his blessing and tears of transport shall be a sufficient consolation to me for the contempt of all mankind.[10]

Without question, then, Beccaria's idealism spread to the new world and was accepted by those who shortly thereafter would become founders of a new nation, the United States of America.

At the same time, other writers adopted the thoughts and values of Beccaria, thereby contributing to the dissemination of his ideas to an ever wider audience. In France, Pastoret drew up a list of 120 capital offenses and proposed a reorganization of the French laws following Beccaria's principles, favoring noncapital penalties.[11] Other French writers such as De la Madeleine, Marat, and later Condorcet advanced similar arguments. Von Sonnenfels, a professor in Vienna, argued against torture as well as the death penalty.[12] So did Amalry in Holland, Mello Freire in Portugal, and notable thinkers such as Campomanes, Jovellanos, and Lardizabal in Spain. In Italy in 1777, Beccaria's friend Piètro Verri drafted an article opposing torture, in which he demonstrated the absurdity of confessions.[13] Paolo Risi had written a similar treatise in 1766,[14] two years after Beccaria's *Essay*. In Naples, Filangieri condemned secret accusations and horrible prison conditions in his book, *Science of Legislation*.[15] Renazzi argued in his work, "The Elements of Criminal Law,"[16] that penalties should be graduated according to the severity of each offense. The Italian legal scholars of the time such as Cremani, Defalco, and Nani argued that ancient Roman laws should be replaced by less oppressive new legislation.

In 1771, the English legal scholar William Eden (later Lord Auckland) wrote, after acknowledging his debt to Beccaria, that:

The great object of the lawgiver is the prevention of crimes. . . . Vengeance belongeth to no man. . . . Lenity should be the guardian of moderate governments. . . . The excess of penalty flatters the imagination with the hope of impunity. . . . The acerbity of justice deadens its execution. . . . Penal laws are to check the arm of wickedness, but not to wage war with the natural sentiments of the heart. . . . Obsolete and useless statutes should be repealed, for they debilitate the authority of such as still exist and are necessary. . . . Nothing but the evident result of absolute necessity can authorize the destruction of mankind by the hand of man. The infliction of death is not, therefore, to be considered in any instance as a mode of punishment, but merely as our last melancholy resource in the extermination of those from society, whose continuance among their fellow citizens is become inconsistent with the public safety.[17]

Henry Home (also Lord Kames), a Scottish jurist, opposed capital punishment beginning in 1758 and continued that argument in his book, *Historical Law-Tracts*, published in 1776.[18] Lord Mansfield, William Blackstone, and other leading eighteenth-century English legal scholars praised Beccaria, but none more so than Jeremy Bentham who wrote of Beccaria as:

my master, first evangelist of reason, who has raised thy Italy so much above England and also France . . . thou who speakest reason on laws, whilst in France they speak only jargon (which, however, is reason itself compared with the English jargon), thou who hast made such frequent and useful excursions in the paths of utility.[19]

On the other hand, paradoxically, England seemed moved more by Beccaria's stand against pardons than his posture against capital punishment. In 1770, Sir William Meredith introduced a bill into Parliament calling for appointment of a committee to investigate capital offenses, remarking:

Our criminal code breathes the spirit of Draco, whose laws were written in blood. In a well-regulated state nothing is more requisite than to proportion punishment to the crime, and thereby satisfy the mind of the people that equal justice is administered to every delinquent. At present, however, the crimes of larceny and petty theft, as well as of treason and murder, are alike punished with death. . . . From seeing the number of criminals who are pardoned, people are induced to commit offences under the idea that they can do so with impunity.[20]

In 1784, Archdeacon William Paley defended the practice of carrying out executions in his book entitled *Moral and Political Philosophy*, as did Martin Madan the following year in his *Thoughts on Executive Justice*. Fearing the impact on crime of too many pardons, the English crown curtailed its lenient clemency policy, and in England executions were carried out at a higher rate during the last decade of the eighteenth century than they had been at any time since the Enlightenment.

Beccaria had a less confusing impact upon justice on the continent of Europe. In Russia, Empress Catherine II tried unsuccessfully to have Beccaria visit her court. In 1766, she convened a commission and directed it to compile an all-new criminal code, the *Instructions*, for which she wrote personally in her own hand, clearly influenced by Beccaria:

The political liberty of a Citizen is the Peace of Mind arising from the Consciousness, that every Individual enjoys his peculiar Safety; and in order that the People might attain this Liberty, the Laws ought to be so framed, that no one Citizen should stand in Fear of another; but that all of them should stand in Fear of the same Laws. —Every Punishment, which is not inflicted through Necessity, is tyrannical. —Experience teaches, that, in those Countries where Punishments are mild, they operate with the same Efficacy upon the Minds of the Citizens, as the most severe in other Places. —It is unjust to punish a Thief, who robs on the High-way, in the same Manner as another, who not only robs, but commits Murder. Every One sees clearly that some Difference ought to be made in their Punishment, for the Sake of the general Safety.[21]

After setting the tone of her new code, Catherine II went on to become much more specific concerning the amount of punishment and the method of its infliction, again drawing almost entirely from Beccaria:

All punishments, by which the human Body might be maimed, ought to be abolished. —We ought to hear what the Defendant has to say. . . . He ought therefore either to answer for himself, or choose any other Person to speak in his Behalf. —The usage of Torture is contrary to all Dictates of Nature and Reason; even Mankind itself cries out against it, and demands loudly the total Abolition of it. —(Torture) is a sure method of condemning an *innocent* Person of a weakly Constitution, and of acquitting a *wicked* Wretch, who depends upon the Robustness of his Frame. —To make an Oath too cheap by frequent Practice, is to weaken the Obligation of it, and to destroy its Efficacy. . . . — When the Defendant is condemned, it is not the Judges who inflict the Punishment upon him, but the Law. —Nothing is so dangerous, as this general Axiom: *The Spirit of the Law ought to be considered, and not the Letter.* —By making the *penal* Laws always *clearly* intelligible, *Word by Word*, everyone may calculate truly, and know exactly the inconveniences of a bad Action. — We may admit the Testimony of *any Person*, who has *no Reason* to be a false Witness. By these Means the *Credibility* of the Evidence, will be *greater* or *less*, *in Proportion* to the Hatred, or Friendship, or Connections, or Differences, *subsisting* between the *Witness* and the *Party* accused. In a Reign of Peace and Tranquility . . . there can be *no* Necessity for *taking away the Life* of a Citizen. —It is better to *prevent* Crimes, than to *punish* them. —The *most sure*, but, at the same time, the *most difficult* Expedient to mend the morals of the People, is a perfect System of Education. —That the Punishment should not seem to proceed from the Violence of one, or many, who rise up against a Citizen, it ought to be public, as speedy as the Good of the Community requires, and as moderate as possible; and according to the Circumstances, proportioned to the Crime, and precisely *expressed* in the Laws. —All this will never please those Flatterers, who are daily instilling this pernicious Maxim into all the Soverigns on Earth, *That their People are created for them only*. But We think, and esteem it Our Glory to declare, "That We are created for Our People. . . ." [22]

Catherine appointed 652 members to her commission, representing all classes from each province of Russia. War with the Turks prevented the full implementation of Catherine the Great's *Instructions*, but most of her basic Beccarian principles were fulfilled in Russia.

The Swedish Parliament approved sweeping criminal law reforms on Janury 20, 1779, inspired by King Gustavus III, who admired Beccaria. Sweden abolished torture formally in 1786, having abandoned that practice years earlier. In Prussia, Emperor Frederick II abolished torture upon coming to the throne, then devoted most of his reign to the task of drafting a completely revised set of laws, civil and criminal. On September 5, 1777, he wrote to Voltaire: "Beccaria has left nothing to glean after him; we need only to follow what he has so wisely indicted." [23] Frederick the Great died in 1786, but in 1794 his new code of laws went into effect as the General Prussian Territorial Code, which restricted capital punishment to a very few serious crimes. Maria Theresa had opposed Beccarian reforms in Austria, and these were absent from her code of 1769. She did abolish torture in 1776, however, influenced by Sonnenfels. Her successor, Emperor Josef II, initiated the drafting of a new criminal code for Austria in 1787, and it limited capital punishment to treason.

As France moved steadily toward revolution, some of Beccaria's reforms were implemented. King Louis XVI abolished "preparatory" torture in 1780 and "preliminary" torture in 1788. As part of his edict of May 8, 1788, also, Louis required criminal convictions to be accompanied by written reasons supporting guilt of the accused; ruled that the death penalty must be the unanimous vote of three judges instead of a majority vote of two; and gave persons acquitted of a criminal charge the right to seek reparations for injury to their reputations.[24] These reforms did not avert revolution, for within two months the Estates General was convened on July 8, 1788, and the end of the French monarchy approached.

The power passed to the "citizens," who delivered *Cahiers* to their representatives demanding, among other things, equality under the law, abolition of crimes against morals and religion, suppression of the discretionary powers of judges, the assistance of counsel during criminal proceedings, trial by jury open to the public, termination of an ancient tradition requiring an accused to deny his guilt under oath, and elimination of punishments imposed against a convicted offender's family. On October 8-9, 1789, the Constituent Assembly approved the principles contained in the Declaration of the Rights of Man dated August 26, 1789, which had originated from Beccaria's *Essay* almost verbatim: "The law has the right to prohibit only actions harmful to society and the law shall inflict only such punishments as are strictly and clearly necessary, and no one shall be punished, except in virtue of a law enacted before the offense and legally applied."[25] The laws enacted on October 8-9, 1789, opened trials to the public and allowed the assistance of counsel.

In 1790, laws punishing an accused's relatives were repealed, as were laws that had permitted the general confiscation of property from a convicted offender. The Penal Code of October 6, 1791, prescribed punishments according to the seriousness of each crime. This was modified in 1795 by the Code of Misdemeanors and Punishments, which contained 646 articles, many taken directly from Beccaria.

The United States Constitution contains Beccarian principles, also, and was drafted in the 1787 Convention. Chief examples of Beccaria's influence within the Constitution proper are: Article I, section 9, which provides that "No Bill of Attainder or ex post facto Law shall be passed (by Congress)"; in Article I, section 10, which provides that "No State shall . . . grant Letters of Marque and Reprisal . . . pass any Bill of Attainder [or] ex post facto Law"; Article III, section 2, which provides: "The Trial of all Crimes, except in Cases of Impeachment, shall be by Jury; and such Trial shall be held in the State where the said Crimes shall have been committed"; and in Article III, section 3, which provides: "The Congress shall have Power to declare the Punishment of Treason, but no Attainder of Treason shall work Corruption of Blood, or Forfeiture [of property] except during the Life of the Person attained."

Writing in No. 78 of *The Federalist*, published in 1788, Alexander Hamilton observed that:

The complete independence of the courts of justice is peculiarly essential in a limited Constitution. By a limited Constitution, I understand one which contains certain specified exceptions to the legislative authority; such, for instance, as that it shall pass no bills of attainder, no ex-post-facto laws, and the like. Limitations of this kind can be preserved in practice no other way than through the medium of courts of justice, whose duty it must be to declare all acts contrary to the manifest tenor of the Constitution void. Without this, all the reservations of particular rights or privileges would amount to nothing.[26]

Unlike Beccaria, however, Hamilton and the other founders of the United States Constitution viewed the role of the judiciary as being to interpret, not merely to carry out, the laws. Thus, also in No. 78 of *The Federalist*, Hamilton continued:

The interpretation of the laws is the proper and peculiar province of the courts. A constitution is, in fact, and must be regarded by the judges, as a fundamental law. It therefore belongs to them to ascertain its meaning, as well as the meaning of any particular act proceeding from the legislative body. If there should happen to be an irreconcilable variance between the two, that which has the superior obligation and validity ought, of course, to be preferred; or, in other words, the Constitution ought to be preferred to the statute, the intention of the people to the intention of their agents.

But, returning to basic Beccarian tenets, Hamilton qualified his point:

Nor does the conclusion by any means suppose a superiority of the judicial to the legislative power. It only supposes that the power of the people is superior to both; and that where the will of the legislature, declared in its statutes, stands in opposition to that of the people, declared in the Constitution, the judges ought to be governed by the latter rather than the former. They ought to regulate their decisions by the fundamental laws, rather than by those which are not fundamental. . . .

The courts must declare the sense of the law; and if they should be disposed to exercise WILL instead of JUDGMENT, the consequence would equally be the substitution of their pleasure to that of the legislative body. The observation, if it proves anything, would prove that there ought to be no judges distinct from that body.

If, then, the courts of justice are to be considered as the bulwarks of a limited Constitution against the legislative encroachments, this consideration will
afford a strong argument for the permanent tenure of judicial offices, since nothing
will contribute so much as this to that independent spirit in the judges which
must be essential to the faithful performance of so arduous a duty.[27]

Additional examples of Beccaria's philosophy emerge within the Bill
of Rights, or first ten amendments to the United States Constitution,
proposed in 1789 and ratified in 1791. The Sixth and Eighth Amendments epitomize Beccaria's stance:

[Amendment VI] In all criminal prosecutions, the accused shall enjoy the right
to a speedy and public trial, by an impartial jury of the State and district wherein
the crime shall have been committed, which district shall have been previously
ascertained by law, and to be informed of the nature and cause of the accusation; to be confronted with the witnesses against him; to have compulsory process for obtaining witnesses in his favor, and to have the Assistance of Counsel
for his defence.
[Amendment VIII] Excessive bail shall not be required, nor excessive fines imposed, nor cruel and unusual punishments inflicted.

Other eighteenth-century idealists besides Beccaria influenced the design
of the new American federation, including Montesquieu particularly, at
all levels of government. For instance, each of the original thirteen states
followed the separation of powers doctrine and made their courts distinct from the legislative and executive authorities.[28]

Each of the original states reduced the number of crimes for which
capital punishment could be imposed, also. On March 25, 1794, the
Pennsylvania General Assembly passed An Act for the Better Preventing of Crimes and for Abolishing and Punishment of Death in Certain
Cases, through which this state abolished capital punishment except for
first-degree murder.[29] In 1785, Thomas Jefferson introduced his Bill of
Proportioning Crimes and Punishments in Cases heretofore Capital before the Virginia House of Delegates. He had drafted the bill in 1778,
but even in 1785 it failed to pass the first time it was introduced, which
Jefferson explained in his autobiography:

Beccaria, and other writers on crimes and punishments, had satisfied the reasonable world of the unrightfulness and inefficacy of the punishment of crimes
by death; and hard labor on roads, canals and other public works had been suggested as a proper substitute. The Revisors had adopted these opinions; but the
general idea of our country had not yet advanced to that point. The bill, therefore, was lost in the House of Delegates by a majority of a single vote. . . .

[M]eanwhile, the public opinion was ripening, by time, reflection, and by the example of Pennsylvania. . . . In 1796 [the Virginia] legislature resumed the subject, and passed the law for amending the penals of the Commonwealth.[30]

Jefferson agreed with Beccaria on another point as well: that in a judicial system having moderate laws, the executive authority does not need to pardon convicted criminal offenders. He wrote: "[W]hen laws are made as mild as they should be, . . . pardons are absurd. The principle of Beccaria is sound. Let the legislators be merciful, but the executors of the law inexorable."[31] Jefferson did not favor wide discretion in law enforcement.

In 1791, Beccaria himself was offered a role in the drafting of actual laws. When the Austrian Code of 1787 was enacted, Emperor Josef II had decided not to implement it in Lombardy, the Italian province with Milan as its capital which Austria ruled and where Beccaria lived. When Josef decided in 1791 to appoint a commission to recommend what portions of the Austrian Code should be extended to Lombardy, he named Beccaria as well as Paolo Nisi to the commission. While the full commission was being assembled, Beccaria was invited to submit his personal critique of the Austrian Code of 1787, which he did in 1791 under the title of *Brief Reflections*.[32] A year later, in 1792, the commission divided into two factions, and both submitted reports on their conflicting views of punishment. Beccaria joined in one of these reports[33] with two other commission members, Risi and Gallarati-Scotti.

In his *Brief Reflections*, Beccaria distinguished major crimes (*delitti*) from minor offenses (*delitti politici*) and noted that whereas the former tend to destroy society, the latter only damage it. Therefore, Beccaria recommended, the principal objective of punishment for major crimes should be deterrence of others besides the convicted offender, while the fundamental purpose of punishment for minor ones should be to correct the individual wrongdoer. Consequently, he favored long prison terms to be served under harsh conditions by persons convicted of a major crime but light and unembarrassing penalties for those who committed minor offenses. Thus, Beccaria opposed the Austrian Code in his *Brief Reflections* because the same penalties (such as flogging and the pillory) were imposable for both major and minor offenses, the only difference being in the duration and intensity of the punishment. Beccaria felt that penalties which disgraced the minor offender were likely to make him into a major offender.

Unlike his *Essay on Crimes and Punishment*, where Beccaria insisted that punishments should be based upon the severity of the offense exclusively, without regard for the offender's social position, in his *Brief*

Reflections Beccaria seemed to argue that social background should be a factor in punishing minor crimes, because flogging would dishearten a well-bred person and bring shame upon his family, and therefore this punishment would hurt a person of higher social class more than it would someone of lower class. Because the Milanese people were not prone to violence, Beccaria reasoned, education would be preferable to punishment; but imprisonment rather than flogging should be the punishment for minor crimes, although minor offenders should be confined separately from major criminals. In the ultimate analysis, Beccaria deemed the Austrian Code too lenient toward persons who committed major offenses repeatedly, but he favored its practice of treating as minor offenders persons convicted for the first time of committing serious crimes such as robbery.

Beccaria remarked about the Austrian Code's treatment of sexual offenders, such as those convicted of adultery and prostitution. He did not oppose the Austrian Code's classification of adultery as a minor crime, nor its provision making adultery a crime only at the request of the injured spouse and then only when the injured spouse was innocent of similar behavior. Beccaria did oppose the Austrian Code's criminalization of prostitution, which he considered a "necessary evil," particularly in the cities. Perhaps this explains why Beccaria stressed in his *Brief Reflections* that an adulterous wife could do more social harm to her husband, by encountering risk of illegitimate pregnancy, than an adulterous husband could do to his wife by sleeping with a loose woman.

When the commission did meet to discuss the new Lombard Code, its membership divided essentially over the wisdom and vlaue of the death penalty. Beccaria continued to assert, as he had done in his *Essay*, that capital punishment is appropriate only for an offender whose influence is strong enough to permit his escape even from a heavily guarded prison. As an alternative, Beccaria argued for the construction of prisons, preferably near the larger cities where a dense population could observe imprisonment on a daily basis. Commission members who disagreed with Beccaria's strong stand against capital punishment seemed to fear that, if they abolished the death penalty, heinous criminals from other countries might travel to Lombardy to carry out their depredations. These members voted to permit capital punishment in cases of serious crime where absolute certainty existed as to the offender's guilt, in order to foreclose the possibility that the offender might escape and hurt or kill innocent people in the future. The commission met in several sessions but never reached any substantive agreement and dissolved as neighboring France entered revolution. Beccaria died in 1794 at the age of fifty-six. He had been inspirational as a lawgiver, and the ideals that he articulated exploded during the Enlightenment to be written into stone for all time, much as the molten lava flowing from an active volcano bursts into flames and afterwards flows toward the sea, forming igneous rock as it cools. Beccaria's brief opportunity as a lawmaker ended without bearing tangible fruit and failed to survive the test of history.

What H. G. Wells wrote of Voltaire and eighteenth-century historian Edward Gibbon he might as well have said of all eighteenth-century idealists, Beccaria included:

The ideal they sustained was the ideal of a polite and polished world in which men—men of quality that is, for no others counted—would be ashamed to be cruel or gross or enthusiastic, in which the appointments of life would be spacious and elegant, and the fear of ridicule the potent auxiliary of the law in maintaining the decorum and harmonies of life. Voltaire had in him the possibility of a passionate hatred of injustice, and his intervention on behalf of a persecuted or ill-used man are the high lights of his long and complicated life-story. . . . In an interregnum incommoded with an abundance of sleek parsons and sly priests it was hard to realize what fires had once blazed in the heart of Christianity, and what fires of political and religious passion might still blaze in the hearts of men.[34]

But Beccaria was not alone among eighteenth-century idealists in having a desire to reform the criminal justice system. The shortcomings Beccaria witnessed in the prosecution and punishment of offenders others witnessed in the prevention of crime. Policing the cities of the eighteenth century proved to be ineffective, and the demand arose for the reform of the police, also.

Police Reform

Under the Statute of Winchester, enacted by Parliament in the year 1285, London had been divided into twenty-four wards, each supervised by an alderman and protected by six watchmen. Curfew was one hour after sunset every night, at which time the gates to the city closed and so did the doors to its taverns. London was reasonably protected until the eighteenth century, when new dangers arose. The industrial revolution precipitated a meteoric rise in commerce throughout England, a period also when that country's population doubled from 6 to 12 million persons. With an increase in trade came an increase in the size of towns. Populations migrated toward the cities, such as London and Birmingham, in search of work. As the density of urban populations swelled, housing became difficult to obtain and street crime became rampant, perpetrated by what some historians have labeled as a "criminal class" of offenders who lived in slum areas called "rookeries" on the out-skirts of London.[35] In 1663, the Court of Common Council enacted leg-islation to employ one thousand watchmen or bellmen, who would work a sunset-to-sunrise shift within the city of London itself looking out for fires. These men, often drunken, shuffled along the darkened streets car-rying long staves and dimly lit lanterns, calling out the time and weather conditions periodically. They were known as the Charlies, after King Charles II during whose reign their jobs had been created. Because they were criers and not accustomed to secrecy, the whereabouts of these watchmen became known in advance to criminals in the streets, who avoided the Charlies and went on with their unlawful activities, un-daunted.

Crime flourished even more in the areas outside of the city of Lon-don, where the Charlies were not empowered to venture at all. If Lon-don had poor policing, its outskirts had no policing. Over a million peo-ple inhabited these outskirts that consisted of 152 separate parishes by the end of the eighteenth century. Law enforcement was relegated among a hierarchy of feudal authorities such as the lord high steward, high bail-iff, burgesses, court of burgesses, court leet, and annoyance jury. In 1662, one area adjacent to London known as Westminster (the site of Parlia-ment itself) passed its own Improvement Act, establishing the Commis-sioners of Scotland Yard as a new force of watchmen. Other parishes followed suit. Nevertheless, people who traveled into or away from London were attacked routinely by marauders who lived openly and no-toriously in the areas immediately adjacent to the city's boundaries.

Henry Fielding became chief magistrate of Bow Street in 1748, and three years later he published an ambitious pamphlet entitled *An Enquiry into the Causes of the Late Increase of Robbers*, which he said he in-tended to use "to rouse the civil power from its present lethargic state." To Fielding, the principal reason for major crime in the streets was the existence of an apathetical and a corrupt judiciary. Also, he believed the population was unaware of the degree to which crime had become sys-tematic. To remedy the lack of public understanding of the problem he perceived, Fielding published *The Covent Garden* as a semiweekly jour-nal throughout 1752, in which he printed accounts of various criminal cases and gave descriptions of known robbers.[36] When Henry Fielding died at the age of forty-seven, he was succeeded by his brother, John, in 1754. For the next twenty-five years, John Fielding endeavored to carry out his late brother Henry's ideals, during the course of which he published assorted pamphlets such as *A Plan for Preventing Robberies within Twenty Miles of London*. In that pamphlet, John Fielding sug-gested to metropolitan residents that they band together in groups of twenty

to generate a central data bank containing information on local criminals. Also, he published regular broadsheets that detailed the descriptions of known criminal offenders, entitled *The Quarterly Pursuit of
Criminals* and *The Weekly Pursuit*. On occasion, Fielding would publish
a supplement, known as *The Extraordinary Pursuit*. These broadsheets,
or handbills, he attached to the doors or walls of public buildings such
as churches and inns. In 1763, John Fielding established an eight-man
horse patrol to guard the roads leading to London at night, but funding
ran out and this effort lasted less than one year. John Fielding was knighted
in 1761. The significance of the contributions by Henry and Sir John
Fielding, Sir Leon Radzinowicz has noted:

as educators of public opinion, lies in the single-minded determination with which,
over a period of nearly thirty years, they strove to demonstrate to their contemporaries how serious were the dangers which threatened to engulf [England]
and how pressing was the need for discarding fragmentary remedies in favour
of a larger plan.[37]

The alternative was anarchy.

London was beset by a wave of massive violence, known as the Gordon riots, that lasted for a week during the summer of 1780. A sweeping discontent sent violent mobs on a rampage. The mobs started fires
throughout the city, being stopped only when the army intervened at the
personal command of King George III. The watchmen were ineffective
in maintaining order. Among the property destroyed by fire during the
riots was the Bow Street archive of Sir John Fielding, a repository of
criminal justice information. The decade of the 1780s was turbulent in
England, with the American Revolution underway and the French Revolution becoming inevitable. Citizens disagreed as to how law could be
restored in the streets. Some favored volunteer organizations of armed
civilians. There was little consensus in Parliament on any issue in 1783
when William Pitt became prime minister of a coalition party heavily
fragmented. In 1785, Pitt's solicitor-general introduced into Parliament
a bill drafted by the Bow Street magistrates that called for creation of a
unified District of the Metropolis consisting of the City of London and
its outskirts. A board of three commissioners was to be appointed by the
king, under which a chief constable would be appointed for each of nine
divisions. The chief constable would supervise a force of petty constables who would become "ministerial officers of the peace" and patrol
their divisions on foot and horseback. Magistrates would be stripped of
authority over policing and would continue only as judicial officers; but
they revolted to retain their dual powers, and Pitt's government re-

lented. When the bill was withdrawn in Parliament, major reform of the police was destined not to occur in London for another forty-four years.

In the interim, minor police reforms occurred in London. The Middlesex Justices Act of 1792 added seven magistrates' offices to the metropolitan area besides the one at Bow Street. Three magistrates would work out of an office, each being paid four hundred pounds a year. A magistrate's office could hire six full-time constables, at a salary of twelve shillings per man per week. By 1797, the informal police organization known as the Bow Street Runners that Henry Fielding had started in 1750 had grown to a force of about seventy men. In 1798, West Indian merchants financed creation of the Marine Police Establishment, a force of about sixty salaried officers whose duty became to protect commerce along the river docks. By 1800, about one hundred twenty full-time officers worked the greater London area.

Where England had dallied, Ireland had rallied, however, and William Pitt's 1785 bill was enacted almost verbatim by the Irish Parliament in 1786. F. W. Maitland remarked a century later that "[a] full history of the new police would probably lay its first scene in Ireland, and begin with the Dublin Police Act passed by the Irish Parliament in 1786."[38] In Boston, policing had been the responsibility of constables and watchmen since 1634, young men over eighteen years old having been subject to being drafted for either duty.[39] Civil and criminal warrants were executed in Boston by the county sheriff since 1692.[40] By statute enacted in 1801, Boston alone among Massachusetts towns was required by law to keep the watch continuously, because of its "size and the character of its population."[41] By the close of the eighteenth century, therefore, as towns grew into cities in England and America, citizens came to appreciate the need for full-time policing of their communities, but they lacked much sense as to how to fulfill this need.

Prison Reform

Implementation of idealist prison reform ideas followed from the theoretical framework of Beccaria and Karl Christian Friedrich Krause, whose manuscript, *Das System der Rechtsphilosophie*, written in the 1820s, German criminologist Karl Roeder revised and caused to be republished in 1874. Inspired directly by Beccaria, Alexander Maconochie and John Haviland came to create major penal institutions in the early nineteenth century. Maconochie, a retired Royal Navy captain of Scottish ancestry, accompanied Arctic explorer Sir John Franklin to Tasmania in 1837 when Franklin became lieutenant governor of Van Diemen's Land, an English prison colony there. At the same time, England released its Molesworth

Committee report in which the system of transporting convicts to Australia was praised. Although Franklin was in charge of the prisoners England transported to Tasmania, Maconochie criticized the system of transportation severely, for which Franklin dismissed him as his private secretary. While continuing to reside in Tasmania, Maconochie published many of his thoughts on penology, such as *Thoughts on Convict Management* in 1838 and its *Supplement*[42] the following year. At about the same time, in Philadelphia, John Haviland, a young architect without an abundance of private clients, designed American prisons. From 1823 until 1836, he supervised construction of Pennsylvania's Eastern Penitentiary, known as Cherry Hill, in Philadelphia. Subsequently, in the late 1830s Haviland designed New York City's nineteenth century judicial center known as the Tombs because it resembled an Egyptian pyramid; the Dauphin county jail in Harrisburg, Pennsylvania in 1840; the Berks County jail in Reading, Pennsylvania in 1846; and the Lancaster County jail in Lancaster, Pennsylvania in 1849. Haviland died suddenly in 1852.

Haviland's designs for Pennsylvania prisons were inspired by Quaker precepts as well as Beccaria. As early as 1682, William Penn instituted a Quaker penal code for Pennsylvania that prioritized reform of criminal offenders over their punishment.[43] The Act of 1821, known as the Eastern Penitentiary Act, authorized erection of a prison on Cherry Hill to alleviate overcrowding at the Walnut Street Jail, but provided expressly that "the principle of solitary confinement of the prisoners be preserved and maintained."[44] The correctional philosophy of Alexander Maconochie, also, stemmed from Quaker origins, at least in part. Two Quakers, James Backhouse and George Washington Walker, resided in Van Diemen's Land in 1837 with Maconochie and influenced him greatly.[45] By 1839, England tired of Maconochie's criticism of its traditional colonial prisons, and appointed him superintendent of the prison at Norfolk Island where Maconochie was invited to test his prison reform proposals himself. There, Maconochie implemented a system that required prisoners to complete a certain number of tasks, as opposed to serving a fixed number of months, as the precondition to their release. By 1844 when Maconochie returned to England, he had dismantled the gallows at Norfolk, abolished the traditional requirement that prisoners must cringe in front of guards, permitted prisoners to use cutlery utensils while dining, allowed prisoners to earn the right to wear clothes other than prison uniforms, and constructed both churches and schools for prisoners to attend. Maconochie's reforms whereby convicts were encouraged to prove their self-improvement via deeds became known as the "Mark System," and is said to have been a precursor of what today we call the indeterminate sentence.

The basic axioms of Maconochie's Mark System were set forth in his 1846 book, *Crime and Punishment*, and are as follows:

(i) Sentences should not be for imprisonment for a period of time, but for the performance of a determined and specified quantity of labor; in brief, time sentences should be abolished, and task sentences substituted;

(ii) The quantity of labour a prisoner must perform should be expressed in a number of marks which he must earn, by improvement in conduct, frugality of living, and habits of industry, before he can be released;

(iii) Whilst in prison a prisoner should earn everything he receives; all else should be added to his debt of marks;

(iv) When qualified by discipline to do so he should work in association with a small number of other prisoners, forming a group of six or seven, and the whole group should be answerable for the conduct and labour of each member of it;

(v) In the final stage, a prisoner, whilst still obliged to earn his daily tally of marks, should be given a proprietary interest in his own labour and be subject to a less rigorous discipline in order to prepare him for release into society.

In 1849, Maconochie became governor of the Birmingham Borough Prison, but was dismissed within two years amidst allegations that he was too lenient in disciplining some of the less tractable prisoners. He died in 1860, but among his disciples was Sir Walter Crofton who headed the board of directors of the Irish Prison System and upon whose thought the New York Prison Association predicated much of its philosophy under Enoch Wines and Theodore Dwight in the middle of the nineteenth century.[46]

A firm supporter of the Pennsylvania prison system in the latter years of the nineteenth century, even after that system had gone out of fashion in America, was Karl Roeder. While Krause had demanded education of prisoners, arguing that punishment is nothing more than a right to educate the subliterate, Roeder expanded upon Krause's *Rechtsphilosophie* in both editions of his *Grundzüge des Naturrechts oder der Rechtsphilosophie*, that of 1846 and that of 1863.[47] Among those who influenced Roeder, besides Krause, were Francis Lieber, Nicolaus Heinrich Julius, and Alexis de Tocqueville, all of whom had visited the Philadelphia prison system and then written about it,[48] which Roeder read. In the end, Roeder came to advocate a system of punishment that could "heal the will" of the criminal offender by improving each offender's capacity for "moral resistance." Thus, the convicted criminal owes and must pay a moral debt to God and to society, according to Roeder, in order to atone for his crimes. Through Roeder's influence, a variety of German states constructed solitary confinement-style prisons, patterned after Cherry Hill, beginning with Prussia in 1832 at Insterburg and continuing with Berlin's Moabit prison in 1849.

At the Third Congress dedicated to Charities, Correction and Philanthropy, held in Frankfurt in 1857, Roeder argued that reform alone, rather than the traditional *three* elements of punishment (expiation, deterrence and reformation) was an acceptable purpose of punishment.[49] Moreover, Roeder contended that complete solitary confinement is necessary for reform and must not be commuted except for children under the age of twelve and adult prisoners who are terminally ill. Roeder's exception for children is consistent with his belief that offenders under the age of fourteen should be kept segregated from adult prisoners.[50] Perhaps the most perfect European counterpart of Philadelphia's Cherry Hill (Eastern State) Prison was the Bruchal Prison built at Baden in 1848 and opened in 1851. The German Criminal Code of 1871 required that each prisoner spend the first three years of a sentence in solitary confinement, another example of Karl Roeder's influence and of unadulterated idealism unaffected by the pragmatic consideration that, to work and pay for his keep, a prisoner cannot remain in solitary confinement for too long.

NOTES

1. In this article, published on Friday, February 1, 1788, in the NEW YORK PACKET, Madison wrote that Montesquieu relied heavily on the British Constitution.

2. See TRATTO DEI DÉLITTI È DELLA PÈNA 12-13 (6th ed. 1776), where Beccaria, in the closing paragraph to his introduction, pays tribute to Montesquieu's influence.

3. L. Radzinowicz, IDEOLOGY AND CRIME 4 (1966).

4. C. Phillipson, THREE CRIMINAL LAW REFORMERS: BECCARIA, BENTHAM, ROMILLY chap. 3 (1923).

5. See Plato, *Protagonist*, 324: "No one punishes a malefactor under the notion, or for the reason, that he has done wrong,—only the unreasoning fury of a beast acts in that way. No, he that would inflict rational punishment does not retaliate for a past offence, which cannot be undone; he has regard to the future, and desires that he who is punished and those who have witnessed his punishment may be deterred from offending thereafter." See also, Plato, *Laws*, xi, 934: "Not that he is punished because he did wrong, for that which is done can never be undone, but in order that in future times, he, and those who see him corrected, may utterly hate injustice, or at any rate abate much of their evil-doing."

6. See Seneca, *De ira*, i, 19: "Nemo prudens punit quia peccatum est, sed ne peccetur. Revocari enim praeteria non possunt, futura prohibentur." See also *Id.*, ii, 31.

7. *Supra*, note 4 at 66, n. 3.

8. *Id.* at 69.

9. 298-316. See also G. Chinard, ed., THE COMMONPLACE BOOK OF THOMAS JEFFERSON: A REPERTORY OF HIS IDEAS ON GOVERNMENT 38-39 (1939).

10. See Kidder, HISTORY OF THE BOSTON MASSACRE 232 (1968).

11. Pastoret, DES LOIS PENALES (1790).

12. J. von Sonnenfels, *Ueber die Abschaffung dur Tortur*; French tr. in J. Brissot de Warville, BIBLIOTHEQUE PHILOSOPHIQUE DU LEGISLATEUR, DU POLITIQUE, DU JURISCONSULTE (1783).

13. OSSERVAZIONI SULLA TORTURA (1804).

14. *Animadversiones ad criminalem jurisprudentiam pertinentes.*

15. SCIENZA DELLA LEGISLAZIONE (1780).

16. ELEMENTA JURIS CRIMINALIS (1773–81).

17. PRINCIPLES OF PENAL LAW 6-22 (1771).

18. H. Home (Lord Kames), HISTORICAL LAW-TRACTS: CRIMINAL LAW (1776).

19. From manuscript in University College, London, cited in E. Halevy, LA FORMATION DU RADICALISME PHILOSOPHIQUE 30 (1901).

20. See Fletcher, MONTESQUIEU AND ENGLISH POLITICS (1750–1800) 190 (1939). This bill failed to pass in the House of Lords.

21. See W. Reddaway, DOCUMENTS OF CATHERINE THE GREAT: THE CORRESPONDENCE WITH VOLTAIRE AND THE INSTRUCTIONS OF 1767 215-309 (Eng. tr. of 1768).

22. *Id.*

23. See M. Maestro, CESARE BECCARIA AND THE ORIGINS OF PENAL REFORM 134 (1973).

24. A. Esmein, HISTORIE DE LA PROCEDURE CRIMINELLE EN FRANCE 400-403 (1913).

25. K. Bar, A HISTORY OF CONTINENTAL CRIMINAL LAW 320 (1968).

26. In the same article, Hamilton wrote also that "there is no liberty, if the power of judging be not separated from the legislative and executive powers" and, in a related footnote, remarked: "The celebrated Montesquieu nothing." *Spirit of Laws* 186.

27. So, the United States Congress enacted the Judiciary Act of September 24, 1789, 1 Stat. 73, which authorized the appointment of federal judges for life, as well as judicial review of legislation.

28. See B. Poore, THE FEDERAL AND STATE CONSTITUTIONS, COLONIAL CHARTERS AND OTHER ORGANIC LAWS OF THE UNITED STATES 18 *et seq.* (1878).

29. Robert J. Turnbull wrote: "Several circumstances combined to make the proposed alteration expedient, and among others the small and valuable gift of

the immortal Beccaria to the world had its due weight; for on the framing of the new constitution of Pennsylvania, in 1776, the legislature was directed to proceed as soon as might be to the reformation of the penal laws and to invent punishments less sanguinary and better proportioned to the various degrees of criminality." A VISIT TO THE PHILADELPHIA PRISON 6 (1796).

30. Padover, S. ed, THE COMPLETE JEFFERSON 67 (1943).

31. Jefferson made this remark in a comment to an article entitled, "États Unis," prepared for the ENCYCLOPEDIE METHODIQUE. See Padover, ed., THE COMPLETE JEFFERSON 61 (1943).

32. The critique is entitled, "Brevi riflessioni intorno al codice generale sopra i delitti e le pene, per cio che riguarda i delitti politici." See Beccaria, OPERE 705-18 (2nd Romagnoli ed., 1804).

33. See *Id.*, 735-41. The report of the other commission members appears in C. Cantu, BECCARIA È IL DIRITTO PENALE 357-74 (1862).

34. H. G. Wells, THE OUTLINE OF HISTORY 678 (1961 ed.).

35. See J. Tobias, URBAN CRIME IN VICTORIAN ENGLAND (1967,1972).

36. See T. Critchley, A HISTORY OF POLICE IN ENGLAND AND WALES 32-34 (1967).

37. L. Radzinowicz, A HISTORY OF ENGLISH CRIMINAL LAW 14 (1956).

38. F. Maitland, JUSTICE AND POLICE 108 (1885).

39. R. Lane, POLICING THE CITY, BOSTON 1822–1885 9-10 (1967). Constables received two dollars per day for court attendance. *Id.* at 9. The duty of the volunteer watchmen was to "see that all disturbances and disorders in the night shall be prevented and suppressed." Thus, watchmen could "examine all persons, whom they [had] reason to suspect of any unlawful design, and to demand of them their business . . . and whither they [were] going; [and] enter any house of ill-fame for the purpose of suppressing any riot or disturbance." *Id.* at 10. Also, watchmen guarded the community against fires at night and lighted street lamps. *Id.* at 11.

40. *Id.* at 7.

41. *Id.* at 11.

42. SUPPLEMENT TO THOUGHTS ON CONVICT MANAGEMENT (1839).

43. Penn's code was repealed after his death, but solitary confinement as a means of fostering meditation among prisoners continued as the underlying principle in eighteenth and nineteenth century Pennsylvania prisons.

44. See T. McElwee, A CONCISE HISTORY OF THE EASTERN PENITENTIARY 144 (1835).

45. See A. Maconochie, GENERAL VIEWS REGARDING THE SOCIAL SYSTEM OF CONVICT MANAGEMENT (1839).

46. See Z. Brockway, FIFTY YEARS OF PRISON SERVICE (1912; reprinted 1969).

47. See also K. Roeder, DIE HERRSCHENDEN GRUNDLEHREN VON

VERBRECHEN UND STRAFE IN IHREN INNEREN WIDERSPRÜCHEN (1867).

48. See F. Lieber, *On the Penitentiary System in the United States*, in F. Lieber, MISCELLANEOUS WRITINGS (1881); N. Julius, DAS AMERI-KANISCHE BESSERUNGSSYSTE (1833); and G. de Beaumont and A. de Toqueville, DU SYSTÈME PÉNITENTIAIRE AUX ETATS-UNIS (1845).

49. See CONGRES INTERNATIONAL DE BIENFAISANCE DE FRANC-FORT-SUR-LE-MEIN, SESSION DE 1857 372-377, 396-399, 401-413 (1858).

50. See K. Roeder, STRAFVOLLZUG IM GEIST DES RECHTS 118-120 (1863).

4

Utilitarianism after the Mechanical Revolution

Eighteenth-century idealism inspired widespread popular desire for social change in general and, particularly, for alternatives to torture and death as penalties for criminal behavior. At the death of Beccaria in 1794, however, few practical substitutes for capital punishment existed where a serious offense had been committed because the dungeons in use up to that time were not designed to confine large numbers of people for long periods, having been intended for use merely as short-term jails to facilitate inquisition and execution. Within two decades after Beccaria's death, on the contrary, it became possible to construct fortress-style penitentiaries that could house hundreds of convicts whose factory labor could produce goods to be sold in commerce and, thus, to defray the burgeoning cost of keeping prisoners in confinement.

What made the vital difference was the adaptation of the steam engine for several uses, during a short time span that has become known since as the mechanical revolution. More than any other single idea or invention, the steam engine contributed to emergence of the prison system as we know it today. The utilitarian movement paralleled expanded use of the steam engine, first in England, then onward to the European continent and finally to America. Much of the utilitarian movement's vast impact upon the criminal justice system was catalyzed by expanded usage of steam power. Ample evidence suggests, for instance, that technology for constructing large prisons as factories, made possible by the steam engine, ushered in the goal of reforming the criminal offender through hard labor. Even Beccaria had not envisioned the prisoner as being a productive laborer. Only comparatively recently have we come to articulate the important question whether, historically, we built prisons because we needed them to house offenders or whether we convicted people of criminal offenses because we needed able bodies to do cheap labor and fill what otherwise would be empty prison cells.

UTILITARIANISM AS A PHILOSOPHY OF CRIMINOLOGY

The Steam Engine and the Industrial Revolution: Impact on Corrections Practices

The Enlightenment produced scientific as well as philosophical inquiries, and, during much of the eighteenth century, work progressed on ways to harness steam power efficiently. Scientists Denis Papin in France and Thomas Savery in England had designed model engines using steam power in their laboratories prior to 1712, but to be practical the steam engine had to be constructed of rolled sheet iron, made via a process developed in 1728. Thomas Newcomen invented an "atmospheric engine" utilizing atmospheric pressure against a vacuum created by the condensation of steam to drive a piston working a cylinder. In 1769, James Watt patented a variation of the Newcomen atmospheric engine, this one having a condenser separate from its pump, considered a major improvement. In 1781, Watt secured a second patent for a more sophisticated steam engine using a double-action system whereby steam was admitted first to one side of a piston, then to the other, being released into a condenser from each side when not driving the piston, thus creating a rotary motion. At that point, Watt's steam engine fulfilled a vital need, powering a pump capable of draining Cornish coal mines of excess water during the winter season and thereby enabling the production of coal in amounts large enough for conversion into coke. Coke generated sufficient heat to permit the smelting of iron, eventually into the harder, lighter, but stronger substance known as steel.

In 1783, British factories started producing rods and bars made of rolled iron, and these items were necessary to the creation of prison cells as we know them today. Although the Bessemer conversion process of transforming iron into steel was not perfected until 1856, and the open-hearth steel production furnace did not appear until 1864, some steel was available in the early nineteenth century, and its lighter weight and greater strength than iron enabled the construction of multiple cell tiers, six to ten stories tall, reached by narrow walkways called galleys, characteristic of fortress-style prisons modeled after the one built in 1819 at Auburn, New York.

By 1785, Watt's steam engine was put to use powering a cotton mill at Nottingham, England. This touched off what has become known since as the industrial revolution. Steam replaced water as the power source for turning factory machinery, and diversified industries sprang up in growing cities. In 1804, Richard Trevithick adapted Watt's steam engine to power a railroad locomotive, which George Stephenson rede-

signed and made into a commercial success in 1814. In 1807, Robert
Fulton launched his steamboat, *Clermont*, on the Hudson River north of
New York City. In 1825, the first English railway opened between
Stockton and Darlington, cutting transportation time by a factor of ten.
Within a decade, trains entered regular service across the European continent and along the eastern United States, all powered by steam and
fueled by coal. Steamboats and steam locomotives speeded up the process of transporting coal and iron ore from mines to factories, thereby
bringing the industrial revolution into full swing and beginning the modern age of technology.

Steam served as the source of power also for constructing the high
walls surrounding the fortress-style prisons that sprung up across the
eastern half of the United States during the first half of the nineteenth
century, and as the power source of converting raw materials into finished products within prison factories, vital to rendering early prisons
economically self-sufficient. Had the early prisons, particularly the ones
in America, not been economically self-sufficient, as undoubtedly they
would not have been without the steam engine, they would not have
proved useful enough to endure the test of popular approval, and consequently these prisons would not have been replicated as they have been
around the world.

In the 1840s, steam locomotives were transporting increasingly large
numbers of convicted criminal offenders from new and densely populated cities having high crimes rates to prisons situated in rural areas
where otherwise underemployed residents enlisted their services eagerly
as guards. Convict labor and the concept of a prison as a factory accompanied the industrial revolution in the United States and contributed in
no small measure to the success the industrial revolution achieved in the
countryside. Within two decades, prisons that had been constructed as
experiments in sparsely populated farm regions precipitated the growth
of new towns in the vicinities of the prisons. Towns sprung up around
American prisons much as villages had grown around European castles
a century or more earlier. In America, as in Europe, towns outgrew the
walls of the original fortresses that had inspired their origins and growth,
and expanded over wider terrains into sprawling cities.

Ideas and Influence of Jeremy Bentham

Utilitarianism became a new philosophy in 1672, with publication of
Richard Cumberland's book, *De legibus naturae*, and reached its full
expression by 1739 when David Hume wrote *A Treatise of Human Nature*. Thus, utilitarianism anteceded even the idealism of the French encyclopedists by more than half a century, although early utilitarianism

and idealism overlapped. The first utilitarian philosophers did not focus extensively on criminal laws, much less on criminology. This changed with Jeremy Bentham, from 1776 when his long literary career began until his death in 1832.

Bentham's early inspirations came primarily from Claude Adrien Helvetius' work, *De l'Esprit*, published in 1758, which set forth a new set of ethics that suggested that all human actions are motivated by self-interest, even those actions that are strictly moral. Helvetius claimed that an action's morality should be judged in terms of its usefulness to the community and that both education and legislation harmonize individual egoism and the good of the community by means of rewards and punishments. Bentham had read *De l'Esprit* and other utilitarian works such as Barrington's *Observations of the Statutes* (1766) and Joseph Priestley's *Essay on Government* (1768) when, in 1776, he began to write the work that afterwards he considered to be his best, *The Critical Elements of Jurisprudence*. He completed that in 1780 but failed to publish it until 1789, perhaps on account of the same shyness that caused him to abandon the practice of law with his father out of an unconquerable fear of rebuke from judges in the courtroom. Throughout most of his life, Bentham embarked on literary projects only to lay them aside and begin some other work before returning much later to complete the efforts he had undertaken earlier.

At the time when Bentham finished his first major work, *A Fragment on Government*, in 1776, he was twenty-eight years old, or two years older than Beccaria had been in 1764 when he wrote his *Essay on Crimes and Punishment*. Like Beccaria, Bentham achieved fame and widespread respect during his lifetime. Whereas Beccaria's esteem stemmed principally from a single book that he wrote while very young, Bentham's derived slowly over a long life span that embraced a changing world and produced a number of books. Born ten years after Beccaria, Bentham lived twenty-eight years longer than did Beccaria before he died in 1832 at the age of eighty-four. Many of Bentham's ideas in law and criminology he conceived during or after the mechanical revolution that began at about the time when Beccaria died in 1794. More than half of Bentham's professional career took place in the first three decades of the nineteenth century, which Beccaria never lived to see.

The Scope of Bentham's Influence: Police, Courts, and Corrections

Bentham's influence extended to all three areas of the criminal justice system: to the police, in the form of his influence over development of

London's metropolitan police system; to the courts, in the form of the Pannomion Code he proposed to President James Madison for implementation in the United States; and to corrections, in the form of his celebrated Panopticon House design for a prison model, some characteristics of which became embodied in the early prisons of New England, New York, and Pennsylvania. Bentham's law models were enacted into the statutes of only a few American states, and then only in part, but they were adopted to a larger extent by Australia, Canada, France, Germany, Greece, Portugal, Spain, and a number of South American countries. Bentham's contract labor system for prison industries received widespread acceptance, and some twenty-one states plus the District of Columbia and territories of the United States[1] had adopted this system for at least some of the prisons or jails they maintained in 1886. Pervasive throughout the ideas of Jeremy Bentham is his bottom-line "greatest happiness principle," through which he argued that pleasure and happiness are equivalents and that the ethical goal of a society should be to achieve the most happiness for the largest segment of its population. Sir Henry Maine noted while writing during the middle of the nineteenth century that almost all legal forms effected up to then in that century could be traced to the influence of Bentham.[2]

The Policing System. The structure of police changed in the early years of the nineteenth century, both in England and in the United States, due largely to the utilitarians. Between 1795 and 1800, Jeremy Bentham corresponded with Patrick Colquhoun, and together they formulated plans for altering London's metropolitan police system.[3] In 1795, Colquhoun published *A Treatise on the Police of Metropolis*, the first systematic survey of police practices to be conducted anywhere. Concerning London, Colquhoun wrote:

The watchmen destined to guard the lives and properties of the inhabitants residing in near eight thousand streets, lanes, courts, and alleys, and about 162,000 houses . . . are under the direction of no less than above seventy different Trusts; regulated by perhaps double the number of local acts of Parliament . . . under which the directors, guardians, governors, trustees, or vestries, according to the title they assume, are authorised to act, each attending only to their own particular Ward, Parish, Hamlet, Liberty, or Precinct.

In his preface to the sixth edition of his *Treatise*, published in 1800, Colquhoun declared that:

[P]olice in [England] may be considered as a new science; the properties of which consist not in the judicial powers which lead to punishment and which belong to the magistrates alone; but the prevention and detection of crimes; and

in those other functions which relate to internal regulations for the well order
and comfort of civil society.[4]

What Colquhoun proposed was a paid professional police force for each
local geographic section within the metropolitan London area, responsible to a board of five police commissioners. His plan was very similar
to the one introduced unsuccessfully into Parliament by the government
of Prime Minister William Pitt in 1785. In setting forth his plan,
Colquhoun followed three ideas advanced earlier by Henry and Sir John
Fielding: (1) the central police board should organize an intelligence service to gather information on crimes and offenders; (2) it should maintain a register of known criminal offenders and criminal groups; and (3)
it should publish a police gazette to facilitate detection of crimes and to
promote the moral education of the community by publicizing punishments such as "whipping, the pillory, the hulks, transportation, and public
execution."[5] In another monograph, *Treatise on the Commerce and Police of the River Thames*, published in 1800, Colquhoun estimated there
were ten thousand thieves, prostitutes, and other criminals who stole over
a half-million pounds annually from the riverside docks. Bentham collaborated with Colquhoun in drafting a bill in Parliament that became
the Thames River Police Act of 1800, with minor changes.

The Thames River Police Act embodied many utilitarian principles,
both in its substance and in the way it was drafted. The purpose of the
bill was "to do that for the whole which could never be effectual when
applied only to a part,"[6] an aim utilitarian to the core. The purpose of
the bill was recited in even greater detail:

To establish a kind of Police which shall be an immediate connection with the
whole property on the River give universal protection by enlarging the Civil
Force and by extending the preventive Plan to every point of danger with all
the improvements which experience has suggested. . . . By so doing a strong
and Energetic Police will be obtained pervading the whole River. By such a
measure it will be assigned to somebody instead of nobody to watch over the
immense property at all times exposed to danger in the Port of London.[7]

Thus, the bill contained evidence of a desire to make specific officers of
the police accountable for patrolling targeted crime areas, the objective
being to prevent crime in advance of its occurrence insofar as possible.
To further enhance the preventive design of the bill, it mandated regis-
tration and licensing of "lumpers," the name used at the time for long-
shoremen who unloaded boats from England's colonies. The bill went
further yet, empowering river police to apprehend suspicious persons,

the antecedent of our "stop and frisk" laws; and to conduct warrantless searches and seizures "in case of suspicion" that a boat carried contraband, the antecedent of our field searches condoned where the police act on probable cause. The bill required shipmasters, on penalty of a fine, to keep locked their ships' holds when not unloading from them. To increase the operations ability of the river police, the bill provided that such fines, as well as fines imposed as punishments on thieves and other criminals caught along the docks, be allocated in half to the river police. Only in the 1980s has the United States begun to use revenue generated from one investigation to finance another, usually in its war on drugs. Persons who contributed to the conviction of criminals shared the other half of fines received.

The Thames River Police bill was utilitarian in the way it was drafted, also, as seen in the cautious approach taken by Jeremy Bentham in resisting the temptation to include so much within the bill that Parliament would reject it. Much later, Bentham explained with characteristic lack of modesty:

A bill was necessary. Colquhoun had found the facts. I ventured to supply the law. I drew the bill, leaving out as much of the customary surplusage as I durst. In the procedure clause, for giving execution and effect to the law, I ventured as far as I durst, and further than any one had ventured before. . . . At my humble request, a learned gentleman . . . received it . . . and, without the change of a word, it became law.[8]

The Thames River Police Act had its critics, nonetheless, some of whom challenged its "specimens of preventive legislation" as being "entirely repugnant . . . to the spirit of English government."[9]

Once the Thames River Police Act was passed in 1800, Parliament revised it periodically, six times through 1829, each time extending progressively the powers the police enjoyed in England. Policing expanded throughout other parts of metropolitan London, also. By 1811, when Sir Richard Ford served as chief magistrate at Bow Street, a mounted patrol of sixty men, becoming known as the Bow Street Runners, rode along the major highways within twenty miles of London, thus fulfilling yet another idea advanced by Sir John Fielding half a century earlier. By 1821, the Unmounted Horse Patrol became operationalized as the training unit for their mounted counterparts from Bow Street. The Bow Street patrols became the first uniformed police in England when, during 1822, upon forming a daylight division to curb daytime street robberies, they donned blue coats and trousers, black hats, Wellington boots, and scarlet waistcoats from which derived their nickname: Robin Redbreasts. By 1828, 450 paid police patrolled metropolitan London.

Between 1822 and 1830, Jeremy Bentham wrote his last major work, *The Constitutional Code*, in which he stressed the need for a preventive police force under centralized governmental control.[10] Edwin Chadwick, Bentham's colleague and friend, consolidated utilitarian ideas on centralized and preventative policing in testimony he gave during 1828 before the Select Committee on the Police of the Metropolis that British Home Secretary Sir Robert Peel had convened. In April 1829, Peel introduced into Parliament his Bill for Improving the Police in and near the Metropolis. The Duke of Wellington supported the bill as Britain's prime minister, and it passed. The act took effect on July 19, 1829, as the Metropolitan Police Act, and established a single metropolitan police district across a seven-mile radius from the center of London. The new police force would be headquartered in an old fortress known as Scotland Yard, the name by which the police force itself would become famous. Army Colonel Charles Rowan was appointed the first chief superintendent of the metropolitan police force. The force was divided into seventeen police divisions, each manned by 165 officers. A division was commanded by a superintendent, under whom four inspectors supervised sixteen sergeants and a sergeant watched over nine constables who became known affectionately as "Bobbies" after Sir Robert Peel, the home secretary, to whom the chief superintendent reported. True to utilitarian principles, Peel declared that efficiency was the paramount objective of the new Metropolitan Police Force and that "the chief prerequisite of an efficient police" was "unity of design and responsibility of its agents."[11] The Bobbies accomplished this aim much more so than had their watchmen predecessors, the Charlies, and gained to respect of the people whom they served.

According to Jeremy Bentham, police business encompasses eight major functions:

1. Prevention of crimes
2. Prevention of calamities
3. Prevention of endemic diseases
4. Assisting in charity
5. Facilitating interior communications
6. Supervising public amusements
7. Gathering intelligence and information
8. Gathering and maintaining public census data.[12]

In addition, Bentham proposed creation of an insurance fund to be used both to finance police operations and to idemnify victims of crime where

their offenders were unknown or insolvent.[13] Utilitarians were very concerned about the identification of suspicious persons, and Bentham recommended that every British subject should use a first and last name.
He wanted everyone to use both names on all legal documents, together
with their birthdates and birthplaces. As a final precaution to target recidivist offenders, Bentham advocated the tattooing of everyone's first
and last name on his or her wrists, following the custom of English sail-
ors at the time.[14]

Edwin Chadwick, afterwards knighted, added his own input to the
utilitarian ideas of Bentham. The transcript of his testimony before the
Select Committee during 1828 was lost before the committee submitted
its report, so Chadwick published his thoughts privately and added af-
terthoughts to his original testimony. Chadwick's boldest proposal was
the abolition of the grand jury, because he feared suspicious persons
perjured their testimony before gullible grand jurors and avoided indictment.[15] He startled England by advocating that anyone's failure to report a crime he knew about should become a crime in itself.[16] Chadwick
urged that the London police *Gazette* be expanded to include information pertinent to all crimes known to the police, rather than only the most
serious, and be distributed the next morning to every Bobby as well as
to pawnbrokers and tavern keepers.[17]

Some historians have noted that the success of the Metropolitan Police drove criminals out of London, necessitating creation of police forces
in surrounding towns by means of the Municipal Corporations Act of
1835, after which criminals retreated to more rural locations, necessitating Parliament's passage of the County Police Act in 1839.[18] That year,
Birmingham saw rioting inspired by the chartist movement, an idealist
effort to improve the lifestyles of workingmen and their families.[19] Birmingham had no police of its own, so London loaned it one hundred
Bobbies, who put down the rioters. Parliament enacted legislation au-
thorizing creation of a central police force for Birmingham, Bolton, and
Manchester, notwithstanding "home rule" objections. By August 27,
1829, centralized police were empowered to patrol the streets of England's largest cities, and did so.

After additional chartist uprisings, Parliament passed the Parish Constable Act in 1842, and for many years thereafter England enjoyed a
dual system of policing by municipal and county constables, who feuded
over jurisdictional limits. This system spread to and has lasted in the
United States, also. Sir Edwin Chadwick testified again before a second
Select Committee in 1854, this one assembled by Lord Palmerston as
British home secretary. Shortly afterwards, he became prime minister,
but his successor as home secretary, Sir George Grey, tried three times

between 1854 and 1856 to gain passage of legislation that would strengthen centralized police control, being motivated by Chadwick to do so. Failing twice, Grey succeeded on a third try, and the County and Borough Police Act of 1856 lasted one hundred years. Under it, 226 police forces emerged across England, some with as few as a single constable. Borough constables were given countywide jurisdiction, and county constables were permitted to perform official acts inside of boroughs.

Legislation and Punishment

To Jeremy Bentham, as to most utilitarians, the fundamental purpose of legislation should be to deter crime, by both direct and indirect means. For instance, Bentham argued that, indirectly, legislation might contribute to crime prevention either by minimizing the availability of knowledge necessry for commission of the crime or by eliminating the offender's power or will to commit it.[20] Indirectly, legislation might impact crime, according to Bentham, by endeavoring insofar as possible:

1. To change the course of dangerous desires, and direct the inclinations toward amusements comfortable to the public interest.
2. To arrange so that a given desire may be satisfied without injury, or with the least possible injury.
3. To avoid furnishing encouragements to crime.
4. To increase responsibility in proportion as temptation increases.
5. To diminish the sensibility to temptation.
6. To strengthen the impression of punishments upon the imagination.
7. To facilitate knowledge of the fact of an offence.
8. To prevent an offence by giving to many persons an immediate interest to prevent it.
9. To facilitate the means of recognizing and finding individuals.
10. To increase the difficulty of escape.
11. To diminish the uncertainty of prosecutions and punishments.
12. To prohibit accessory offences, in order to prevent the principal offence.[21]

Bentham felt that "the culture of honour, the employment of the impulse of religion, and the use to be made of the power of instruction and education"[22] could assist legislation in reducing crime through indirect means.

Directly, legislation may deter crime, according to Bentham, as long as the punishment fits the crime. According to Coleman Phillipson, Bentham felt punishment would work as long as:

1. The evils of the punishment . . . be made to exceed the advantage of the offence. . . .

2. The less certain a punishment is the severer it should be; the greater the certainty the less the severity. . . .

3. When two offences are in conjunction, the greater should receive heavier punishment, so that the offender may have a motive to stop at the lesser. . . . Equal punishment for unequal offences often conduces to the commission of the greater offence.

4. The greater the offence the more reason is there to hazard a severe punishment in the hope of preventing it. . . . [T]he infliction of a penalty is a certain cost to procure an uncertain gain. To apply a heavy punishment for a slight offence is to pay very dearly for the chance of avoiding a small evil.

5. The same punishment for the same offence should not be inflicted on all offenders. Regard should be paid to their different sensibility. The same nominal punishment is not the same real punishment.[23]

Bentham argued that "[a]ge, sex, rank, fortune, and many other circumstances ought to modify the punishments inflicted for the same offence," reasoning as follows:

If the offence is a corporal injury, the same pecuniary punishment would be a trifle to the rich, and oppressive to the poor. The same punishment that would brand with ignominy a man of a certain rank would not produce even the slightest stain in case the offender belonged to an inferior class. The same imprisonment would be ruin to a man of business, death to an infirm old man, and eternal disgrace to a woman, while it would be next to nothing to an individual placed under other circumstances.[24]

However, Bentham warned that "the proportion between punishments and offences ought not to be so mathematically followed up as to render the laws subtle, complicated, and obscure."[25] He demanded "brevity" and "simplicity" in order to make the punishment all the more "striking" to the public to maximize its deterrent impact.

So that punishment would be *proportionate* to the crime, Bentham suggested twelve essential qualities he deemed it should possess:

1. *variability*, or susceptibility of adjustment to the gravity of each peculiar offense

2. *equability*, meaning that a punishment should exert the same effect on similarly situated offenders after being adapted to each offender's "sensibility"

3. *commensurability*, where the more serious offenses would be punished more severely

4. *characteristicalness*, in that a punishment should be analogous to the underlying offense so that both the offender and the onlooking community may witness and remember the relationship between the two

5. *exemplarity*, so that the public will not fail to perceive punishment for what it is

6. *frugality*, to the extent that punishment will not denigrate the seriousness of a crime

7. *remissibility*, so that upon discovery of an offender's innocence the punishment will not be irreparable

8. *subservience to reformation*, to the extent that different types of inmates in confinement should be housed separately according to their character and habits

9. *efficacy with respect to disablement*, in that mutilations lead too frequently to death of the offender when capital punishment is unnecessary

10. *serviency to compensation*, so that the offender is able to indemnify his victim for harm done

11. *popularity*, so that a punishment will not shock the conscience of the community which, in turn in protest, might set free a guilty person

12. *simplicity of description* so that the average citizen will understand the punishment and be deterred by it.[26]

To achieve the purposes of punishment, Bentham argued, different crimes mandate different penalties. He identified eleven kinds of punishment:

1. *capital*, or death, which he deemed inefficient because it was unpopular (except for murder), although he conceded death might be appropriate for the leader of a rebellion against the state

2. *afflictive*, including fasting and whipping, which he thought to be suitable only for serious offenses because such punishments cannot be applied with mitigation

3. *indelible*, such as amputation or branding, which Bentham argued should be abolished but, if retained, be limited to dangerous offenders or rare offenses such as counterfeiting (he recommended branding the face of a counterfeiter with the image of a coin)

4. *ignominious*, such as the pillory, which Bentham declared to be the least equitable of all punishments, because the defenseless offender's fate remained in the hands of capricious onlookers who had the power to stone him to death

5. *penitential*, involving community censure but not infamy, which he favored where the offender outraged the public morals

6. *chronic*, such as imprisonment that he urged, as well as banishment and transporation beyond the seas, Bentham favoring the former but castigating the latter because many transportees died aboard ship of diseases incurred during the voyage

7. simply *restrictive*, such as revocation of a professional license

8. simply *compulsive*, as when a probationer is required to visit a probation officer periodically

9. *pecuniary*, where an offender is fined, which Bentham stressed would be valueless unless proportioned to an offender's financial resources

10. *quasi-pecuniary*, where an offender is deprived of services

11. *characteristic*, such as requiring prisoners to wear striped uniforms as a reminder of their status.[27]

Bentham favored imprisonment strongly, provided confinement could be geared toward the offender's reform.

Utilitarians have been concerned that an offender receive his just desserts and that the punishment fit the crime. Bentham articulated two "evils" according to which the seriousness of a criminal offense might be measured: evil of the first order, measured according to actual harm done to the victim, such as personal disgrace, physical anguish, or reduction in value of property; and evil of the second order, measured by the amount of public alarm in response to the offender's crime, taking into account factors such as the offender's state of mind when he perpetrated the crime, the amount of public trust that afforded the offender an opportunity to commit the crime, and the condition of the victim after the crime, in addition to the harm done to the victim during the crime.[28] Bentham divided crime victims into classes, also, such as purely private, affecting only the individual harmed; reflective, affecting only the offender himself; semipublic, affecting a portion of the community; and public, affecting much of the entire community.[29]

Jeremy Bentham wrote that:

Nature has placed mankind under the governance of two soverign masters, pain and pleasure. . . . [T]hey govern us in all we do, in all we think: every effort we can make to throw off our subjection will serve but to demonstrate and confirm it.[30]

He devised a sort of moral calculus for predicting whether any given person would commit a particular crime, according to the assumption that every act a person commits he evaluates in terms of the likelihood that performing that act will cause pleasure instead of pain. Among the many factors Bentham argued may be considered in balancing pleasure against pain are skill, benevolence, and piety as examples of pleasure, and desire, disappointment, and hunger or thirst as examples of pain.[31] Of course it followed then logically to Bentham and his followers that, to deter or prevent crime, potential criminal offenders must be made to internalize that the amount of pain to be derived from crime would exceed the amount of pleasure.

Bentham favored imprisonment as the proper punishment for a number of crimes, but he opposed typical prisons of his time that kept the inmate idle and in isolation. Confinement should not be designed to make the prisoner repent, Bentham thought, but to make him work. As usual, Bentham had in mind a complex system of incarceration that involved detailed architecture of the prison itself, to be known as the Panópticon House.[32] Such a prison would contain three essential characteristics, Coleman Phillipson wrote:

[F]irst, the construction of a circular or polygonal building, having cells on each story in the circumference, all visible from the governor's lodge in the centre;

[S]econdly, management by contract, so that the contractor, taking the profits of the prisoners' labour, would identify his interest with his duty; and

[T]hirdly, responsibility and magisterial supervision of the manager, who would be bound to insure the lives and safe custody of those entrusted to him.[33]

Bentham insisted that the Panópticon House be erected in the vicinity of a large city so it would be exemplary by being a visible reminder to everyone that crime does not pay. Bentham described the planned result:

The appearance of the building, the singularity of its shape, the walls and ditches by which it would be surrounded, the guards stationed at its gate, would all excite ideas of restraint and punishment. . . . The public would be allowed to contrast the labour of the free man and that of a prisoner, . . . the enjoyment of the innocent and the privations of the criminal. . . . At the same time the *real* punishment would be less than the apparent.[34]

Thus, the Panópticon House would frighten the public on the outside without harming the prisoners on the inside. Bentham envisioned the "governor," or warden, would impose strict discipline on all inmates, teach them useful trades which they could apply upon release in the free world, and reward them immediately for their labor, which Bentham deemed to be "the only resource against *ennui*" (boredom).[35] Bentham wanted prisoners to receive the fair market value of their services, which he said should be banked until their release and given to them at that time to afford them a fresh start in society.[36] He viewed the Panópticon House as a benevolent alternative to the disease and famine that awaited prisoners who were transported beyond the seas in the holds of ships, and this view was accurate, at least during Bentham's lifetime if not afterwards.

England never constructed the Panópticon House because Parliament objected to its cost. France built a modified Panópticon prison at Lyons, called Rouanne Prison, designed by celebrated architect Pierre Gabriel Buginet; and three modified Panópticon prisons were erected in the United States, of which one remains today.[37] Due in large part to Bentham's influence and the popularity of the utilitarian movement in America, New York constructed a prison at Auburn in 1819, designed by architect John Cray, where prisoners would work at hard labor. Citizens could visit the prison and see the prisoners at work by paying a fee of twenty-five cents to the warden.[38] Among the labor the Auburn prisoners performed was the physical expansion of their facility to accommodate more prisoners. By 1825, when space ran out at Auburn, New York built a second prison at Ossining, modeled after Auburn, this one to be known as Sing Sing. Elam Lynds was the warden, first at Auburn, then at Sing Sing, and he maintained the strict regimentation Bentham advocated, forbidding any prisoner from talking with any other prisoner and flogging obstinate prisoners with a "cat" made of six wire strands.[39]

The Auburn system that compelled prisoners to do work triumphed over a rival American system that emerged at about the same time in Philadelphia. Quakers who controlled eastern Pennsylvania politics at the time opened their Eastern State Penitentiary at Philadelphia in 1829, designed by architect John Haviland. Known as Cherry Hill because the land on which it stood had been a cherry orchard earlier, this prison operated in marked contrast to the Bentham and Auburn models. Instead of being forced to work, prisoners were forced to do nothing but sit alone in solitary cells and repent their sins. No prisoner ever saw another prisoner, and prisoners were blindfolded when being led into or out of the institution. Inmates performed small chores within individual cells, but not for profit. Little wonder, then, that the Quaker or Philadelphia model failed to survive the test of efficiency.[40] The survival of the Auburn prison model and the failure of the Philadelphia Quaker one reflect the success of utilitarianism over pure idealism in the setting of early American corrections. As new territories became settled, new states entered the union, and the American population migrated westward throughout the nineteenth century, more prisons were built, virtually all of them patterned after Auburn and reflecting the Puritan work ethic so important to Bentham and the utilitarians.

As rivalries continued to exist between the Philadelphia and Auburn prison systems, two penologists emerged to favor in general the latter over the former: Edward Livingston and Charles Lucas. Called America's greatest penologist by William Tallack,[41] Edward Livingston was the brother of Robert Livingston who participated with Thomas Jefferson in drafting the American Declaration of Independence. Charles Lucas was the inspector-general of French prisons from 1830 until his retirement in 1865, after having published his three-volume work, *The Penitentiary System in Europe and the United States*[42] between 1828 and 1830 for which the French Academy of Moral and Political Science awarded him the Monthyon Prize. Earlier, in 1826, the Count de Sellon of Geneva and the Societé de la Moralité Cretienne of Paris offered separate prizes to the winner of public competitions on the subject of capital punishment, its efficacy and legitimacy. Lucas, an abolitionist, won both prizes. Also an abolitionist, Livingston's early manuscript burned shortly after its completion, although subsequently he reconstructed it substantially from memory. His collected works include it.

Somewhat paradoxically, Charles Lucas devoted nearly all of his professional life towards eliminating transportation as punishment for crime and replacing it with imprisonment;[43] but with Frédéric Auguste Demetz he co-founded two "agricultural" colonies to which youthful offenders under age sixteen were banished.[44] Demetz and Lucas compared the results of the two colonies, one of which Demetz managed as a congregate system, the other of which Lucas managed as an Auburn system. Beginning in 1837, Lucas proposed a system of sentencing that included both minimum and maximum sentences, as follows:

under 5 years
 5 - 10 years
10 - 15 years
15 - 20 years
20 - 25 years[45]

Lucas proposed that a "disciplinary board" be invested with discretion to evaluate each inmate's progress during imprisonment, according to the prisoner's "moral improvement," in order that actual length of sentence could be indeterminate. Thus, as Lucas wrote, "the control of experience in prison would repair . . . errors, one of which would have unduly extended the captivity of a man who was not dangerous any more, and the other would have given back to society a man still dangerous."[46] In order for each new prisoner to be classified fairly, Lucas proposed what he called "moral screening" to separate, for instance, "social criminality'' emobdied in the occasional offender from ''scholarly or erudite criminality'' that, Lucas contended, prisoners learned during confinement. Lucas proposed that correctional officers be trained as professionals, in the same way Bentham had desired police officers to be trained.[47]

Thus, Charles Lucas viewed the reformation of the convict as a person as being paramount to punishment of the crime:

. . . [T]he degree of perversity of a crime changes with each actor since the intentionality is different. . . . [R]eformation is more or less rapid according to this degree of perversity; thus the length of punishment should be proportionate to the actor's perversity and not to his violation as such, because, for two offenders having committed the same crime, a certain amount of corrective detention will be necessary for one and another amount for the other. But when punishment is proportionate to the criminal act only, we are opened each day to detain a reformed man and to release an unregenerated man. Repressive justice should then be focused on agents and not on acts.[48]

Utilitarian tenets are evident within Lucas' philosophy, then, as he urges punishment to fit the offender, not the crime. Prison space should not be wasted, nor the lives of convicts interrupted, for longer than necessary to reform the individual.

Edward Livingston, also, was concerned with matching an offender's sentence to meet his reform, particularly when reform included mastery of occupational skills, which Livingston deemed would require a minimum of two years' confinement.[49] Livingston recommended that early release, or parole, be determined by five persons sitting as a board of inspectors. For the offender who has not learned or cannot learn a job skill, Livingston advised counties to create houses of correction where such persons could be employed working for the government while in confinement, and in this way the system of jails as factories emerged throughout America.[50] Livingston was invited to draft a comprehensive code for Louisiana that would include not just a penal code but also rules for sentencing and correctional management.[51] Louisiana failed to enact Livingston's code, just as Lombardy failed to enact Beccaria's, and the English Parliament failed to enact Bentham's. Livingston departed that state to serve with President Andrew Jackson as secretary of state and minister to France.

Prisons fulfilled the prophecy of efficiency for a short moment in history, when prisons were new and still healthful places in which to live and when prison factories could produce finished products as good as those manufactured by free enterprises. Those conditions did not last for long, however. Because of limited space behind prison walls, prison industries were limited in the kinds of products they could manufacture, unlike free enterprises. At the beginning of the industrial revolution, most factories were like prisons. Within fifty years or less, on the contrary, free enterprises had expanded geometrically, whereas prisons had expanded only arithmetically if they expanded at all. States were unwilling to recapitalize prison work facilities frequently enough to make them competitive with outside industries. Outside of prisons, labor and management joined in opposition to the competition from prison labor, and the growing influence of organized labor made prison industries impolitic within the industrialized states where they had flourished. As the decades passed, moreover, and the original prisons built in the early nineteenth century grew older, they became infested with diseases, just as had the ancient fortress towns of Europe succumbed to plagues, and droves of prisoners died during epidemics.[52] By the close of the nineteenth century, imprisonment would become about as hazardous to a prisoner's health as Bentham had proclaimed ships used to transport convicts across the ocean had been several generations earlier. Prisons ceased to be efficient because they failed to keep pace with progress.

NOTES

1. These states include: Connecticut, Illinois, Indiana, Iowa, Kansas, Maryland, Massachusetts, Michigan, Minnesota, New Hampshire, New York, Ohio, Oregon, Pennsylvania, Rhode Island, South Carolina, Texas, Vermont, Virginia, Washington, and Wisconsin. U.S. Commissioner of Labor, SECOND ANNUAL REPORT, CONVICT LABOR 8-28, table 1 (1887). Dakota Territory used the contract labor system, also. *Id.*

2. Maine wrote:

It is impossible to overrate the importance to a nation or profession of having a distinct object to aim at in the pursuit of improvement. The secret of Bentham's immense influence in England during the past thirty years is his success in placing such an object before the country. He gave us a clear rule of reform. . . . Bentham made the good of the community take precedence of every other object, and thus gave escape to a current which had long been trying to find its way outwards.

H. Maine, ANCIENT LAW 78-79 (1861).

3. J. Bowring, ed., THE WORKS OF JEREMY BENTHAM 329 (1843).

4. P. Colquhoun, A TREATISE ON THE POLICE OF THE METROPOLIS 213 (5th ed., 1797).

5. T. Critchley, A HISTORY OF POLICE IN ENGLAND AND WALES 39-40 (1967).

6. L. Radzinowicz, A HISTORY OF ENGLISH CRIMINAL LAW 380 (1956), quoting from 78 J. CT. COM. COUN. 189-90 (February 21, 1799).

7. *Id*. The "immense property" consisted mostly of raw materials being unloaded from ships that had sailed to England from India, the Far East, and the New World.

8. *Id*. at 387-88, quoting from J. Bentham, WORKS 335. Actually, the bill adopted on July 11, 1800, was different in detail from the one Bentham and Colquhoun had drafted in February 1799, as Radzinowicz pointed out, *id*., at 388.

9. See *Powers of Justices of Peace*, 5 NEW EDINBURGH REV. 315-36 (1823).

10. Bentham proposed the role of a "preventive service minister" to fulfill the following functions: "locative, suppletive, directive, procurative, custoditive, applicative, reparative, transformative, eliminative, statistic, recordative, publicative, officially-informative, melioration-suggestive." 9 J. Bentham, THE CONSTITUTIONAL CODE 213, 439-41 (1830).

11. *Supra*, note 5 at 50, quoting from 21 PARL. DEB., N.S. 872-77 (April 15, 1829).

12. See L. Radzinowicz, A HISTORY OF ENGLISH CRIMINAL LAW 434 (1956).

13. *Id*., citing J. Bentham, PRINCIPLES OF PENAL LAW 580.

14. *Id*., citing PRINCIPLES OF PENAL LAW 557-58. These suggestions became implemented a hundred years later by the German Nazis.

15. *Id*. at 463-64. The Supreme Court of the United States followed this recommendation, implicitly, when it ruled that states have no federal constitutional obligation to initiate criminal prosecutions by grand jury indictment. HURTADO v. CALIFORNIA, 110 U.S. 516 (1884), some fifty years later.

16. Chadwick desired revival of an old English crime, misprison of felony. *Id*. at 465, n. 4.

17. Chadwick thought police managers could use an accurate chart of daily criminal activity to redeploy street officers into high crime areas. *Id*. at 460-62. Such is common today.

18. At least one historian, Critchley, has contended that "[t]his attractive theory bears no relation to the facts." *Supra*, note 5 at 58.

19. Chartism promised the English workingman "that all shall have a good house to live in with a garden back and front, just as the occupier likes, good clothing to keep him warm and to make him look respectable, and plenty of good food and drink to make him look and feel happy." *Id*. at 76, quoting G. Harvey's LONDON DEMOCRAT (April 27, 1839).

20. See C. Phillipson, THREE CRIMINAL LAW REFORMERS: BECCARIA, BENTHAM, ROMILLY 218 (1923).

21. J. Bentham, treatise, *Principles of a Penal Code*, IV, in J. Bowring, ed., *Supra*, n. 3 at 533.

22. *Id*.

23. *Supra*, note 20 at 204-5.

24. *Supra*, note 21, chap. 6.

25. *Id*.

26. *Id.*, chap. 7.

27. *Supra*, note 20 at 207. Bentham advised poignantly: "Search out . . . the motives of offences, and generally you will recognize the dominant passion of the offender, and you may punish him . . . with the instrument of his own sin." *Supra*, note 21, chap. 7.

28. *Supra*, note 20 at 196-97.

29. *Id.* at 196.

30. J. Bentham, A FRAGMENT ON GOVERNMENT AND AN INTRO-DUCTION TO THE PRINCIPLE OF MORALS AND LEGISLATION 21 (W. Harrison, ed., 1967).

31. *Id.* at 152.

32. *Supra*, note 21 at 498-503.

33. *Supra*, note 20 at 212.

34. *Supra*, note 21 at 498-503. See also J. Bentham, PANÓPTICON OR INSPECTION HOUSE (1791).

35. *Supra*, note 20 at 212.

36. *Supra*, note 21 at 498-503. Bentham wrote: "In this privileged asylum, [prisoners] would have different degrees of liberty, a choice of their occupations, the entire profit of their labour, with fixed and moderate charges for their board and lodging, and the right of going and returning, on leaving a certain sum as security; they would wear no prisoner's uniform, no humiliating badge." *Id.*

37. The three American prisons were: Virginia's prison at Richmond, built in 1800, designed by the architect Latrobe with suggestions from Thomas Jefferson, who had studied Pierre Gabriel Buginet's Roanne design; Pennsylvania's Western State Penitentiary at Pittsburgh, built in 1821, designed by William Strickland; and Illinois' Stateville prison, built between 1916 and 1925, which is in use today. See H. Barnes and N. Teeters, NEW HORIZONS IN CRIMINOLOGY 335, n. 16 (3rd ed. 1959). Pennsylvania's Western Penitentiary was rebuilt in 1882.

38. See W. Lewis, FROM NEWGATE TO DANNEMORA 124 (1965), citing Herre, "A History of Auburn Prison from the Beginning to about 1867" (Ed.D. dissertation, Pennsylvania State University, 1950).

39. M. Wilson, THE CRIME OF PUNISHMENT 224 (1931). See also L. Lawes, CELL 202 (1935). Lewis E. Lawes was a reform warden at Sing Sing.

40. See N. Teeters and J. Shearer, THE PRISON AT PHILADELPHIA: CHERRY HILL (1957). This despite the prediction of French visitors Gustave de Beaumont and Alexis de Tocqueville that "[n]o salutary system can possibly exist without the separation of the criminals." ON THE PENITENTIARY SYSTEM IN THE UNITED STATES, ETC. 21 (1833).

41. W. Tallack, PENOLOGICAL AND PREVENTIVE PRINCIPLES 117 (1889).

42. This work was published as C. Lucas, DU SYSTÈME PÉNITEN-TIAIRE EN EUROPE ET AUX ETATS-UNIS.

43. Lucas wrote: "Societies must absorb their criminality and not throw it

out arbitrarily on an unknown land.'' C. Lucas, DU SYSTÈME PÉNAL ET DU SYSTÈME RÉPRESSIF EN GÉNÉRAL, DE LA PEINE DE MORT EN PARTICULAR 336 (1827).

44. The two communities became known as Mettray, formed in 1839 by Demetz, that followed a congregate (modified Cherry Hill system) and Val d'Yèvre, founded in 1843 by Lucas, that followed an Auburn system.

45. A prisoner could be reclassified after the first two years of imprisonment, and then again annually to each lower range of sentence.

46. *Supra*, note 43 at 308.

47. *Supra*, note 42 at 308.

48. *Id*. at 281-282.

49. See E. Livingston, 2 THE COMPLETE WORKS OF EDWARD LIVINGSTON ON CRIMINAL JURISPRUDENCE 577-584 (1873; reprinted 1968).

50. *Id*. at 541-543.

51. See E. Smith, *Edward Livingston and His Criminal Code*, 39 J. SOC.SCI. 27 (1901).

52. See B. McKelvey, AMERICAN PRISONS (1972).

5

Positivism after the Rise of Science

Most historians have agreed that the rise of modern science was complete, except for organic chemistry,[1] by the end of the seventeenth century. By then, Copernicus, Galileo, Kepler, and Newton had traced the interface of physical forces visible to the naked eye. By then, also, Bacon, Descartes, Liebniz, and Locke had articulated the methods and assumptions on which modern science rests. It took another century for the scientific method to become firmly rooted into a separate school of philosophy, however, and this feat has been credited generally to Auguste Comte. In 1826, Comte prepared to vociferate the core of what would become his six-volume *Cours de philosophic positive* (Course in Positive Philosophy), published between 1830 and 1842. Essential to Comte's *Cours* was the "Law of Three States" which he expounded, drawing from earlier works by the French writer Saint-Simon and economist A. R. T. Turgot. Comte argued that the history of civilization ascends through three levels, or stages: the theological, the metaphysical, and the positive. In the most primitive of these, the theological state, Comte observed that men ascribe goodness, wickedness, and change either to divine or demonological origin. In the metaphysical state, a second, transitional stage, he noted that abstract terminology such as "ideas" and "forces" replace the supernatural as the popular explanation of causation. It is not until man reaches the third and highest stage, the positive state, Comte concluded, that man casts aside both theological and metaphysical explanations in favor of scientific descriptions of causation.[2] At that point, man discards the question *why* in favor of asking *how* things occur and seeks to answer the latter question by using simple mathematical equations.

THE EARLY POSITIVISTS

A positivist influence of sorts over criminology antecedes the era of Comte and is evident from as far back as 1586 when Jean Baptists della Porte published *The Human Physiognomy*, in which he asserted that a thief may be identifiable by his characteristically small ears and nose, bushy eyebrows, mobile eyes and sharp vision, lips that are large and remain open, plus long and slender fingers. Thorston Sellin is said to have called della Porte the "first criminologist."[3] Physiognomy came to be an accepted discipline of study during the eighteenth century when Hohan Caspar Lavater published his four-volume work on the subject, entitled *Physiognomical Fragments*, in 1775. Lavater attempted to draw a nexus between the "fragments" of a person's face (e.g., the chin, ears, eyes, nose) and that person's behavioral tendencies.[4]

On July 1, 1858, Charles Darwin and Alfred Russel Wallace delivered a joint paper before the Linneaean Society at London, following which in 1859 Darwin published *The Origin of the Species*.[5] Darwin theorized that evolution occurs by natural selection following survival of the fittest species and fittest members within each species. He shocked the world with this declaration, because the Bible maintains that God created each order of life separately.[6] Darwin shocked the world even more in 1871 when he published *The Descent of Man*,[7] suggesting with impressive documentation that man's ancestors were animals of a lower order forming a continuous linkage between the most primitive forms of life and man. He outraged religious leaders who maintained God had created man in His own image.[8] Positivism in the biological sciences came of age with Darwin, and positivist criminology took shape soon afterwards. Darwin remarked incisively within *The Descent of Man*: "With mankind some of the worst dispositions which occasionally without any assignable cause make their appearance in families, may perhaps be reversions to a savage state, from which we are not removed by many generations."[9] Five years later, in 1876, Cesare Lombroso published *L'Uomo delinquente* (*The Criminal Man*) in which he proposed that criminals are "born" as "atavistic" or biological "throwbacks" to an earlier and lower form of life.

Cesare Lombroso

Lombroso, an Italian army psychiatrist, embarked upon a systemmatic search for the causes of criminal behavior, which he assumed resulted from a characteristic present in the criminal's body but absent from the bodies of other people. Lombroso took precise measurements of various bodily organs (notably, the brain, skull, skeleton, viscera) of some three thousand Italian soldiers, then compared each soldier's measurements with his observable behavioral traits. Lombroso took similar measurements from some six thousand living prisoners and autopsied nearly four hundred dead ones.[10] In 1870, at thirty-five years of age, Lombroso autopsied a man named Vilella who was reputed to have been a famous bandit. Inside Vilella's skull, Lombroso discovered a remarkable depression that he called the middle occipital fossa. Nearby, he noticed the hypertrophy (overdevelopment) of the vermis in Vilella's brain, a known characteristic of lower primates. Based on this evidence, Lombroso concluded that Vilella's skull bore the characteristics of an order lower than man, that Vilella had been born before his time, and that, indeed, through Vilella Lombroso had found Atavus.

Years later, writing an introduction to a 1911 book authored by his daughter, Gina Lombroso Ferrero, Cesare Lombroso told what the autopsy of Vilella's skull had meant to him:

This was not merely an idea, but a revelation. At the sight of that skull, I seemed to see all of a sudden, lighted up as a vast plain under a flaming sky, the problem of the nature of the criminal—an atavistic being who reproduces in his person the ferocious instincts of primitive humanity and the inferior animals. Thus were explained anatomically the enormous jaws, high cheekbones, prominent superciliar arches, solitary lines in the palms, extreme size of the orbits, handle-shaped or sessile ears found in criminals, savages, and apes, insensibility to pain, extremely acute sight, tattooing, excessive idleness, love of orgies, and the irresistible craving for evil for its own sake, the desire not only to extinguish life in the victim, but to mutilate the corpse, tear its flesh, and drink its blood.[11]

"At the sight of these strange anomalies," Lombroso concluded in a famous address delivered in 1906, "the problem of the nature of the origin of the criminal seemed to be resolved; the characteristics of primitive men and of inferior animals must be reproduced in our times."[12] Lombroso devoted most of his research effort toward the study of physiognomy, and found that: "many criminals have outstanding ears, abundant hair, a sparse beard, enormous frontal sinuses and jaws, a square and projecting chin, broad cheekbones, frequent gestures, in fact a type resembling the Mongolian and sometimes the Negro."[13] As Lombroso proceeded with his research, the list of his "anomalies" increased substantially, as did the pages he needed to describe his findings. L'Uomo delinquente increased from a first edition of 252 pages to a fifth edition of more than 1,900 pages in three volumes.[14] Among the "anomalies," however, Lombroso seemed preoccupied with tattooing which, he in-

sisted, "is in fact one of the essential characteristics of primitive man
and of the man who is still living in a savage stage."[15] From their apparent fondness for tattooing, Lombroso inferred that criminals were less
sensitive to pain than ordinary people are,[16] an inference Lombroso expanded as he came to believe criminals possessed fewer sensory powers
in general than a normal person.[17] Lombroso came to argue that a criminal man displays a lack of moral as well as physical sensitivity,[18] evident from the criminal's seeming lack of concern for the suffering of his
victim.

In summarizing his anatomical observations and comparing the
"anomalies" he observed on living prisoners with those identified by
autopsying dead ones, Lombroso contended:

The study of the living, in short, confirms, although less exactly and less constantly, this frequency of microcephalies, of asymmetries, of oblique orbis, or
prognathisms, of frontal sinuses. . . . It shows new analogies between the insane, savages, and criminals. The prognathism, the hair abundant, black and
frizzled, the sparse beard, the oblique eyes; the small skull, the developed jaw
and zygomas, the retreating forehead, the voluminous ears, . . . are new characteristics added to the characteristics observed in the dead which bring the European criminals nearer to the Australian and Mongolian type; while the strabism, the cranial asymmetries and the serious histological anomalies, the
osteomates, the meningitic lesions, hepatic and cardiac, also show us in the
criminal a man abnormal before birth, by arrest of development or by disease
acquired from different organs, above all, from the nerve centers, as in the insane; and make him a person who is in truth chronically ill.[19]

During the course of his research, however, Lombroso commenced to
separate the born criminal from at least three other classes of criminals:
the criminal by passion, the insane criminal, and the occasional criminal, the latter being subdivisible into four subcategories: the pseudocriminal, the criminaloid, the habitual criminal, and the epileptoid.

The Born Criminal. Lombroso believed that the born criminal represented a distinct anthropological type of person, but he felt further that
this type was analogous to two other types of persons, the "moral imbecile" and the epileptic. While Lombroso argued that every born criminal is both a moral imbecile and an epileptic, he cautioned that not every
moral imbecile and not every epileptic are born criminals.[20] Apparently,
Lombroso considered both moral imbecility and epilepsy to be caused
either by heredity or trauma, and so an inconsistency of sorts lingers in
his usage of the word "born." Lombroso interchanged the terms "moral
imbecility" and "moral insanity" as he described the traits of people
whom he had studied, and explained:

The objection has justly been made against this fusion that the cases of true moral insanity that I have been able to study are too restrictive in number. That is true; but it is after all very natural; for, precisely because moral imbeciles are born criminals, they are not found as frequently in the asylum as in the prison; and it is also for that reason that it is not easy to establish a comparison. But there exists in epilepsy a uniting bond much more important, much more comprehensible, which can be studied upon a great scale, that unites and bases the moral imbecile and the born criminal in the same natural family.[21]

Lombroso went much further, however, and asserted:

Criminality is therefore an atavistic phenomenon which is provoked by morbid causes of which the fundamental manifestation is epilepsy. It is very true that criminality can be provoked by other diseases (hysteria, alcoholism, paralysis, insanity, phrenastenia, etc.), but it is epilepsy which gives to it, by its frequency, by its gravity, the most extended basis.[22]

Clearly, the two stages can be seen in the development of Lombroso's theory of the "criminal man." Early in his research, Lombroso saw Atavus solely as a savage, having been literally "born" as a primate lower than man. In a subsequent stage, Lombroso came to perceive a "criminal man" as being both atavistic (a biological throwback) and a degenerate, as Lombroso admitted: "The studies which form the first part of this volume accord admirably with those which have been developed in the second and third parts of the first volume to make us see in the criminal a savage and at the same time a sick man."[23] It was only after Lombroso's second stage, after he recognized degeneracy as a possible cause of criminality, that he articulated classes of criminals besides the "born criminal."

The Criminal by Passion. The first class of criminal that Lombroso identified in addition to his "born criminal" was the "criminal by passion," whom Lombroso distinguished by the ferocity, impetuousness, and suddenness of his criminal behavior. He calculated that the criminal by passion is more likely to be female than male, usually is young, and possesses few anomalies of the skull plus a good overall physiognomy. Consequently, Lombroso saw in this category of offender some likelihood of reformation but also the danger of suicide, perhaps both on account of this offender's high propensity for repentance. All criminals by passion have been excited by a propensity for violence, according to Lombroso, but the violence could be triggered by rage or by political zeal.[24] Lombroso explained:

The passions which excite these criminals are not those which rise gradually in the organism, as avarice and ambition, but those which burst forth unexpect-

edly, as anger, platonic or filial love, offended honor; which are usually generous passions and often sublime. On the other hand, those which predominate
in ordinary criminals are the most ignoble and the most ferocious, as vengeance, cupidity, carnal love, and drunkenness.[25]

Lombroso found traces of epilepsy and "impulsive insanity" even in
the criminal by passion.

The Insane Criminal. The "insane criminal" shared with the "born
criminal" many physical traits of degeneracy, according to Lombroso,
including particularly "outstanding ears, frontal sinuses, a voluminous
jaw and zygoma, a ferocious look or strabism, a thin upper lip."[26] Examples of the insane criminal recognized by Lombroso were kleptoman-
iacs, dipsomaniacs (habitual drunkards), homicidal monomaniacs, nym-
phomaniacs, and pederasts (adults having a sexual desire for children),
as well as "hysterical criminals" and "criminal mattoid."

The Occasional Criminal. The third and final class of criminal whom
Lombroso came to recognize as being separate from the "born criminal" he called the "occasional criminal" but subdivided into four subcategories, the first of which he termed the pseudocriminal. As the name
implies, these persons, Lombroso contended, should not be thought of
as being criminals at all but are so labeled because of deficiencies in the
law. He said the crimes committed by the pseudocriminal, such as assault in self-defense or theft to sustain one's family, are "rather juridical
than real, because they are created by imperfections of the law rather
than by those of men: they do not awaken any fear for the future, and
they do not disturb the moral sense of the masses."[27]

The second subcategory of the occasional criminal Lombroso termed
the criminaloid, typified by the person who is tempted toward a crime
over a period of time and, being weak, finally succumbs. Lombroso offered as examples of the criminaloid the fiduciary such as a banker or a
lawyer who is entrusted with money belonging to other people, the busi-
nessman who possesses the ongoing opportunity to perpetrate a fraud,
and the wife who may become perverted over time by association with
an evil husband. Lombroso explained:

These are individuals who constitute the gradations between the born criminal
and the honest man, or, better still, a variety of born criminal who has indeed
a special organic tendency but one which is less intense, who has therefore only
a touch of degeneracy; that is why I will call them *criminaloids*. But it is natural that in them the importance of the occasion determining the crime should
be decisive, while it is not so for the born criminal, for whom it is a circumstance with which he can dispense and with which he often does dispense, as,
for example, in cases of *brutal mischievousness*.[28]

Lombroso concluded that the criminaloid is predisposed to wrongdoing by a temptation to imitate evil conduct of the born criminal.[29]

The third of four subcategories of the occasional criminal Lombroso called the habitual criminal, who proceeds into a lifestyle of crime not by a single circumstance but by a group of circumstances pervading his early life. Lombroso offered as examples members of organized crime families such as the Neopolitan Cammora, the Sicilian Mafia, and the Spanish Black Hand. Lombroso observed:

The greatest number of these individuals is furnished by those who—normal from birth and without tendencies for a peculiar constitution for crime—not having found in the early education of parents, schools, etc., this force which provokes, or, better said, facilitates the passage from this physiological criminality—which we have seen belongs properly to an early age—to a normal, honest life, fall continually lower into the primitive tendency towards evil.[30]

Lombroso saw in the habitual criminal entry into a criminal career through conditioning rather than heredity.

The fourth and final subcategory of the occasional criminal Lombroso referred to as the epileptoid, or person suffering from a latent epilepsy that may become manifested at any time. This kinetic criminality may remain dormant throughout the lifetime of the epileptoid, however. In this fashion, Lombroso became forced to concede that not every criminal was truly atavistic, as he seemed to have contended originally. Lombroso wrote in the 1895 edition of *L'Homme Criminel*:

In this edition I have demonstrated that in addition to the characteristics truly atavistic there are acquired and entirely pathological characteristics; facial asymmetry, for example, which does not exist in the savage, strabism, inequality of the ears, dischromatopsy, unilateral paresia, irresistible impulses, the need of doing evil for the sake of evil, etc., and this sinister gayety which is noticeable in the professional slang of criminals and which, alternating with a certain religiousness, is found so often in epileptics. There may be added meningitis and softening of the brain, which certainly do not result from atavism.[31]

By the close of his professional career, therefore, Lombroso thought that degeneracy as well as atavism caused criminality, and he even admitted that an entirely normal person could become a criminal by passion or a pseudocriminal under exceptional circumstances.

Lombroso's last major book, entitled *Crime: Its Causes and Remedies*, published posthumously in 1911, two years after his death at the age of seventy-four, had been written with a North American readership in mind. Throughout the first half of that book, Lombroso discussed the aetiology or source of crime as including almost every inducement imaginable. He had come full circle from 1876 when he singled out biological atavism as being the only cause of criminal behavior. Among the causes listed in Lombroso's 1911 table of contents are:

[a]Long-heads and Round-heads

Lombroso concluded in his 1911 book that "[e]very crime has its origin in a multiplicity of causes, often intertwined and confused, each of which we must, in obedience to the necessities of thought and speech, investigate singly. This multiplicity is generally the rule with human phenomena, to which one can almost never assign a single cause unrelated to others."[32]

Lombroso began his 1911 book with the argument that "[t]he influence which is most apt to produce a disposition toward rebellion and crime is that of a relatively moderate degree of heat."[33] He explained this by suggesting that heat excites the body's nervous centers, much as alcohol does, but without producing apathy. He expounded on a cyclical theory peculiar to his final work:

History records no example of tropical people that has not fallen into subjection. Great heat leads to overproduction, which in turn become the cause, first, of an unequal distribution of wealth, and then, as a consequence, of great inequality in the distribution of political and social power.[34]

He found, furthermore, that in both the northern and southern hemispheres, both political uprisings and violent crimes occur most frequently in summer, next frequently spring.[35] As Lombroso's twilight years witnessed his acceptance of the environment as exerting much impact on crime, they witnessed also his acceptance of human interactions as exerting some impact on crime. A great deal of the change in Lombroso's line of thought seems to have come from association with his son-in-law, Guglielmo Ferrero, whom Lombroso cited with praise in his last book:

The types of civilization which man has hitherto produced, according to Guglielmo Ferrero, are two: the type characterized by violence, and that characterized by fraud. They are distinguished by the form which the struggle for existence takes. In the primitive civilization the struggle is carried on purely by force, and wealth and power are achieved by arms, at the expense either of foreigners or of weaker fellow-citizens. Commercial competition between the two peoples is carried on through armies and fleets. . . . Judicial contests are decided by the duel. In the civilization characterized by fraud, on the other hand, the struggle for existence is carried on by cunning and deceit, and the wager of battle is replaced by legal chicanery; political power is obtained, no longer at the point of the sword, but by money; money is extracted from the pockets of others by tricks and mysterious maneuvers, such as the operations of the stock-exchange.[36]

Lombroso admitted the distinction between Ferrero's two types of civilizations is not absolute, and that characteristics of each may be found in the same society.

Because "pathology, in the social field as in the physical, follows the pathway of physiology," Lombroso reasoned, therefore:

[T]here are two forms of criminality manifesting themselves in our day side by side: atavistic criminality, which is a return on the part of certain individuals of morbid constitution to the violent means of the struggle for existence now suppressed by civilization, such as homicide, robbery, and rape; and "evolutive" criminality, which is no less perverted in intent but more civilized in the means employed, for in place of violence it uses trickery and deceit.[37]

Throughout much of Lombroso's last book, he seems to have concluded that certain ethnic peoples had become more "evolutive" than others. He offered as examples Jews who are moneylenders, counterfeiters, and smugglers, and Gypsies who are con artists and petty thieves, no matter into what country they migrate.[38]

The theories of Cesare Lombroso changed drastically over his long professional career from initial publication of *The Criminal Man* in 1876 to his death in 1909. He founded the "Italian school" of criminology and remained the principal spokesman of positivist criminology even after the turn of the twentieth century when, by all outward appearances, he seems to have stopped being a positivist at all. Lombroso the psychiatrist was complemented by two legal scholars, Raffaele Garofalo and Enrico Ferri, as the dominant participants in the Italian school. Baron Raffaele Garofalo, an Italian nobleman as Beccaria had been before him, was seventeen years younger than Lombroso, born in 1852, and educated to become a magistrate. He rose to sit on several regional appellate courts before being appointed to the senate of the Kingdom of Italy. Enrico Ferri was four years younger than Garofalo, studied under Lombroso and became his finest pupil, then taught and practiced criminal law. He succeeded the "classical" criminologist Francesco Carrara as the principal criminology professor at the University of Pisa in 1890, but three years later the university dismissed him for his socialist views. Ferri served as a deputy elected to the lower chamber of the Italian Parliament and as the founding editor of *Avanti*, a socialist newspaper. Both Garofalo and Ferri lived well into the difficult period between the two world wars, Ferri dying in 1929 and Garofalo in 1934. Because they lived in Italy during the time when Benito Mussolini rose to dictatorship there, both Ferri and Garofalo, but, pardoxically, especially Garofalo, received criticism for adapting to fascism.[39] Consequently but unjustifiably, positivist criminology has been associated with fascism and genocide.

Neither Garofalo nor Ferri exhibited Lombroso's concern for targeting the causes of criminal behavior, perhaps because they were lawyers while Lombroso was a physician. On the other hand, Lombroso devoted ample attention toward both criminal procedures in the courts and the treatment of the convicted offender in confinement. Garofalo and Ferri predicated a good deal of their strategies for criminal procedure and penology upon Lombroso's theory of crime's causation, but Lombroso based many of his ideas on criminal procedures and penology upon those set forth by Garofalo and Ferri. Lombroso began to consider these topics seriously only at the end of his life when he was quite familiar with the notions produced by Garofalo and Ferri.

Raffaele Garofalo

Garofalo's major work began as a brochure entitled, "Concerning a Positive Criterion of Punishment," which he published in 1880 at the age of twenty-eight. That brochure evolved into his book, *Criminology*, published at Naples in 1885, at Turin in 1891, and, following substantial revision, translated into French in 1905 and into English in 1914. Garofalo wrote various other works, notably *Criminal Attempt by Insufficient Means* (1882),[40] *The True Manner of Trial and Sentence* (1882),[41] *Indemnification of Crime Victims* (1887),[42] and *Concerning International Solidarity in the War against Crime* (1909).[43] Garofalo pioneered the concept of social defense, and viewed the major purpose of penology as being able to restrain the criminal from recidivating in order to protect society, rather than to reform or rehabilitate the offender so that he will be a better person. One of Garofalo's most famous statements is that "[o]ur efforts . . . are to be directed, not to measuring the quantum of harm to be inflicted on the criminal, but to determining the kind of restraint best fitted to the peculiarities of his nature[:]"

"What!" some one may exclaim. "Would you make no distinction in punishment between the man who has stolen twenty francs and the man who has stolen but twenty centimes?"

My answer is that I do not know, for the question is one which cannot be decided abstractly. The thing important here to determine is—which one of these two thieves has the greater criminal aptitude, and is thus the greater danger to society? It may well be the former, but it may quite as well be the latter.

What we are aiming at is not to fix the quantum of suffering occasioned by the offense, on the basis of the value of what has been stolen, but to designate the repressive means which shall be exactly appropriate, that is to say, the obstacle capable of averting the danger. The problem then can be formulated in but one way. "By what means are we to determine the offender's degree of constant perversity and the degree of sociability which he still retains?"[44]

Garofalo proceeded then to identify criteria the court should consider to answer that question.

To determine the best kind of restraint for a given criminal offender, Garofalo recommended that a judge consider the "objective" circumstances of the crime (such as whether the offender "ought to be classed as a thief from instinct, from idleness, from the effect of a neglected and depraved childhood, from the effect of bad company, or simply because of the evil examples of his family surroundings") as well as the previous history of the offender (such as "his family and social relationships[,] . . . age, . . . the education which he has received, his occupations, and his general aim in life").[45] Garofalo suggested a pre-sentence investigation should be conducted to instruct a sentencing judge as to the offender's "moral anomaly," so that the jurist might project how well the offender could be expected to "adapt" to alternative means of "repression." An initial sentencing decision, Garofalo urged, has to be to decide whether the offender's "elimination" is necessary for the safety of the community and, if so, if it has to be permanent or only temporary, as well as what means should be employed to achieve it.

"Elimination" of an offender could be achieved in various ways, Garofalo argued, such as by (1) death, (2) "relegation" (transportation) out of the country, and (3)imprisonment.[46] Permanent elimination would include capital punishment as well as transportation or imprisonment for life, but also the less drastic alternative of expelling an offender permanently from his profession or trade, if without membership therein he could not repeat a particular crime such as embezzlement. Repression without elimination would be preferable, Garofalo agreed, when possible without risk of recidivism. One form of such "repression" he called "enforced reparation," where the offender both indemnifies the victim of his crime and a fine to the state.[47]

Four categories of criminals, each meriting different punishment, are articulated by Garofalo: (1) extreme criminals, (2) impulsive criminals, (3) professional malefactors, and (4) endemic criminals. By extreme criminals, Garofalo referred to "men wholly destitute of moral sense and capable alike of murder or theft" who are "too improvident, too brutalized, of too little sensibility, to appreciate the disgrace of prison, or to feel the suffering, moral rather than physical, which loss of liberty entails."[48] For them, he reasoned, death is the only suitable penalty. *"But its inflection must be swift and certain.* When too seldom applied, it begins to lose its effect upon them."[49]

The second class of offender, impulsive criminals, Garofalo believed might benefit from imprisonment, even if insane. Among this group Garofalo included people whose criminality results from their "temperament, from neurosis, or as the effect of alcoholic excitation," but with them, also, he urged that "[t]o produce the requisite impression, the threatened harm must be serious and immediate."[50] Garofalo elaborated:

If every one were convinced that to strike another with the hand meant the instant loss of that hand, many supposedly irresistible impulses would cease to be irresistible: perhaps the very word which describes this act would disappear from our active vocabulary.

It is no answer to say that the barbarous punishments of the Middle Ages were not more efficacious than the punishments of the present day. . . . [T]here was then a greater uncertainty of punishment. Numerous ways of escaping it existed, such as immunities, the right of asylum, and the protection of the great nobles. Then, too, the irregular working of the police system and the defective administration of justice in that day must be taken into account.[51]

Garofalo took exception, therefore, to the "efficacious" argument of Jeremy Bentham and the utilitarians (see Chapter 4) while at the same time, implicitly, praising the improvement of policing achieved by the force of utilitarianism.

The third class of offender Garofalo labeled the professional malefactor, whose crimes legislation cannot prevent, he argued, because this criminal calculates fairly accurately his risk of detection and apprehension: "They boldly face the danger, because in this trade, as in any other, some risk must be run—and there are much more hazardous trades which do not lack craftsmen. Yet here, as elsewhere, the smaller the risk and the more certain the reward, the greater the supply of recruits."[52] This class of offender has to be "eliminated," Garofalo warned, apparently through lengthy imprisonment or transportation out of the country. On the other hand, Garofalo felt that laws could prevent the conduct of endemic criminals, and that harsh punishments for this class of offender may become counterproductive. Garofalo offered as an example gun control ("disarmament") legislation enacted in 1854 on Corsica which resulted in a substantial decrease of its murder rate prior to repeal of the law fourteen years later in 1868, after which the murder rate rose again.[53]

Consistent with his belief that punishment should be "swift and certain," Garofalo opposed the tradition of permitting convicted offenders to remain free pending the appeal of their convictions or sentences to higher courts. In fact, he seems to have opposed the right of appeal itself, at least implied:

[A]ccording to the Italian procedure nearly all persons accused of misdemeanors ["délits"] are entitled to provisional liberty, and consequently to remain at large not only during the judicial investigation ["instruction"], but until the termination of proceedings for review in the Court of Cassation—and the convicted prisoner seldom fails to invoke the action of the last-mentioned court. This feature manifestly robs a criminal prosecution of much of its terror. . . . [T]he sentences imposed are for terms of imprisonment much too short, and even these short sentences the pardoning power is too ready to commute. The result wears the appearance of a semiimpunity.[54]

Italy's Court of Cassation at the time functioned as the national court of last resort in criminal matters, and an appeal to it took as long as similar appeals require today to be processed through the Supreme Court of the United States of America.

Nor did Garofalo enjoy much respect for juries, which he thought reflected popular biases and ignorance. Instead, he preferred trial before a judge. His reasoning, not surprisingly, reflects his years on the bench:

However conclusive the evidence against the accused, however unimpeachable its character, its whole effect may vanish before some sudden impression which the art of a skillful advocate is capable of producing on the minds of the jurors. Every one admits, and foremost of all the legal profession, that the result of a [jury] trial . . . depends on sheer chance. . . .

The injustices committed by the jury, for the most part, are due in reality to its ignorance, whether because of its inability to grasp the meaning of many legal terms and to appreciate the true significance and connection of the often numerous questions which are propounded to it, or because of the lack of necessary aptitude for or experience in the critical labor of examining the evidence and weighing the arguments for and against, in a case where the fact of guilt does not appear at the first glance. Sometimes the jurors bring in a verdict of acquittal, as a protest against the government. . . . "In short, whether it is due to his nervous sensibility or artistic impressionability, I am unable to see how the Italian, when called upon to act as judge, can help being emotionally affected, unless he has undergone a special training to prepare him for this function."

The permanent judge, it is true, is not always beyond the reach of corruption: he may also be accessible to fear or other influences. But he has a name to preserve, an honorable position to retain; from prudence, from necessity, he acquires courage and firmness, for the slightest breath of suspicion may suffice to accomplish his ruin. Hence, scandals from this cause will never be common, nor of so startling a nature as those which the jury every day compels us to witness.[55]

Garofalo favored the statement he quoted from a British judge in India: the only way to reform the jury is to abolish it![56]

Garofalo paralleled Beccaria in protesting the head of government's prerogative to grant amnesty, clemency, or pardon to the convicted criminal offender.[57] He favored a form of preventive detention before trial where the interests of justice warranted it, as:

(1) Where it is probable that the accused will be sentenced to a punishment heavy enough to make it an object to him to take to flight or go into hiding—because the punishment in question is for him the greater of the two evils.

(2) Where the case is one of striking ["coups"] or wounding ["blessures"], until the victim has fully recovered from the effect of his injuries.

(3) Where it is probable that the person injured will resort to bloodshed to take revenge upon the aggressor.

(4) Where the accused is a recidivist, habitual offender, or person without visible means of support or fixed place of abode.

(5) Where the accused is a thief or swindler who has been taken in the act.

(6) And finally, in all cases where there is danger of the accused intimidating or suborning the injured person or the witnesses, or in any way hindering or thwarting the judicial investigation.[58]

To remedy what Garofalo considered to be "defects of existing criminal procedures," he proposed certain "principles" as a basis for an international penal code, both substantive and procedural [see the appendix to this chapter].

One of Garofalo's most important thoughts was his proposal for what he called a "rational system of punishment,"[59] where the penalty inflicted would be in proportion of the risk of future danger the offender would pose to society. Thus, Garofalo established the positivist notion of punishment to achieve social defense and rejected both the Christian ideal of moral responsibility and the Beccarian argument that punishment should be meted out in proportion to the seriousness of the offense. Garofalo wanted an offender to be measured for punishment in terms of his *temibilita*, or frightfulness. He asked: "Are we not obliged to say that against the individual whose manifest total absence of free will make him incapable of controlling himself or resisting his vicious impulses, society requires increased, instead of lessened, protection!"[60] He answered:

Be it so: if the injury inflicted is necessary for the preservation of society, let abstract justice take such offenses as it may. The entire world affords a continual spectacle of similar injustices. Men suffer because of mental and physical defects, because of an unfortunate situation in life, which they are without power to change. The child who is deficient in memory or attention will never receive good marks at school. However great a source of mortification he may find it, he will always remain at the foot of his class. . . . Must we call these injustices? Is the law itself unjust, when it condemns the children to poverty because of the debts of the father?[61]

In this way, Garofalo explained, "the criminal will undergo the punishment which has been merited, not by a doubtful faculty of his mind, but by all that which constitutes his personality, namely, his psychic organisms, his instincts, and his character."[62]

Enrico Ferri

At the age of twenty-one, in 1877, Enrico Ferri published a 476-page dissertation entitled *The Denial of Free Will and the Theory of Imputability*,[63] a copy of which he sent to Lombroso who declared it was not "positivist enough."[64] Ferri went on to study in France, gathering statistical data and learning the German language, after which he won a docentship to study criminology under Lombroso at the University of Turin. During this period, Lombroso and Ferri became close friends and, as Thorsten Sellin noted, each influenced the other.[65] In 1881, Ferri published *New Horizons of Criminal Law and Penal Procedure*,[66] but three years later, with its second edition, he changed the title to *Criminal Sociology*.[67] In 1884, also, Ferri published *The Homicide-Suicide*,[68] in which he first classified criminals into four types: the born criminal, the insane, the occasional criminal, and the criminal by passion, in the tradition of Lombroso. He added to insane a subcategory, the Mattoide or semi-insane, in his *Criminal Sociology*, and also a fifth category, the habitual criminal.[69]

Ferri cautioned that his classifications of criminals did not explain the causes of crime. As early as 1881 when Ferri published his "Studies on Criminality in France between 1824 and 1878,"[70] he recognized three different factors as being the chief causes of criminal behavior: anthropological causes, including the offender's age, race, and sex, plus his physical and psychic anomalies; telluric conditions, such as climate and temperature, the fertility of the soil in a given geographic area, and meteoric conditions; and social causes, among them the offender's education, profession, religion, and socioeconomic status, and an area's population density, industrial conditions, and type of government.[71] Charles A. Ellwood said in his introduction to Ferri's 1917 American edition of *Criminal Sociology*:

In a word, Ferri finds that crime is a product practically of all the forces in the universe, though these forces manifest themselves in varying proportions in different crimes and criminals. To Lombroso he would give chief credit for . . . the importance of the anthropologic factors, and it is especially in the born-criminal, he thinks, that the importance of [this] factor becomes manifest. To writers of the socialist school he would give credit for calling attention to the importance of social and economic factors, and these are seen especially in the occasional and habitual criminals; while to staticians like Quetelet he would give credit for . . . telluric factors like climate, seen especially in crimes of passion.[72]

Ferri's editions grew in size as they grew in number, as had Lombroso's. The first Italian edition of *Criminal Sociology* had consisted of 160 pages in 1884, while the fifth Italian edition contained 1,000 pages by 1900.[73]

Among the most important contributions to criminology Ferri made in his *Criminal Sociology* was his "law of criminal saturation," which Ferri described himself as follows:

[C]rime, whether natural or legal, continues to increase in the aggregate with more or less of an annual variation which tends to accumulate, in a long period, into a series of real criminal waves. From this we see that the level of crime each year is determined by the different conditions of the physical and social environment combined with the congenital tendencies and accidental impulses of individuals, in accordance with a law, which, in analogy to the law of chemistry, I have called the law of criminal saturation. As a given volume of water at a definite temperature will dissolve a fixed quantity of chemical substance and not an atom more or less; so in a given social environment with definite individual and physical conditions, a fixed number of delicts [crimes], no more and no less, can be committed.[74]

During some periods of time, however, Ferri saw a "criminal supersaturation" or crime "wave," such as (according to Ferri) during periods of election in America and during periods of economic or social crises or times of famine elsewhere.[75] Moreover, Ferri witnessed what he termed a "periodical movement of crime" across Europe and a "periodical growth of crime," which he said fluctuated at intervals of approximately five years.[76] Ferri viewed crime as following a seesaw pattern:

[T]here is an approximately constant law which we note in the crime of all countries whereby there is an alternation in the annual movement of crimes against property with the movement of those against the person: as the one increases— the other decreases. This is because the most efficient and most variable general factors (abundance of food and mildness of climate) which decrease attempts against property increase the number of violent and sexual crimes: Attacks on property being much more numerous than crimes against the person contributed more in fixing the level of annual delinquency.[77]

Ferri conceded, however, that, notwithstanding periodic oscillations, the crime rate tends to increase in most countries, a fact he attributed at least in part to increasing birth rates and immigration patterns.[78] Ferri noted that, for instance, the United States reported one convict for every 1,647 inhabitants in 1850, but that rate increased to one convict for every 1,342 inhabitants by 1860, one for every 1,171 by 1870, one for every 855 by 1880, and one convict for every 757 inhabitants by 1890.[79] He noted similar increases in the crime rates of European countries as their populations increased during the nineteenth century, explaining: "This increase of population is a natural and inherent cause of the increase in crime by increasing the number of relations, of things, and of persons in a denser population on the same territory and especially in urban centers."[80] In this respect, clearly, Enrico Ferri commenced to accept social ecology as exerting a significant impact upon criminal behavior, a concept that seems insolubrious with the original works of the Italian positivist criminologists, Ferri himself included.

In the third part to *Criminal Sociology*, Ferri summarized the "positive theory of penal responsibility," in which he denied that man possesses "free will," the abuse of which by a criminal had been Beccaria's justification for punishment. Ferri explained:

The habitual reasoning by which public sentiment, traditional philosophy, and classical criminal science justify the right to punish man for his misdeeds is reducible to this: man possesses free choice or moral liberty; he can will either good or evil—and hence, if he chooses evil he is responsible for his choice and should be punished for it. . . . The positivist criminal school does not accept this. . . . [P]ositivistic physio-psychology has completely destroyed the belief in free choice or moral liberty, in which, it demonstrates, we should recognize observation. . . . [E]ven accepting this criterion of individual responsibility, insurmountable theoretical and practical difficulties are met in applying it to each particular case, and the field is left open to a mass of exceptions.[81]

According to Ferri, it is inaccurate to think of the human mind as being divisible into several faculties, such as memory, intelligence, and "will," because:

If we look to positivistic psychology for a less fantastic and less naive notion of the mental faculties, we find that these so-called faculties are but syntheses, works of the mind corresponding to no real entity. . . . [M]emory and intelligence are but the subjective abstract and general sum of all the particular thoughts which we have had either in our own existence or as an inheritance from our ancestors. Nor does a memory exist. There are only isolated acts of memory in the same way that an intelligence does not exist, there being only isolated thoughts, and so on. In like manner the will is but the abstract synthesis of all of the volitional acts which we have performed. Hence the will does not exist as an autonomous being which from time to time issues volitional commands. . . . The volitional deliberation resulting from the above-mentioned physio-psychological process of every human act, is not the cause of the movement; it is but the consciousness of this very movement which is being executed, not by virtue of the volitional command, but merely by the process of reciprocal transformation of physical and physio-psychological forces.[82]

Thus, Ferri concluded, the difference between a "voluntary" and an "involuntary" act is nothing more than the presence or absence of that consciousness, which has nothing to do with "moral liberty" or "free choice."[83]

Ferri identified four "evolutionary phases" of law during the course of which various excuses were generated to justify penalties. These phases were: the primitive, during which the wronged victim took instantaneous vindictive action; the religious, during which a punishment was viewed as being divine vengeance; the ethical, where the punishment was designed to make the offender repent his sins; and the juridical, where the offender is deemed to have violated a law by the exercise of his "free will."[84] Ferri desired to inaugurate a fifth phase, where "punishment will no longer be retribution for a moral fault by a proportionate chastisement . . . but a sum of preventive and repressive social measures" designed to protect society.[85] He called this fifth phase the social phase.

Ferri's punishments were intended not to be based on moral responsibility of the offender. He urged "the complete withdrawal from the punitive agency of every criterion of responsibility or moral culpability," and he advocated "substituting a more positive criterion which . . . cannot be contested solely on account of differences of religious or philosophical beliefs or mental habits."[86] This, he suggested, would be accomplished by means of physical, biological, and social sanctions:

The man or animal that, even unconsciously, involuntarily, or by constraint, violates the laws of nature, finds in nature itself an irresistible reaction or sanction. He who leans too far out of a window, even with the most moral or benevolent intention, falls. This is the physical sanction. Whoever eats too much, gets indigestion, becomes ill and suffers. . . . This is the biological sanction. A passer-by who in his absentmindedness and without intent to injure, jostles another, evokes in the latter a reaction either in words or acts. [This is the social sanction.][87]

Ferri articulated a variety of social sanctions, ranging from public opinion to economic reparation to violence, which he considered may be applied in relation to "social selection":

Society is a natural living organism and as every animal body lives by a continual process of assimilation and disassimilation tending to the well-being of the individual, the very first conditions of its existence, so likewise human society can neither exist nor prosper without the ceaseless labor of natural assimilation (birth) or artificial assimilation (immigration) and of equally natural disassimilation (deaths) or necessarily artificial disassimilation (emigration and segregation of anti-social individuals, incapable of assimilation because of contagious disease, insanity, and crime). Thus, this function of social preservation against criminality comes into its place among the forms of social selection that have had and still have so large a part in the evolution of humanity.[88]

Consequently, Ferri contended that "[a]t all events, a place must be made in the preservative clinic of crime, as in the clinics of ordinary diseases and insanity, for the social elimination of those who are least adapted to life."[89] Against that premise, Ferri concluded that:

[P]enal justice, first deprived of any other character than that of a function of social preservation, must view crime as the effect of individual anomalies and as a symptom of social pathology necessarily postulating the removal of anti-social individuals by isolating the infectious elements and disinfecting the environment in which the germs develop.[90]

Thus, Ferri came to argue that *moral* culpability is an "impossible basis for defense of society" and must be replaced by "social accountability."[91] Ferri remarked:

Having established that . . . society cannot be denied the right of self-preservation irrespective of the moral responsibility of the individual, the sole foundation of criminal science, and of the agency corresponding to it, must be social accountability. . . . "Man's acts may be imputed to him and, hence, he is responsible for them because he lives in society."[92]

Evidently, the "positive theory of penal responsibility" embraced strict liability whereby one became punishable for anything he did in violation of the law, regardless of his state of mind at the time.

Ferri favored imprisonment for an *indeterminate* period of time as punishment for crime.[93] He conceded that corporal punishment, although in many cases it may "produce excellent effect," is repugnant to principles of humanity and "too easily abused."[94] In this first edition of *Criminal Sociology*, Ferri wrote that "the period of segregation must not be determined by the judge, but, on the contrary, it is in the province of the [correctional] establishment . . . to decide upon a lifelong or temporary detention, depending upon a psychoanthropological study of the prisoner."[95] In addition, Ferri insisted that an offender should pay reparations in three forms:

I. As an obligation of the delinquent to the injured party;

II. As a punishment in place of imprisonment for petty crimes committed by occasional delinquents;

III. As a function of the State in the direct interest of the injured party and in the direct but no less real interest of social defense.[96]

In this way, apparently, Ferri wanted the offender to indemnify the individual victim financially but also to pay a penalty in the nature of a fine to the state, sharing this view held by Raffaele Garofalo and other positivist criminologists.

Prisons should not be "places of ease," Ferri warned, and in prison "the obligation to work must be universal and absolute."[97] He seemed to be mindful of the difficulty posed when prisoners try to compete in the marketplace with free labor. He recommended that prisoners work in those industries that compete least directly with free labor and that they be paid full compensation for their work after board, clothing, lodging, and victim indemnification have been deducted.[98] In this way, Ferri shared Bentham's view that prison should offer the inmate an opportunity to work and receive market value for his services. In addition, Ferri thought that prisons should function also as "hospitals where delinquency is treated"[99] and that insane criminals should be housed in asylums.[100]

Ferri did not oppose capital punishment in theory, although in practice he felt it had become a sham because so few offenders were executed. Consider his views:

It is my belief that the death penalty is prescribed by Nature in every part of the Universe and in all phases of universal life. It does not seem to me to be in absolute contradiction with personal rights, because when the death of another is absolutely necessary, it is perfectly just, as a case of self-defense, whether individual or social. . . . Furthermore, the universal law of evolution shows that the progress of every living species is due to a continual selection brought about by the death of those less fit for the struggle of existence, and this selection can, in humanity, and even, to a certain point, in animals, be effected artificially out of respect to the laws of life under the same conditions as it works naturally. It, therefore, conforms not only to the laws of justice, but to those of nature, that society should effect an artificial selection within itself, destroying the elements harmful to its existence—anti-social, non-assimilable, and deleterious human beings. . . .

On the other hand, the utility and defensive efficacy of capital punishment is problematical, for when a man commits a crime he is either carried away by a sudden passion and thinks nothing, or else he acts with premeditation, and what determines his course in the latter case is not a hypothetical comparison between the capital punishment and life imprisonment, but the hope of impunity. . . . Statistics show that the variation in the number of capital crimes is independent of the number of condemnations and executions. . . .

In the last analysis, capital punishment, in its monosyllabic simplicity, is only an easy panacea, and under its head, it certainly does not solve a problem as complex as that of dangerous criminality. . . . [Capital punishment] must be applied seriously and requires the courage of putting [the offender] to death. . . . [T]he power of intimidation of penalties in general, without excepting capital punishment, is entirely insignificant as far as born-criminals are concerned, and is lessened still further by the fact that the people get accustomed to the idea of capital punishment. . . . [T]en or twelve executions a year will not cure criminality. Furthermore, those few and tardy executions embody all of the disadvantages of the death penalty, and none of its advantages, by awakening, on the one hand, a compassion on the part of the good person and a certain antipathy for the law, and, on the other hand, the ferocious instincts of the masses. . . .

To be logical, we must . . . execute more than fifteen hundred a year. . . . Capital punishment, as it exists today, is a mere scarecrow—and the criminals are like the birds—at first they believe it real, but soon they play in the shadow of the scaffold.[101]

Benito Mussolini asked Enrico Ferri to draft a new penal code for Italy, which the latter submitted as the Ferri Draft of 1921. The Italian Chamber of Deputies rejected it, largely because it departed too abruptly from the classical tradition of Beccaria, so ingrained in the Italian culture. Nevertheless, the Ferri Draft incorporated the jurisprudence and penology of its author and the Italian school of positivist criminology. For this reason, it is important intellectually. With the failure of the Ferri Draft in 1922, one may argue, the Italian school of positivist criminology ceased to have much of an impact except among its most ardent proponents.

DECLINE OF THE ITALIAN SCHOOL OF CRIMINOLOGY

Good reasons can be advanced as to why the Italian school of criminology began to decline a generation before its eventual fall in 1922, almost from the beginning of the twentieth century. In 1866, (Gregor) Johann Mendel had published two genetic "laws"[102] pertaining to the hybridization of plants, which became popular again toward the end of the nineteenth century. Against Mendel's "laws" as background, scientists conducted hybrid experiments, particularly on the primrose. Three geneticists, Karl Correns, Hugo deVries, and Erich Tschermak, published independent results of their hybrid experiments in 1900. The next year, in 1901, deVries published volume one of *The Mutation Theory*, the second volume appearing in 1903. According to deVries' naturalistic theory of mutation, any living thing (plant or animal) is a mosaic of independent characteristics that vary discontinuously.[103] So, new varieties and subspecies of life emerge by mutation as hybrid breeding occurs, and parents transmit to their offspring both desirable characteristics and less desirable ones, including congenital defects and diseases. In this respect, nearly all living things may be considered "throwbacks" in one way or another, although, to be sure, some are more seriously "atavistic" than others.

Three years after Mendel published his laws and a decade after Darwin's *The Origin of the Species* emerged, English anthropologist Francis Galton published *Hereditary Genius* (1869), in which he applied Darwin's theory of physical evolution to the individual's intellectual development. In 1883, Galton published *Inquiries into Human Faculty* in which he coined the word "eugenics" to describe his theory for controlling hereditary defects through planned breeding. He founded the Eugenics (Education) Society at London in 1908, for which he was knighted. Karl Pearson, one of Sir Francis Galton's students, utilized various new statistical measures to study resemblance among family members. In 1901, Charles Buckman Goring began to take precise measurements of more than three thousand inmates at English prisons and to compare them with control groups he thought represented the general noncriminal population, such as students from Cambridge and Oxford Universities, British soldiers, and hospital patients. Karl Pearson assisted Goring, and together they used statistical techniques that were sophisticated for the time.

Charles Buckman Goring

In 1913, Goring published his famous work, *The English Convict: A Statistical Study*, in which he set out both to disprove Lombroso's theory that criminals may be identified through their physical characteristics and to prove his own theory that criminals may be targeted statistically by measuring the prison histories of family members. Table 1 reconstructs the table that Goring constructed in support of his thesis.[104] Goring's notion that imprisonment of a close relative may induce one's criminality (i.e., from father to son, one brother to another) is one kind of an environmentalist theory, albeit in an early form. Goring wrote that his data "forced" him to hypothesize "the possible existence of a character in all men which, in the absence of a better term, we call the crim-

Table 1.
Goring's Table of Physical Resemblances and Criminality Patterns within Families.

Characteristic	Approximate Correlations	
	Parental Resemblance (Father-Son)	*Fraternal Resemblance (Brothers)*
Ordinary physical traits and features	.60	.45
Inherited defects, insanity, and mental disease	.60	.45
General criminality as measured by imprisonment	.60	.45
Offences involving damage to property	.45	.46
Sexual offences	.45	.23
Crimes of stealing and burglary	.60	.55
Crimes of violence to person	.50	.46
Crimes of fraud	.15	.17

inal 'diathesis' . . . a constitutional proclivity'' and which, whether mental, moral, or physical, is sufficiently potent to determine even ''the fate of imprisonment.'' [105] After studying some thirty-seven physical traits and six mental traits, however, Goring's correlations supported both environmental and hereditary theories of criminal causation.

Nevertheless, Goring included that Lombroso's positivist criminology was ''an organized system of self-evident confusion whose parallel is only to be found in the astrology, alchemy, and other credulities of the Middle Ages.'' [106] Yet, Goring's primary criticism was of Lombroso's methods rather than of his theory itself, as to the theory Goring having conceded: ''I shall accept it as the foundation of criminology, but shall nonetheless condemn Lombroso as a traitor to science. . . . If to disregard the laws of scientific procedure be to commit a grave offence, there has been no greater scientific criminal than Lombroso.'' [107] Upon rejecting Lombroso's biological determinism as not having been proven satisfactorily, Goring went on to maintain nevertheless that criminal behavior is inherited in the form of ''defective intelligence,'' which he said could be controlled eugenically by curtailing the reproduction of families exhibiting traits such as ''feeblemindedness, epilepsy, insanity, and defective social instincts.'' [108]

Goring's principal contribution to criminology was his use of a biometric method to study behavioral characteristics of prisoners. As statistician Karl Pearson expounded, writing the introduction to *The English Convict*, Goring avoided the bias and sentimentality of earlier criminologists such as Lombroso, primarily because Goring had no theory of his own to advance. Instead, Pearson contended, Goring gathered the facts ''and analyzed them by the modern statistico-mathematical method. . . . That material was unprecedented in criminal literature.'' [109] To that extent, of course, Pearson was correct, and Goring's impact on the future of criminology was lasting. Six years later, Pearson went on to prophesize further when introducing Goring's abridged edition:

[O]ne of the chief merits of Goring's work will be that by its very nature it compels those who would controvert it from the scientific side to collect better material and to adopt practically Goring's methods of procedure. They may or may not be successful. Strange as it may seem, the contradiction of his conclusions would be a small matter compared with the fundamental fact that Goring's methods have ploughed deeply the ground, and traced firmly the lines on which the scientific criminologist of the future will be compelled to work. [110]

As Goring criticized Lombroso, however, so have others taken exception to Goring himself. [111] Harvard anthropologist Earnest Albert Hooton became Goring's chief critic who set out to avenge Goring's refutation of Lombroso, because Hooton felt Goring had been "prejudiced against Lombroso and all of his theories."[112]

Earnest Albert Hooton

In 1927, Hooton embarked upon a formidable project, well-funded and assisted by many Harvard students, intended to prove once and for all the truth of Lombroso's theories. Hooton sampled 13,873 criminals and 3,203 controls from the general male population, drawing both sample groups from ten states.[113] He studied what he called "Old American" whites as well as other white males who were foreign-born or whose parents had been foreign-born, together with "Negroes" and people whom he called "Negroids."[114] Hooton obtained some 107 measurements of each subject's physical characteristics, including most which Lombroso had studied, such as ear protrusion, eye folds, forehead, lips, jaw angles, and tattooing.[115] Finally, in 1939, Hooton published the results of his twelve-year "Harvard study" in two different ways: a three-volume edition entitled *The American Criminal: An Anthropological Study*, designed for the scholarly community, and a single-volume book, *Crime and the Man*, in which he condensed the larger work "to epitomize the [survey] results . . . in a way which will be tolerable for intelligent and determined readers who are interested in human behavior but not in statistics."[116] In other words, Hooton directed his condensed book at the lay reader, hoping for the widespread popularity Beccaria, Lombroso, and a number of other criminologists before and after Hooton enjoyed. Hooton hoped in vain.

If Goring found Lombroso's research to be lacking in scientific method, undoubtedly he would have been more horrified by Hooton's inquiry. Hooton's control groups consisted of what Stephen Schafer has called "a fantastic conglomeration of noncriminal civilians"[117] who included officers of the Massachusetts militia; outpatients from the Massachusetts General Hospital; Harvard University students; Nashville, Tennessee firemen; and patrons of a bath house. Most control-group members had one thing in common—they were uncooperative! Robert K. Merton and M. F. Ashley-Montagu remarked that Hooton's control group resembled anthropoid apes more than American criminals.[118] Schafer's observation that "[t]he scientific response to Hooton's work was severely unfavorable"[119] was a profound understatement. Hooton's greatest problem seems to have been that he failed to account for differences among both sample prisoners and sample nonprisoners in different states who were measured by different field investigators and who came from different occupational backgrounds.[120] His greatest error may have been the immodesty of his conclusions in the light of the scant evidence he collected. Hooton argued that physical inferiority is inherited and that prisoners display signs of physical inferiority "in nearly all their bodily measurements" compared to civilians,[121] but his civilian control groups were insufficiently representative of the general population to permit this generalization. Moreover, Hooton concluded that robbers who murder are tall and thin, but men who forge or perpetrate frauds and murder are tall and heavy; that rapists tend to be short and heavy, while "undersized thin men" are most likely to commit thefts and to burglarize.[122]

As George B. Vold noted, however, Hooton typecast prisoners according to the crime for which they were serving a sentence at the time he studied them, and he ignored the possibility that at least some prisoners may have been incarcerated previously as punishment for a quite different crime.[123] Moreover, in concluding that an average prisoner is eleven pounds lighter than an average civilian, Hooton failed to standardize the diets of both groups.[124] Edwin H. Sutherland said that Hooton "must be complimented for using careful statistical procedures . . . and on the thoroughness of his analysis. [His] is a monumental work in size, but unfortunately it makes little contribution to the explanation of criminal behavior."[125] Hooton conducted a rigorous analysis on untrustworthy data. In that sense, he erred in a fashion similar to today's investigators who rely upon computer printouts unfailingly but without questioning the sources of the input data or data collection methods.

One of the curiosities within Hooton's works, particularly *Crime and the Man*, is the set of drawings he made to illustrate his theses and the books. (The following are examples from *Crime and the Man*, Earnest Albert Hooton. Reprinted by permission.)
Hooton explained his decision to include these drawings:

I originally intended to illustrate the lectures and the book with diagrams and graphs, but decided that ordinary graphs are hardly less depressing than tables. So I began to embellish or deface the graphs with nasty little human figures. Beginning thus innocently, I gradually relapsed into an adolescent vice of which I have been free for a quarter of a century—drawing bad pictures.[126]

Unquestionably, it appears, these drawings reflect the anthropological comparisons that ran through Hooton's mind. In that sense, perhaps, a look at Hooton's drawings is the last glimpse we may have of a true positivist's view of "the criminal man."

Hooton warned bluntly that he favored banishing the offender to some remote place rather than to devote efforts toward rehabilitation:

I have not spent the greater part of twelve years in studying criminals from any humanitarian zeal for the rehabilitation of offenders, or from any deep interest

OLD AMERICAN CRIMINALS
MOSAIC OF CRANIAL, FACIAL, METRIC AND MORPHOLOGICAL FEATURES
MASSACHUSETTS

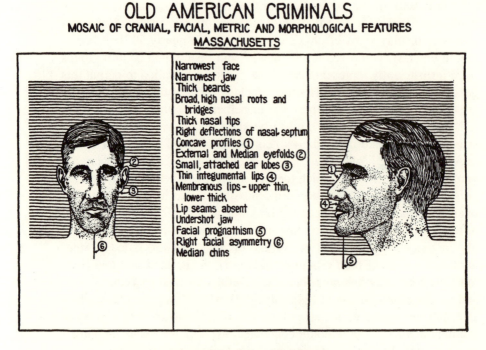

Narrowest face
Narrowest jaw
Thick beards
Broad, high nasal roots and
    bridges
Thick nasal tips
Right deflections of nasal septum
Concave profiles ①
External and Median eyefolds ②
Small, attached ear lobes ③
Thin integumental lips ④
Membranous lips - upper thin,
    lower thick
Lip seams absent
Undershot jaw
Facial prognathism ⑤
Right facial asymmetry ⑥
Median chins

OLD AMERICAN CRIMINALS
MOSAIC OF CRANIAL, FACIAL, METRIC AND MORPHOLOGICAL FEATURES
TENNESSEE

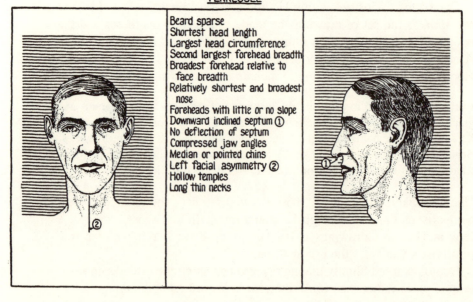

Beard sparse
Shortest head length
Largest head circumference
Second largest forehead breadth
Broadest forehead relative to
    face breadth
Relatively shortest and broadest
    nose
Foreheads with little or no slope
Downward inclined septum ①
No deflection of septum
Compressed jaw angles
Median or pointed chins
Left facial asymmetry ②
Hollow temples
Long thin necks

OLD AMERICAN CRIMINALS
MOSAIC OF CRANIAL, FACIAL, METRIC AND MORPHOLOGICAL FEATURES
KENTUCKY

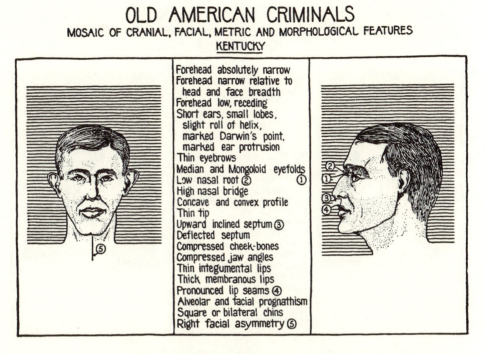

Forehead absolutely narrow
Forehead narrow relative to
  head and face breadth
Forehead low, receding
Short ears, small lobes,
  slight roll of helix,
  marked Darwin's point,
  marked ear protrusion
Thin eyebrows
Median and Mongoloid eyefolds ①
Low nasal root ②
High nasal bridge
Concave and convex profile
Thin tip
Upward inclined septum ③
Deflected septum
Compressed cheek-bones
Compressed jaw angles
Thin integumental lips
Thick membranous lips
Pronounced lip seams ④
Alveolar and facial prognathism
Square or bilateral chins
Right facial asymmetry ⑤

OLD AMERICAN CRIMINALS
MOSAIC OF CRANIAL, FACIAL, METRIC AND MORPHOLOGICAL FEATURES
TEXAS

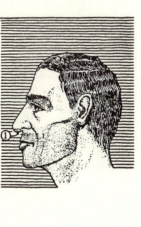

Wavy hair
Heavy beard
Maximum face breadth
Very pronounced cheekbones
Hollow temples
Relatively shortest and broadest
  faces
Nasal profile straight
Broad noses
Thick nasal tips
Downward inclined septum ①
Membranous lips - upper thin,
  lower thick
Full cheeks
Pronounced jaw angles
Bilateral chins
Slight alveolar prognathism
Long ear lobes ②
Pronounced Darwin's point ③
Slight antihelix

OLD AMERICAN CRIMINALS
MOSAIC OF CRANIAL, FACIAL, METRIC AND MORPHOLOGICAL FEATURES
NORTH CAROLINA

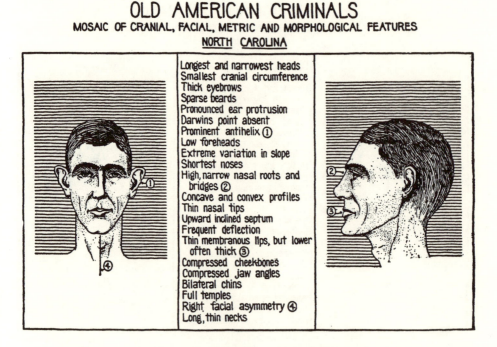

Longest and narrowest heads
Smallest cranial circumference
Thick eyebrows
Sparse beards
Pronounced ear protrusion
Darwins point absent
Prominent antihelix ①
Low foreheads
Extreme variation in slope
Shortest noses
High, narrow nasal roots and
  bridges ②
Concave and convex profiles
Thin nasal tips
Upward inclined septum
Frequent deflection
Thin membranous lips, but lower
  often thick ③
Compressed cheekbones
Compressed jaw angles
Bilateral chins
Full temples
Right facial asymmetry ④
Long, thin necks

OLD AMERICAN CRIMINALS
MOSAIC OF CRANIAL, FACIAL, METRIC AND MORPHOLOGICAL FEATURES
WISCONSIN

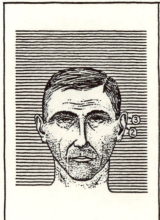

Greatest head breadth
Straight hair
Thick beards
Longest upper faces
Vertical foreheads
Narrow nasal root and bridge
Relatively longest and narrowest
  noses
Concave and convex nasal
  profiles
Thin nasal tips
Upward inclined septum
Deflected septum
Thin cheeks
Thin membranous lips ①
Prominent antihelix ②
Median chins
Lack of asymmetry
Darwin's point absent ③

OLD AMERICAN CRIMINALS
MOSAIC OF CRANIAL, FACIAL, METRIC AND MORPHOLOGICAL FEATURES
ARIZONA, NEW MEXICO, COLORADO

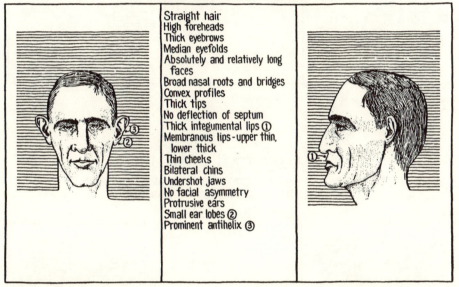

Straight hair
High foreheads
Thick eyebrows
Median eyefolds
Absolutely and relatively long
  faces
Broad nasal roots and bridges
Convex profiles
Thick tips
No deflection of septum
Thick integumental lips ①
Membranous lips-upper thin,
  lower thick
Thin cheeks
Bilateral chins
Undershot jaws
No facial asymmetry
Protrusive ears
Small ear lobes ②
Prominent antihelix ③

OLD AMERICAN CRIMINALS
MOSAIC OF EXCESS METRIC AND MORPHOLOGICAL FEATURES,
INDEPENDENT OF AGE AND STATE SAMPLING
ROBBERS

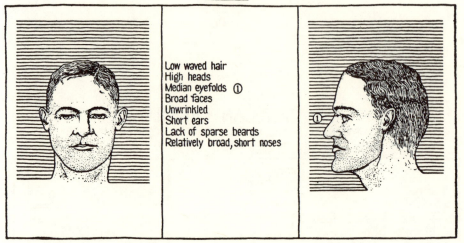

Low waved hair
High heads
Median eyefolds ①
Broad faces
Unwrinkled
Short ears
Lack of sparse beards
Relatively broad, short noses

OLD AMERICAN CRIMINALS
MOSAIC OF EXCESS METRIC AND MORPHOLOGICAL FEATURES,
INDEPENDENT OF AGE AND STATE SAMPLING
BURGLARS AND THIEVES

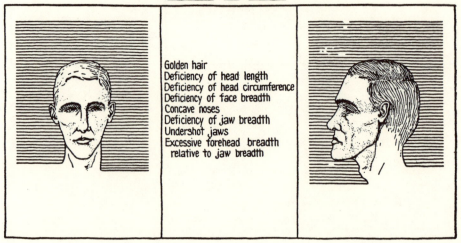

Golden hair
Deficiency of head length
Deficiency of head circumference
Deficiency of face breadth
Concave noses
Deficiency of jaw breadth
Undershot jaws
Excessive forehead breadth
  relative to jaw breadth

OLD AMERICAN CRIMINALS
MOSAIC OF EXCESS METRIC AND MORPHOLOGICAL FEATURES, INDEPENDENT OF AGE AND STATE SAMPLING
FORGERS AND FRAUDS

Thin head hair
Great head circumference
Great head length
No eyefolds
Long face
Nasal bridges of medium height
Deficiency of thin membranous
  lips ①

OLD AMERICAN CRIMINALS
MOSAIC OF EXCESS METRIC AND MORPHOLOGICAL FEATURES, INDEPENDENT OF AGE AND STATE SAMPLING
VERSUS PUBLIC WELFARE

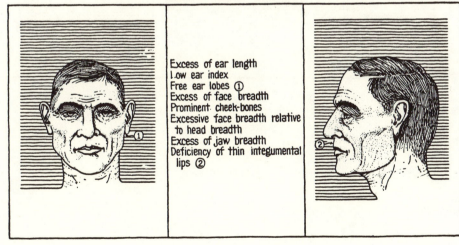

Excess of ear length
Low ear index
Free ear lobes ①
Excess of face breadth
Prominent cheek-bones
Excessive face breadth relative
  to head breadth
Excess of jaw breadth
Deficiency of thin integumental
  lips ②

OLD AMERICAN CRIMINALS
MOSAIC OF METRIC AND MORPHOLOGICAL EXCESSES
OF THREE OCCUPATIONAL TYPES

PROFESSIONAL	*PERSONAL SERVICE*	*CLERICAL*
Second lightest hair Oldest (excess 11.7 years) Heaviest (excess 19.6 pounds) Large head length Large head breadth, round head Excess forehead breadth Excess face breadth High nasal index	Dark hair Deficiency blue eyes Relatively great nose breadth Small and light weight	Lightest hair Darkest eyes Excess head breadth Relatively narrowest nose Small and light weight

BODY-BUILD TYPES

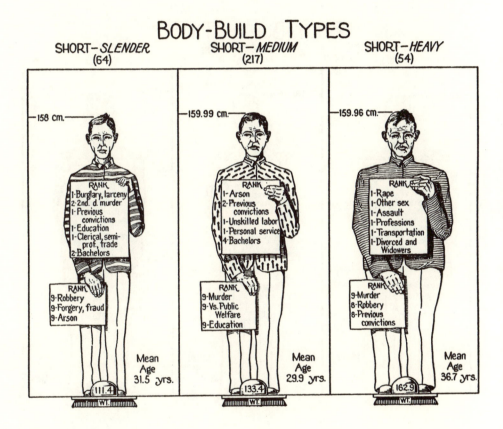

SHORT—*SLENDER*
(64)

SHORT—*MEDIUM*
(217)

SHORT—*HEAVY*
(54)

—158 cm.—

—159.99 cm.—

—159.96 cm.—

RANK
1-Burglary, larceny
2-2nd. d. murder
1-Previous
    convictions
1-Education
1-Clerical, semi-
    prof., trade
2-Bachelors

RANK
1-Arson
2-Previous
    convictions
1-Unskilled labor
1-Personal service
4-Bachelors

RANK
1-Rape
1-Other sex
1-Assault
1-Professions
1-Transportation
1-Divorced and
    Widowers

RANK
9-Robbery
9-Forgery, fraud
9-Arson

RANK
9-Murder
9-Vs. Public
    Welfare
9-Education

RANK
9-Murder
8-Robbery
8-Previous
    convictions

Mean
Age
31.5 yrs.

Mean
Age
29.9 yrs.

Mean
Age
36.7 yrs.

111.4

133.4

162.9

W.T.

W.T.

W.T.

117

BODY-BUILD TYPES

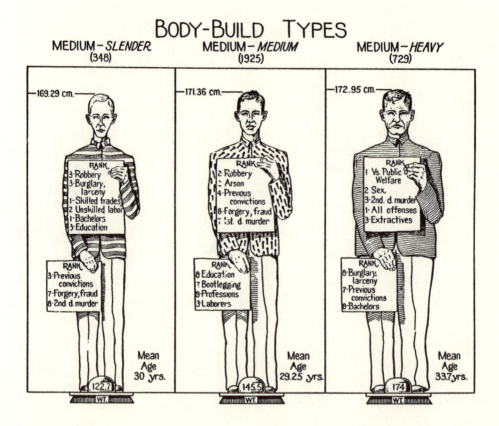

MEDIUM–*SLENDER*
(348)

169.29 cm.

RANK
3·Robbery
3·Burglary, larceny
1·Skilled trades
2·Unskilled labor
1·Bachelors
3·Education

RANK
3·Previous convictions
7·Forgery,fraud
8·2nd. d. murder

Mean Age 30 yrs.

122.7

MEDIUM–*MEDIUM*
(1925)

171.36 cm.

RANK
2·Robbery
2·Arson
4·Previous convictions
8·Forgery, fraud
7·1st. d. murder

RANK
8·Education
7·Bootlegging
9·Professions
3·Laborers

Mean Age 29.25 yrs.

145.5

MEDIUM–*HEAVY*
(729)

172.95 cm.

RANK
1·Vs. Public Welfare
2·Sex
3·2nd. d. murder
1·All offenses
3·Extractives

RANK
8·Burglary, larceny
7·Previous convictions
8·Bachelors

Mean Age 33.7 yrs.

174

WT.

118

BODY-BUILD TYPES

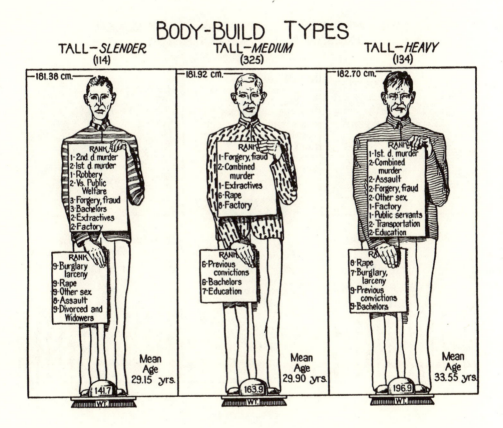

TALL—*SLENDER*
(114)

—181.38 cm.—

RANK
1-2nd. d. murder
2-1st. d. murder
1-Robbery
2-Vs. Public Welfare
3-Forgery, fraud
3-Bachelors
2-Extractives
2-Factory

RANK
9-Burglary larceny
9-Rape
9-Other sex
8-Assault
9-Divorced and Widowers

Mean Age 29.15 yrs.

141.7 WT.

TALL—*MEDIUM*
(325)

—181.92 cm.—

RANK
1-Forgery, fraud
1-Combined murder
1-Extractives
6-Rape
8-Factory

RANK
6-Previous convictions
6-Bachelors
7-Education

Mean Age 29.90 yrs.

163.9 WT.

TALL—*HEAVY*
(134)

—182.70 cm.—

RANK
1-1st. d. murder
2-Combined murder
2-Assault
2-Forgery, fraud
2-Other sex
1-Factory
1-Public servants
2-Transportation
2-Education

RANK
8-Rape
7-Burglary, larceny
9-Previous convictions
9-Bachelors

Mean Age 33.55 yrs.

196.9 WT.

119

SORTING FOR INDIVIDUAL COMBINATIONS OF MORPHOLOGICAL
EXCESSES IN OLD AMERICAN ROBBERS

SIGNIFICANT EXCESSES

No facial asymmetry
Ear protrusion medium
Ear lobes attached ①
Hair color – light brown
Median eyefolds ②
Hair form, low or deep waves
Heavy beard
Darwin's point pronounced ③
Iris-diffused pigment ④

Robbers with no sorting Characters
6 — 1.45%

Robbers with 7 sorting Characters
1 — .24%

5 Characters 7.00%
6 Characters 1.69%
1 Character 10.63%
4 Characters 20.29%
2 Characters 27.05%
3 Characters 31.64%

TOTAL ROBBERS 414

120

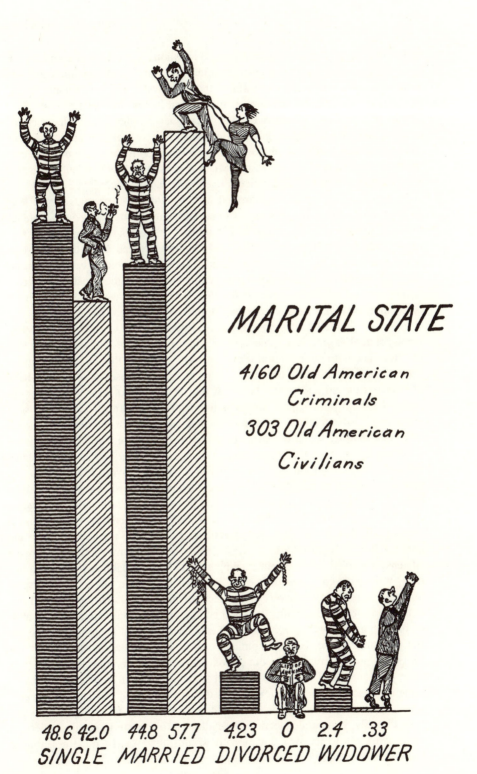

MARITAL STATE

4160 Old American
Criminals
303 Old American
Civilians

| 48.6 | 42.0 | 44.8 | 57.7 | 4.23 | 0 | 2.4 | .33 |
| SINGLE | | MARRIED | | DIVORCED | | WIDOWER | |

in the treatment of incarcerated felons. Such motives are laudable and the efforts of those who engage in criminological work are usually disinterested and sometimes efficacious. More power to their elbows! I wish to disabuse everyone of the idea that the function of the general human biologist is that of the family physician—to comfort or cure individual patients. . . . No scientific criminologist or penologist, however optimistic . . . , has any particular hope of rehabilitating hardened adult criminals *en bloc*. Crime prevention is centered upon the treatment of juveniles and when it gets to be really scientific, it will have to start earlier still and concern itself with familial heredity.

However, I have not fooled around with the study of criminals for so long without developing a few notions as to possible improvements of our penal system. . . . As a primary measure, I think that first offenders ought to be segregated absolutely from recidivists, and carefully studied as to their constitutional endowment and social potentialities. Those who seem to be in any sense reclaimable should be carefully re-educated and taught some vocation, or given an opportunity while in prison to improve their skill in whatever law-abiding occupation they may have chosen and practiced in civilian life. . . .

Either the United States government, or possibly the various state governments, should expropriate some very considerable tract of land—a sizable slab of some state with good natural resources—and establish there a reservation for permanent occupation by paroled delinquents. Such a reservation would have its frontiers closed and would be under the supervision of federal or other officers. I should allow these former delinquents to be almost completely self-governing. Government aid would be at first necessary for building and for establishing industries, but outside capital could be called in. Each paroled delinquent would be given the opportunity to work out a career within this protected area. The population would carry on its own form of government, electing its officials from its own numbers. Married men on parole should be allowed to bring in their wives and families and settle them there. While optimum eugenic considerations would demand that none of these delinquents raise offspring, it seems probable that the processes of genetic selection and recombination would produce from this partially criminalistic stock a good many useful and capable citizens, and even a few of outstanding ability. If the inhabitants of such a territory were allowed to run their own affairs, it is possible that in the course of time they would run them very well, since the more able individuals would rise to the positions of leadership. I should be particularly optimistic about the ability of such a society to develop its own effective means of keeping public order and preventing crime, because criminals are not lenient to criminality when their own ox is gored. Emigrants from prison into such a reservation should be kept there permanently. I am rather inclined to believe that in a generation or two some of these penal reservations might develop into such prosperous and progressive areas that the inhabitants would be unwilling to receive new colonists from the jails. If natural selection were allowed to operate in such a society, it might work out to its own salvation. It would, however, be quite essential to keep out extraneous politicans, criminologists, and uplifters.[127]

Hooton favored the permanent incarceration of "hopeless constitutional inferiors" who "on no account, should be allowed to breed."[128]

Hooton's political philosophy interfaced with his criminology in an interesting manner:

I deem human deterioration to be ultimately responsible not only for crime, but for the evils of war, the oppression of the populace by totalitarian states, and for all of the social cataclysms which are rocking the world and under which civilization is tottering. That man, with all of his pride of intellect, all of his success in manipulating environment and building upon complex civilizations, with all of his boasted science, should be completely impotent to control human behavior and prevent wholesale outbreaks of savagery by entire nations is the most sardonic practical joke perpetrated by organic evolution.

The incredible truth is that man has sought to remedy human ills by tinkering with his mind, by drugging his body, by shuffling his institutions, by trying every sort of government, by killing or enslaving his fellow men, and by the emotional flagellation of various kinds of religion[.] . . .

We can direct and control the progress of human evolution by breeding better types and by the ruthless elimination of inferior types, if only we are willing to

found and to practice a science of human genetics. With sound and progressively evolving human organisms in the majority of our species, problems of human behavior will be minimized, and there will be improved educability. Crime can be eradicated, war can be forgotten.[129]

Eight years before Hooton published his "Harvard study," in 1931, Franz Alexander and Hugo Staub had noted incisively: "The attempt of Lombroso and his school to draw a sharp line between the normal and the criminal comes from the narcissistic wish of the scientist to separate himself and his normal fellow men from the criminal, as if the latter belonged to a different race of beings."[130] Yet, notwithstanding the decline of the positivist viewpoint in criminology during the second, third, and fourth quarters of the twentieth century, the search for the "criminal man" seems to continue undaunted. The major recent example of this is the ongoing effort to link chromosomal disorders (such as an extra "Y" chromosome in some males, known as the "XYY" chromosome[131]) to an abnormally high propensity for violence and, consequently, to a significantly greater involvement in criminal behavior.[132]

Concern about the XYY chromosome began in the early 1960s and reached the height of its popularity in 1965 when Patricia A. Jacobs and two colleagues at a hospital in Carstairs, Scotland, karyotyped 197 prisoners, finding among them 12 who displayed chromosomal anomalies, including 7 who evidenced an XYY chromosome.[133] In the wake of the publicity that followed, various defendants charged with violent offenses such as murder raised a chromosomal anomaly as a defense. Daniel Hugon's XYY chromosome did not gain his acquittal of murder at his Paris trial in 1968, but the next year Lawrence E. Hannell's won him acquittal of murder on grounds of insanity in Australia.[134] The XYY issue has not appeared yet to be successful in the defense of criminal charges in the United States.[135] Although Jacobs' study found the incidence of the extra Y chromosome in 3.5 percent of the prison population studied, more recent research has revealed the occurrence of this phenomenon in a far smaller proportion of the human male population and has indicated that most men who have an extra Y chromosome do not commit violent criminal offenses. For instance, Sarbin and Miller have examined recent studies[136] and concluded:

Contrary to the expectations generated by popular reports and mass media, the studies done thus far are largely in agreement and demonstrate rather conclusively that males of the XYY type are not predictably aggressive. If anything, as a group they are somewhat less aggressive than comparable XY's.[137]

The outstanding difficulty encountered in studying the XYY Syndrome, as it has become known, has been the impossibility of determining how many males in the general human population have the extra Y chromosome[138] and, of these, how peaceable they are.

The search for an explanation of the association, if any, between chromosomal anomaly and criminal behavior remains elusive, much in the same sense as did Lombroso's search for the "criminal man." Scientific inquiry yields new knowledge over time, but sometimes the knowledge gained is not worth the price paid in the course of its quest, and some hypotheses cannot seem to be proven or disproven with any acceptable level of confidence. So goes the search for a criminal man, at least for the moment. A major study that argues in favor of biological influences as predictors of criminal behavior was published in 1985 by Harvard University political scientist James Q. Wilson and Harvard psychologist Richard J. Herrnstein.[139] In *Crime and Human Nature*, Wilson and Herrnstein seem to have undertaken to rehabilitate Earnest A. Hooton much in the same vein that Hooton tried to rehabilitate Caesare Lombroso in the 1930s. On its jacket, the Wilson-Herrnstein book purports to offer a "groundbreaking theory that crime results from individual choice." Inside, the authors are more cautious, but nevertheless they appear to be challenging pragmatist tenets, popular during the past fifty years (see Chapter Seven), that have linked criminality to social experiences. For instance, they offer documentation that identical twins are twice as likely as fraternal ones to have identical delinquency records. The search for "criminal man" never ends.

NOTES

1. This presupposes that criminology is not a science. If it is, as many criminologists (particularly positivist ones) have contended, then at the end of the seventeenth century the rise of modern science was complete except for organic chemistry and criminology!

2. See H. Martineau, tr., THE POSITIVE PHILOSOPHY (1855) and THE POSITIVE PHILOSOPHY OF AUGUSTE COMTE (1893).

3. See S. Schafer, THEORIES IN CRIMINOLOGY 113 (1969).

4. More than twenty people have been mentioned as having conducted empirical studies in criminology in the eighteenth and early nineteenth centuries. See H. Ellis, THE CRIMINAL (2nd ed., 1900).

5. THE ORIGIN OF THE SPECIES BY NATURAL SELECTION, OR THE PRESERVATION OF FAVOURED RACES IN THE STRUGGLE FOR LIFE. Herbert Spencer had already published THE DEVELOPMENT OF HYPOTHESIS in 1852, elaborating on Karl Ernst von Baer's UBER DIE ENTWICKELUNGSGESCHICHTE DER THIERE (History of the Development of Animals) published in 1828 and 1837.

6. Genesis, I:9.

7. THE DESCENT OF MAN AND SELECTION IN RELATION TO SEX.

8. Genesis, I:26. See also the account of the "Scopes monkey trial" in G. Ray, *Six Days or Forever: Tennessee vs. John Thomas Scope's* (Boston: Beacon Press, 1958).

9. *Supra*, note 7 at 137. The next year, in 1872, Darwin published THE EXPRESSION OF THE EMOTIONS IN MAN AND ANIMALS.

10. Lombroso autopsied 383 dead prisoners and wrote:

On considering the results that these 383 skulls give us it is found that the lesions most frequent are: great prominence of the superciliary arches, 58.2 percent; anomaly in the development of the wisdom teeth, 44.6 percent; diminution of the capacity of the skull, 32.5 percent; synostosis of the sutures, 28.9 percent; retreating forehead, 28 percent; hyperostosis of the bones, 28.9 percent; plagiocephaly, 23.1 percent; wormian bones, 22 percent; simplicity of the sutures, 18.4 percent; prominence of the occipital protuberance, 16.6 percent; the middle occipital fossa, 16 percent; symbolic sutures, 13.6 percent; flattening of the occipital, 13.2 percent; osteophytes of the clivus, 10.1 percent; the Inca's or epactal bone, 10.5 percent.

See C. Lombroso, L'HOMME CRIMINEL 155 (1895), translated in M. Parmelee's introduction to C. Lombroso, CRIME: ITS CAUSES AND REMEDIES xiv (1918). Lombroso supervised measurement of 5,907 living prisoners, also. *Id.* at xviii. See also, Y. Rennie, THE SEARCH FOR CRIMINAL MAN (1978). Initially, Lombroso had set out to study the relationship between genius and insanity. See C. Lombroso, GENIO E FOLLIA (1864).

11. C. Lombroso, introduction to G. Ferrero, CRIMINAL MAN ACCORDING TO THE CLASSIFICATION OF CESARE LOMBROSO xv (1911).

12. Opening Address before the Sixth International Congress of Criminal Anthropology, Turin, Italy, April 1906. Lombroso continued there:

Many facts seemed to confirm this hypothesis, above all, the psychology of the criminal, the frequency of tattooing and of professional slang; the passions as much more fleeting as they are more violent, and above all that of vengeance; the lack of foresight which resembles courage and courage which alternates with cowardice, and idleness which alternates with the passion for play and activity.

Id. See also M. Parmelee, *supra*, note 10 at xiv.

13. See C. Lombroso, L'HOMME CRIMINEL 222 (1895), translated in M. Parmelee's introduction to C. Lombroso, CRIME: ITS CAUSES AND REMEDIES xviii (1918).

14. See *supra*, chap. 1, note 12.

15. *Supra*, note 13 at 295; Parmelee's introduction at xix.

16. Lombroso speculated: "The special taste of criminals for a painful operation so long and so full of danger as tattooing, the large number of wounds their bodies present, have led me to suspect in them a physical insensibility greater than amongst most men, an insensibility like that which is encountered in some insane persons and especially in violent lunatics." *Id.* at 310; Parmelee's introduction at xx.

17. Lombroso generalized further:

From all of these facts it could be deduced that nearly all the different kinds of sensibility, tactile, olfactory, and of the taste, are obtuse in the criminal . . . while in the
criminal as in the insane and hysterical the sensibility to metals, to the magnet, and to
the atmosphere is exaggerated. Their physical insensibility recalls quite forcibly that of
savage peoples, who can face, in the initiations to puberty, tortures which a man of the
white race could never endure.

Id. at 346; Parmelee's introduction at xx.

18. Lombroso generalized further:

In general, in criminal man, the moral insensibility is as great as the physical insensibility; undoubtedly the one is the effect of the other. It is not that in him the voice of
sentiment is entirely silent . . . ; but it is certain that the passions which make the heart
of the normal man beat with the greatest force are very feeble in him. The first sentiment
which is extinguished in these beings is that of pity for the suffering of another, and this
happens just because they themselves are insensible to suffering.

Id. at 356; Parmelee's introduction at xx.

19. *Id*. at 262; Parmelee's introduction at xix.

20. *Supra*, note 13; Parmelee's introduction at xxii and xxiii.

21. C. Lombroso, L'HOMME CRIMINEL 49-50 (1895); translated in M.
Parmelee's introduction to C. Lombroso, CRIME: ITS CAUSES AND REM-
EDIES xxiii (1918).

22. *Id*. at 120; Parmelee's introduction at xxiii.

23. *Id*. at 135; Parmelee's introduction at xxiv.

24. Lombroso observed:

In nearly all political criminals by passion we have noticed an exaggerated sensibility,
a veritable hyperesthesia, as in the ordinary criminals by passion; but a powerful intellect, a great altruism lushed them towards ends much higher than those of the latter: it
is never wealth, vanity, the smile of woman (even though eroticism is not lacking in
them, as in Garibaldi, Mazzini, Cavour) which impel them, but rather the great pa-
triotic, religious, scientific ideals.

Id. at 217; Parmelee's introduction at xxv.

25. *Id*. at 165-66; Parmelee's introduction at xxiv.

26. *Id*. at 254.

27. *Id*. at 484. Lombroso confessed that he had delayed publishing the 1895
edition of L'HOMME CRIMINEL because of his uncertainty over how to classify and subclassify the "occasional criminal." *Id*. at 463.

28. *Id*. at 512; Parmelee's introduction at xxvii. (Emphasis added).

29. *Id*. at 485.

30. *Id*. at 534; Parmelee's introduction at xxvii.

31. *Supra*, note 13 at xi and xii; Parmelee's introduction at xxviii.

32. C. Lombroso, CRIME: ITS CAUSES AND REMEDIES 1 (H. Horton,
tr., 1911).

33. *Id*. at 3.

34. *Id*. at 2.

35. *Id*. at 6-7. Lombroso charted the uprisings in Europe throughout the nineteenth century, finding that most began in summer. *Id*. at 6. Most twentieth-century wars have begun in summer also. World War I began in August 1914. Nazi Germany invaded Poland on September 1, 1939. North Korea invaded South Korea on June 25, 1950. North Vietnam attacked two United States destroyers in the Gulf of Tonkin on August 2, 1964. Even if one takes the position that one or all of these invasions were provoked, the climactic significance remains the same.

36. *Id*. at 44-45, citing G. Ferrero, "Violenti e Frodolenti in Romagna," in IL MONDO CRIMINALE ITALIANO (1894).

37. *Id*. at 45, citing as background Sighele, DELINQUENZA SETTARIA (1898).

38. *Id*. at 36-42. Lombroso himself was of Jewish ancestry. As to the Gypsies, Lombroso remarked: "It is to be noted that this race, so low morally and so incapable of cultural and intellectual development, a race that can never carry on any industry, and which in poetry has not got beyond the poorest lyrics, has created in Hungary a marvelous musical art—a new proof of the genius that, mixed with atavism, is to be found in the criminal." See C. Lombroso, "Atavism and Evolution," CONTEMPORARY REVIEW (July 1895).

39. See G. Vold, THEORETICAL CRIMINOLOGY 39 (1958).

40. *Il tentativo criminoso con mezzi inidonei*.

41. *Cio che dovrebbe essere un giudizio penale*.

42. *Riparazione alle vittime del delitto*.

43. *De la solidarite des nations dans la lutte contre la criminalite*. Another major work by Garofalo was *La Superstition socialiste* (The Socialist Superstition; 1895).

44. R. Garofalo, CRIMINOLOGY 299-300 (R. Miller, tr., 1914).

45. *Id*. at 300.

46. *Id*. at 220-21.

47. *Id*. at 227-28. Garofalo "adapted" his "enforced reparation" plan from Herbert Spencer's theory of restitution and liberation. See H. Spencer, "Prison-Ethics," ESSAYS SCIENTIFIC, POLITICAL, AND SPECULATIVE (1873).

48. *Id*. at 191.

49. *Id*. (Emphasis added.)

50. *Id*.

51. *Id*. at 191-92.

52. *Id*. at 192.

53. *Id*. at 192-93, citing Bournet, LA CRIMINALITE EN CORSE (1887).

54. *Id*. at 193-95. "Since 1889 there has been but one Court of Cassation for criminal matters. This sits at Rome and has jurisdiction throughout the kingdom. As in France, it reviews on questions of law only," Garofalo notes. *Id*., n. 3.

55. *Id*. at 356-60, quoting from Turiello, GOVERNO E GOVERNATI (1882).

56. *Id.* at 361, citing the Chief Justice of the High Court of Allahabad as reported in THE TIMES (London) (November 4, 1903).

57. Garofalo explained: "[W]e are unable to conceive by what right the government can pardon an injury occasioned to society as a whole through an act forbidden by the natural laws of the social organism which this very government exists for the purpose of protecting. It is a mystery how this power of pardon has managed to survive all the other irrational prerogatives which have given way before the progress of institutions." *Id.* at 368-69. He continued: "*Amnesty*, that is to say, the wholesale pardoning of an entire class of persons guilty of ordinary crimes, is something which for strangeness cannot be exceeded." *Id.* at 369.

58. *Id.* at 346-47.

59. *Id.*, chap. 4.

60. *Id.* at 273.

61. *Id.* at 305.

62. *Id.* at 307.

63. *La negazione del libero arbitrio e la teoria dell' imputabilita.*

64. *Supra*, note 3 at 129.

65. Sellin wrote: "While Ferri owed much of his system of ideas to the stimulation of Lombroso, he also became the catalyst who synthesized the latter's concepts with those of the sociologist and had no little influence on Lombroso's thinking." T. Sellin, *Enrico Ferri*, in H. Mannheim, ed., PIONEERS IN CRIMINOLOGY 286 (1960).

66. I NOUVI ORIZZONTI DEL DIRITTO E DELLA PROCEDURA PENALE.

67. LA SOCIOLOGIA CRIMINALE.

68. L'OMICIDIO-SUICIDIO.

69. E. Ferri, CRIMINAL SOCIOLOGY 138-46 (J. Kelly and J. Lisle, trs., 1917).

70. STUDI SULLA CRIMINALITA IN FRANCIA DAL 1824 AL 1878.

71. *Supra*, note 69 at xxxi.

72. *Id.*

73. *Id.* at xxiii (editorial preface by William W. Smithers).

74. *Id.* at 209.

75. *Id.* at 211-12.

76. *Id.* at 195-98.

77. *Id.* at 197, citing Ferri, *Das Verbrechen in seiner Abhangigkeit von dem jahrlichen Temperaturwechsel* (1882).

78. *Id.* at 206-8.

79. *Id.* at 205-6.

80. *Id.* at 206. Ferri explained that the crime rate failed to decrease in Ireland despite a 20 percent population *decrease* due to emigration between 1861 and 1894 because of "politico-social agitations in that country." *Id.* at 207.

81. *Id.* at 289.

82. *Id.* at 295.

83. *Id.* at 296. Ferri went on to argue that "free will" is disproven by "statistics"; *id.* at 297; and that it is "denied by science"; *id.* at 298.

84. *Id.* at 317.

85. *Id.* at 318.

86. *Id.* at 339.

87. *Id.* at 343.

88. *Id.* 349-50.

89. *Id.* 350.

90. *Id.* 350-51.

91. *Id.* at 351-56.

92. *Id.* 361-62.

93. *Id.* at 502.

94. *Id.* at 506.

95. E. Ferri, LA SOCIOLOGIA CRIMINALE 45 (1881). (J. Kelly and J. Lisle, trs., *supra*, note 69 at 506, n. 3).

96. *Supra*, note 69 at 509.

97. *Id.* at 519.

98. *Id.* at 520.

99. *Id.* at 518.

100. *Id.* at 522-27.

101. *Id.* at 528-32.

102. Mendel's first "law" was the "law of segregation." He assumed that each plant has two hereditary factors (genes) for each of its traits, one factor inherited from each parent. A "purebreed" has like pairs of genes (dominant: AA; recessive: aa), whereas a hybrid has an unlike pair (Aa). When gamates (eggs or sperm) form in the hybrid, the two members of a pair of genes are separated into two classes (A and a) of equal number. Mendel's second "law" was the "law of purity of gamates." He said that when fertilization occurs in hybrids following the "law of segregation," the random recombination of eggs and sperm affords a ratio of one AA to two Aa to one aa genetic pairs. Because of dominance, the second pair (Aa) resemble the first pair (AA), so that the ratio of dominant to recessive is three to one. Thus, all recessive plants (aa) breed true, as do one-third of the dominant plants (AA). Two-thirds of the dominant plants (AA) segregate again, however. Thus Mendel's "second law": neither gene of an unlike pair is modified by its association with the other in a hybrid; the recessive gene is simply "masked" by the dominant gene.

103. H. deVries, THE MUTATION THEORY (J. Farmer and A. Darbi-shire, trs., 1901–3). Betweeen Darwin and deVries, at least thirty-five authors published studies on criminal anthropology, including H. Wey, CRIMINAL ANTHROPOLOGY, PROC. NAT'L. PRIS. ASSOC. 274-91 (1890), and A. Drahms, THE CRIMINAL: HIS PERSONNEL AND ENVIRONMENT (1900). See A. Fink, THE CAUSES OF CRIME: BIOLOGICAL THEORIES IN THE UNITED STATES, 1800–1915 99-150 (1938).

104. C. Goring, THE ENGLISH CONVICT: A STATISTICAL STUDY 365

(table 177). Goring concluded emphatically: "[*T*]*here is no such thing as a physical criminal type.*" *Id.* at 173. (Emphasis in the original.)

105. *Id.* at 26.

106. *Id.* at 16.

107. *Id.* at 12. Yet, Goring described Lombroso as a "genius, an indefatigable worker, and a man of strong personality, attracting to himself many disciples and co-workers from all countries of Europe." *Id.* at 11.

108. See E. Driver, *Charles Buckman Goring*, in H. Mannheim, ed., PIONEERS IN CRIMINOLOGY 440 (1962).

109. *Supra*, note 104 at 5, 11.

110. *Id.* at xix (1919 ed.).

111. See, *inter alia*, E. Sutherland and D. Cressey, CRIMINOLOGY 120 (10th ed., 1978).

112. E. Hooton, CRIME AND THE MAN 16 (1939).

113. States included Arizona, Colorado, Kentucky, Massachusetts, Missouri, New Mexico, North Carolina, Tennessee, Texas, and Wisconsin.

114. By "Old Americans," Hooton meant people who had "forgotten their European extraction." *Supra*, note 112 at 40. By "Negroid" in contrast to Negro, Hooton referred to persons having both Caucasian and Negro blood "and physical features approximating those of Europeans [who] have been favored in education, in occupation, and in social status, although they do not like to admit it and are none the happier for it." *Id.* at 291.

115. E. Hooton, THE AMERICAN CRIMINAL: AN ANTHROPOLOGICAL STUDY 301-6 (1939).

116. *Supra*, note 112 at vii.

117. *Supra*, note 3 at 187.

118. R. Merton and A. Ashley-Montagu, *Crime and the Anthropologist*, AM. ANTHROPOLOGIST 384-408 (1940).

119. *Supra*, note 3 at 187.

120. Different reviewers of Hooton's books challenged Hooton from various angles. See E. Sutherland's review in J. CRIM. L. & CRIM. 911-14 (1939). For a defense of Hooton, however, see W. Tucker, *Is There Evidence of a Physical Basis for Criminal Behavior?* J. CRIM. L. & CRIM. 427-37 (1940).

121. *Supra*, note 115 at 229.

122. *Supra*, note 112 at 376-78.

123. *Supra*, note 39 at 63 (2nd ed., 1979).

124. *Id.* at 64.

125. See Cohen, Lindesmith, and Schuessler, SUTHERLAND PAPERS 278 (1956).

126. *Supra*, note 112 at viii. He credits one Elmer Rising as having "professionally drawn and admirably executed" the heads! *Id.*

127. *Id.* at 390-92.

128. *Id.* at 392.

129. *Id.* at 393-97.

130. F. Alexander and H. Staub, THE CRIMINAL, THE JUDGE AND THE PUBLIC: A PSYCHOLOGICAL ANALYSIS 33 (1931, published originally as DER VERBRECHER UND SEINE RICHTER).

131. A "normal" female has two X chromosomes, one inherited from her mother and one from her father. A "normal" male has one X and one Y chromosome, the former inherited from his mother and the latter from his father. Some males have an extra X and/or an extra Y chromosome. An "XXY" pattern, or extra X chromosome in a male, known as Klinefelter's Syndrome, is characterized by feeblemindedness and effeminacy. The XYY Syndrome may carry with it excessive tallness, susceptibility to facial acne, or violent tendencies.

132. See N. Maclean, *et al.*, *A Survey of Sex Chromosome Anomalies among 4,515 Mental Defectives*, 1 LANCET 293 (1962); A. Sandburg, *et al.*, *XYY Genotype*, 268 N. E. J. MED. 585 (1963); W. Price, *et al.*, *Criminal Behavior and the XYY Male*, 213 NATURE 815 (1967).

133. P. Jacobs, M. Brunton, and M. Melville, *Aggressive Behavior, Mental Subnormality, and the XYY Male*, 208 NATURE 1351 (1965).

134. Hannell introduced evidence of mental deficiency, abnormal electro-encephalogram reading, and temporal lobe epilepsy, also, which may have enhanced his defense. Hugon received a light penalty. See. Y. Rennie, THE SEARCH FOR CRIMINAL MAN 224 (1978).

135. See Note, *The XYY Snydrome: A Challenge to Our System of Criminal Responsibility*, 16 N. Y. L. FORUM 232 (1970).

136. See W. Price and P. Whatmore, *Behavior Disorders and Pattern of Crime among XYY Males Identified at a Maximum Security Hospital*, 1 BRIT. MED. J. 533 (1967); H. Hunter, *YY Chromosomes and Klinefelter's Syndrome*, 1 LANCET 984 (1966); R. Fox, *The XYY Offender: A Modern Myth?*, 62 J. CRIM. L., CRIM. 199 (1970).

137. T. Sarbin and J. Miller, *Demonism Revisited: The XYY Chromosomal Anomaly*, 5 ISSUES IN CRIM. 199 (1970).

138. Ordinarily, a person may be karyotyped from a small sample of blood, but sampling the blood of a large segment of the male population is a cumbersome task accompanied by lingering ethical problems.

139. Wilson and Herrnstein have indicated they want to free criminology from the "theoretical bias" of sociology, the discipline into which it has been cast by pragmatists.

6

Naturalism and Dysfunction of the Individual's Body or Mind

In the ancient world before the Christian era, four thinkers expounded a philosophy having as its root the assumption that the universe was a void filled by atoms in motion that form the bodies and minds of living things. These thinkers were Leucippus (c. 450), Democritus (460–360), Epicurus (341–270), and Lucretius (98–54). Their philosophy has been become known as materialism, which sets forth the view that all phenomena may be reduced to matter put into motion by energy, consuming time and occupying space. With the rise of modern science during the seventeenth century and afterward, primitive explanations that had formed classical materialism took on a greater degree of sophistication and generated a newer philosophy commonly known as naturalism. As did positivism, naturalism benefited from knowledge derived from experiments using the scientific method. Whereas many positivists had become preoccupied with identifying a singular mathematical formula that could explain the origin of each phenomenon, naturalists have accepted the plurality of all things and events as part of the harmony of nature. They have rejected the positivist notion that any one equation, if known, would unravel the mysteries of creation and behavior.

NATURALISM AND MATERIALISM: THE EARLY THEORIES

A school of medical thought that may be viewed as being naturalistic can be traced to ancient Greece as far back as the time of Pythagoras (580–510), his pupil Alemaeon (550–500), Epedocles of Agrigentum (490–430), and Hippocrates (c. 460–377), all living before the Christian era.[1] Today, Hippocrates is known as the "father of medicine." Pythagoras and Alemaeon identified the thought process as originating in the brain and targeted mental illness as a brain dysfunction.[2] Empedocles explained personality in terms of temperatures such as hot and cold, moist and dry; and in terms of "humors" including blood, phlegm, and both black and yellow biles.[3] Ancient Greek physicians treated "hysteria," as they called mental illness, by administering to such patients substances that induced unpleasant tastes or odors[4] in an effort to "drive" the affliction out of the body. These views prevailed across Europe throughout the Middle Ages. Early in the nineteenth century, French psychiatrist Jean E. D. Esquirol, director of the Salpetriere sanitarium, declared that "[e]verything in [idiots] betrays an organization imperfect or arrested in its development."[5] This developmental model preceded the positivist search for single hereditary disorders and has maintained respect among psychiatrists and psychologists for more than half a century after the demise of positivist popularity.

Professor Ernest Nagel has concluded that two theses seem central to naturalism:

The first is the existential and casual primacy of organized matter in the executive order of nature. This is the assumption that the occurrence of events, qualities and processes, and the characteristic behaviors of various individuals, are contingent on the organization of spatio-temporally located bodies, whose internal structures and external relations determine and limit the appearance and disappearance of everything that happens. . . . Naturalism does not maintain that only what is material exists, since many things noted in experience, for example, modes of action, relations of meaning, dreams, joys, plans, aspirations, are not as such material bodies or organizations of material bodies. What naturalism does assert as a truth about nature is that though *forms* of behavior or *functions* of material systems are indefeasibly parts of nature, forms and functions are not themselves agents in their own realization or in the realization of anything else. In the conception of nature's processes which naturalism affirms, there is no place for the operation of disembodied forces, no place for an immaterial spirit directing the course of events, no place for the survival of personality after the corruption of the body which exhibits it.

The second major contention of naturalism is that the manifest plurality and variety of things, of their qualities and their functions, are an irreducible feature of the cosmos, not a deceptive appearance cloaking some more homogeneous "ultimate reality" or transempirical substance, and that the sequential orders in which events occur or the manifold relations of dependence in which things exist are *contingent* connections, not the embodiments of a fixed and unified pattern of logically necessary links.[6]

He has noted that "naturalism does not dismiss every other conception of the scheme of things as logically impossible; and it does not rule out alternatives to itself on *a priori* grounds."

Naturalism appeared as a philosophy in French literature with publication in 1864 of a novel by Edmond and Jules de Goncourt entitled *Germinie Lacerteux*, which examined the multifaceted vicissitudes of a servant girl's life. Naturalism reached its literary zenith in Emile Zola, beginning with the novel *Therese Raquin* in 1867 and continuing through his cycle of twenty novels, *Rougon-Macquart* (1871–93), which traces the moral and physical decadence of alcoholics, prostitutes, and other degenerates. Zola offered a typically naturalistic explanation of social degeneracy, ascribing it to both hereditary and environmental deficiencies. Naturalism has appeared in the literature of such other writers as Theodore Dreiser, James T. Farrell, and Jack London; in the legal philosophy of Morris R. Cohen; and in the religious philosophy of George Santayana.

The *Naturphilosophie* of Friedrich von Schelling influenced the early thoughts of Sigmund Freud and, consequently, modern psychology. According to von Schelling, nature is dominated by activities, creations, and forces organized in perpetual conflict to the extent that they have become polarized like good and evil, and the mind's reasoning power reflects this unconscious turmoil. *Naturphilosophie* envisions the work of forces that remain hidden from man's intelligence and, therefore, from scientific theory and empirical observations, also. Freud accepted the limitation that most theories about how the mind works cannot be tested empirically, but he continued to generate more theories, anyway. His 1895 book with Josef Breuer, entitled *Studies in Hysteria*, influenced naturalist criminology, as did other works Freud published during his early professional career, such as *The Interpretation of Dreams* (1900) and *The Psychopathology of Everyday Life* (1904). Most concepts of abnormal psychology had been articulated prior to Freud, however, such as the distinction between functional disorders with no biological root and the organic disorders that could be traced to trauma (injury), disease such as syphilis, or senility (old age). Even the notion of the unconscious, popularized by Freud, is said to have been originated by von Hartmann.[7] The psychiatric "typologies" popularized by many of the naturalistic criminologists during the twentieth century (see *infra*, this chapter) had been conceived well in advance of Freud.[8]

When one tries to apply the philosophies of materialism and naturalism to criminology, one encounters some difficulty apportioning early criminological studies between these two similar but different ways of thinking. This difficulty is compounded by the influence of positivism over some of the same early criminologists. Nevertheless, an argument can be made that eighteenth- and nineteenth-century phrenologists were dominated by the tenets of materialism, such as should be evident from the works of Franz Josef Gall and his student, Johann Gaspar Spurzheim.

Unlike the physiognomists such as Johann Kasper Laviter, whose efforts to identify *direct* associations between physical "traits" and criminal behavior seem to reflect a primitive positivism (see Chapter 5), the early phrenologists attempted to identify human personality characteristics from facial expressions *derived* from bodily "traits."[9] Gall investigated the distribution of nerve tracts (the "white matter") in the medulla (lowest part of the brain) as they enter the spinal cord. In 1798, he published a set of lectures in *Neue Deutsche Mercur* which memorialized his theory that intellectual functions originate within particular areas of the brain. Gall labeled this area of inquiry "cranioscopy" or "organology," because to Gall an individual's behavior was the product of how his organs function in harmony, clearly the outgrowth of a materialistic philosophy.

Phrenology

Gall and Spurzheim collaborated on research designed to reveal human character and personality from an *exterior* appraisal of a person's skull, conducted by feeling for protuberances (bumps) or depressions. Spurzheim called this area of study phrenology, in contrast to Gall's earlier and later work on neuroanatomy. Together, Gall and Spurzheim published a four-volume *Anatomie et physiologie du systeme nerveuse* (Anatomy and Physiology of the Nervous System) between 1810 and 1819. Whereas Gall had divided the brain into twenty-six separate organs, or "faculties" as he called them, Spurzheim added eleven more. Each of the thirty-seven "faculties," according to Gall and Spurzheim, presided over a specific intellectual, moral, or sexual "trait" of the individual. The larger the relevant organ, the more pronounced became the "trait" governed by the organ.[10] Traits identified by Gall and Spurzheim included acquisitiveness, amativeness, benevolence, cautiousness, combativeness, conjugality, constructiveness, destructiveness, firmness, ideality, imitativeness, jealousy, philoprogenitiveness (love of offspring), secretiveness, and self-esteem.

Phrenology gained favor among prison administrators in Europe and America during the second half of the nineteenth century. The prison physician at Toulon penitentiary during the 1840s, Hubert Lauvergne, a student of Gall, observed that convicts display "peculiar faces" that reflect their criminal instincts.[11] He said of assassins specifically: "They possess marked protuberances and a peculiar face stamped by the seal of a brutal and impassable instinct. Their heads are large and receding with notable lateral protuberances, enormous jaws and masticatory muscles always in motions."[12] During the half-century between 1855 and

1904, the annual reports of Pennsylvania's Eastern Penitentiary at Philadelphia classified most inmates according to their phrenological profiles,[13] typified by the phrenological typology that prison published for the year 1856:[14]

Propensity	Number	Percent
Jealousy	1	0.2
Combativeness	14	3.4
Amativeness	34	8.2
Destructiveness	72	17.3
Acquisitiveness	205	70.9
Total	326	100.0

Of course, such a typological breakdown might have been predicted, given that at the time most prison inmates were convicted thieves. As Charles Caldwell had explained twenty years earlier in the first American textbook on phrenology: because a person's "will" may control his "passions," therefore "acquisitiveness" is likely to result in one's propensity for theft or robbery, just as "amativeness" may lead to rape, "combativeness" to assault, "destructiveness" to murder or manslaughter, "imitativeness" to counterfeiting, "philoprogenitiveness" to incest, and "secretiveness" to fraud or treason.[15]

A major distinction between Gall's phrenology and Lombroso's positivism rests in Gall's argument that phrenology is not deterministic or fatalistic. In *Des Dispositions innees de l'ame et de l'esprit du materialisme* (On the Innate Dispositions of the Will and the Spirit of Materialism), published in 1811, Gall had stressed that a person's "will" and "spirit" controlled his behavior. Arthur E. Fink explained that the prevailing view among nineteenth-century phrenologists held that a child could overcome "predominant passions" toward delinquency by rigorous training designed to strengthen organs of the brain that controlled desirable "faculties," after which the "faculties" controlling crime and vice would deteriorate through disuse.[16] A minority view among phrenologists paralleled Lombroso's deterministic view of the "born criminal" (see Chapter 5) and held that, because of the underdevelopment of the occiput, a delinquent child is condemned to a "vegetative" life through which he will seek to gratify "material" wants.[17]

Body Physique

Materialism as an underlying philosophy is apparent within the theories of various "constitutionalists" who focused on crime as being the product of physique and its accompanying personality trait. As early as 1826, Leon Rostand divided people into four morphological categories: cerebral, digestive, respiratory, and muscular.[18] Other variations followed[19] with little attention until 1921 when Ernest Kretschmer published his *Korperbau und Charakter* (Physique and Character), a book that became a popular work instantly. Utilizing a personality distinction first advanced by Emil Kraepelin, Kretschmer began by postulating the difference between two personalities—cycloids (the "circular insane") whose emotions alternate between happiness and sadness, and schizoids (the schizophrenic insane) who display multiple personalities. Then, Kretschmer divided human physiques into three types, also: the asthenic or leptosome is thin; the athletic is tall and muscular; the pyknic is short and fat. Correlating physiques with personality, Kretschmer argued that both asthenics and athletics may have schizothyme personalities characterized by either of two extreme conditions—apathy and waywardness or hypersensitivity and overreaction; whereas pyknics are more likely to have cyclothyme personalities, characterized by fluctuations of mood between manic and depressive states. In his latter work, Kretschmer added a fourth type of physique, a "mix" of the first three, which he called the dysplastic, and associated it with two personality subtypes, epileptoids and hysterics, having explosive personalities.[20] By the twenty-sixth edition of his book published in 1955, Kretschmer had concluded on the basis of some 4x4x4 case studies that asthenics are the most likely to perpetrate petty thefts, athletics to commit violent crimes, pyknics to engage in deceptive practices, and dysplastics to offend morality.[21]

A number of biopsychological theories that preceded or followed Kretschmer reflect a materialistic philosophy, also. Among these are Edward Spranger's idealistic life-form typology, classifying people as aesthetic, economical, religious, social, and theoretical types;[22] Richard Mueller-Freinfels' distinction between the intellectual ("man of abstraction," "man of deed," "man of fantasy," and "man of sensibility") and the emotional persona ("man of aggression," "erotic man," and "man of sympathy");[23] W. Jaensch's distinction between B-type juveniles suffering from Basedow's disease (exophthalmic goiter disorder) and T-type juveniles suffering from tetany, which E. R. Jaensch expanded into the difference between "integrated" and "disintegrated" man;[24] and William H. Sheldon's biological delinquents in relation to his constitutional psychiatry.[25]

Sheldon divided delinquents into three types, based largely upon physique in the tradition of Kretschmer. He distinguished between the ectomorph, the mesomorph, and the endomorph, paralleling this typology on three layers of skin (ectoderm, mesoderm, and endoderm). An embryo develops in three stages, and each stage of development is accompanied by the growth of different tissues. During the earliest stage, the inner layer of skin (endoderm) develops, as so digestive viscera. Next, the mesoderm appears along with bones, muscles, and tendons that facilitate motor development. Finally, the ectoderm or outer layer of skin grows, as do appendages of the nervous system. In Sheldon's endoderm, therefore, the digestive viscera are well developed, the bones are small, the skin is velvety, the body may be fat, the personality is extroverted, and the temperament is "viscerotonic" or relaxed. In this mesomorph, by contrast, the bones and muscles are well developed, the limbs and trunk are large, the chest is barreled, and the temperament is "somotonic" because the mesomorph asserts himself by talking and gesturing aggressively. In Sheldon's ectoderm, on the other hand, the body is lean and delicate and has a finely tuned nervous system, the personality is introverted, and the temperament is "cerebrotonic" because the nervous system provokes frequent complaints about allergies, fatigue, insomnia, and noise.

Undoubtedly, Sheldon was influenced by Earnest A. Hooton's somatic-biological orientation (see Chapter 5), as Stephen Schafer noted.[26] Nevertheless, Sheldon's theories are not positivistic. His types of physique are not absolute in any sense but relative and subject to scale. For instance, during the course of his field research, Sheldon rated each subject he studied in terms of the characteristics of each physique on a seven-point scale to determine that person's somatotype. Thus, a person displaying a somatotype of 7-1-3 would be a strong endomorph,[27] whereas one having a somatotype of 3-1-7 would be a strong ectomorph, and someone with a somatotype of 2-7-1 would be a strong mesomorph. Clearly, Sheldon envisioned that every person would possess some characteristics of all three physiques, in a decidedly materialistic tradition.

Sheldon studied some two hundred male youths whose behavior had led to their confinement at the Hayden Goodwill Inn in Boston over some period of time between 1939 and 1949, then compared their physiques with those of a similar number of college men whom he had studied earlier. Sheldon concluded that the delinquent youths were more likely to be mesomorphs and the college men more likely to be ectomorphs, a conclusion George B. Vold has rejected on methodological grounds.[28] Nevertheless, Edwin H. Sutherland replicated Sheldon's study of the delinquent youths, finding that the more delinquent ones in the group showed the strongest mesomorphic characteristics, significantly stronger than the least delinquent youths.[29]

Two Harvard sociologists, Sheldon and Eleanor Glueck, compared physiques of five hundred persistent delinquents and an equal number of

proven nondelinquents whom they had matched for age, ethnic and racial derivation, general intelligence, and residence in lower socioeconomic neighborhoods. They photographed individual participants in each
group, then assessed each snapshot visually to judge the particular subject's predominant physique.[30] In their book, *Physique and Delinquency*, published in 1956, the Gluecks concluded that 60.1 percent of
the delinquents but only 30.7 percent of the nondelinquents were mesomorphs,[31] thus confirming the findings that William H. Sheldon had
reached earlier. The Gluecks explained that:

[Mesomorphs are] more highly characterized by traits particularly suitable to
the commission of acts of aggression (physical strength, energy, insensitivity,
the tendency to express tensions and frustrations in action), together with a relative freedom from such inhibitions to antisocial adventures as feelings of inadequacy, marked submissiveness to authority, emotional instability, and the
like.[32]

However, unlike Sheldon, the Gluecks found also the mesomorphs who
become delinquent are different from mesomorphs who do not become
delinquent in terms of their susceptibility to childhood diseases and in
terms of personality traits such as destructiveness, emotional conflicts
and instability, and feelings of inadequacy.[33] Finally, the Gluecks noticed that mesomorphs who become delinquent differed from their nondelinquent counterparts by having lacked recreational facilities in their
family homes, where the Gluecks saw the absence of planned family
activities.[34] Thus, unlike Sheldon and the other "constitutionalists" in
the strictest sense, the Gluecks considered some sociocultural factors as
they examined delinquency in relation to physique. Therefore, the
Gluecks, unlike the earlier "constitutionalists," seem to reflect the
emergence of a naturalistic philosophy in contrast to a purely materialistic orientation.

Naturalism reaches greater fruition in the biopsychosocial research of
Georgetown University psychologist Juan B. Cortes, conducted during
the 1960s and published in 1972, who concluded that the concept of a
person's physical "constitution" is the product of both genetic and environmental influences. "It is not, therefore, and should not be, heredity
under or over environment, but only and always heredity *and* environment."[35] Cortes tried to overcome some criticism that had been directed
at the Gluecks, such as that their delinquent population had been institutionalized and that the physiques of the subjects they studied had been
assessed visually instead of having been measured precisely.[36] Cortes
somatotyped one hundred delinquent males and an equal number of high

school seniors. Thirty of the delinquents were not institutionalized. He found that 57 percent of the delinquents studied compared with only 19 percent of the nondelinquents exhibited a high degree of mesomorphy,[37] thus confirming the earlier studies conducted by Sheldon and the Gluecks. Then, Cortes asked seventy-three of the boys whose somatotypes were clearest to describe their own temperaments, and he repeated this procedure with one hundred college girls. In each instance, the subjects' self-descriptions of their temperaments correlated significantly with their physique exactly as William H. Sheldon had theorized.[38]

Based upon his study, nothwithstanding its small size, Cortes offered the following conclusion: "Delinquents and possibly criminals differ from nondelinquents and noncriminals in being *physically* more mesomorphic, more energetic and potentially aggressive *temperamentally*, and in showing higher need for achievement and power *motivationally*."[39] Moreover, Cortes noted that nondelinquents "belong to higher social backgrounds" and "possess greater intelligence" than do delinquents.[40] Cortes' study might be referenced as a sort of bridge between a materialist and a naturalist perspective, where somatotype is given great weight but considered together with temperament and motivation. As Julian B. Roebuck has reminded us: "Contrary to the beliefs of many American criminologists, the constitutional school [of criminology] is not dead. Research continues in this area, and it behooves the skeptic whether he be sociologist, psychiatrist or psychologist to at least keep an open mind to it."[41] Nevertheless, more research has been and continues to be conducted to test psychiatric and psychological theories which, in contrast to the purely constitutional theories, may be viewed as being naturalistic as opposed to materialistic. The psychiatric and psychological theories emerged both before and since the constitutional ones.

PSYCHIATRIC AND PSYCHOLOGICAL THEORIES AND PRACTICES

Until well after the eighteenth-century Enlightenment in Europe, persons who displayed signs of being a "fool" or who appeared to the populace as being "deranged" were carted away to asylums, frequently chained to the walls there, and kept out of both sight and mind of their relatives and the rest of society. Little effort was devoted toward studying or treating the mentally ill person until the decade of the 1830s, when French psychiatrist Philippe Pinel removed the chains from his patients at La Bicetre asylum. Another French psychiatrist, Jean Esquirol, followed the same reforms shortly thereafter at the Salpetriere sanitarium.[42] In the 1840s, Dorothea Lynde Dix commenced her untiring efforts to secure removal of "fetters and iron balls" used to keep American mental patients locked in place,[43] such as at New York's Bloomingdale asylum.[44] Subsequently, William Tuke opened his York Retreat for mental patients in England, and Benjamin Rush became known as the "father of American psychiatry" through his efforts to study and treat patients at the Pennsylvania Hospital in Philadelphia. As Karl O. Christiansen has noted, "[a]t the beginning and in the middle of the nineteenth century we find many physicians whose contribution to the legal and criminal psychiatry had decisive significance to the development of criminology."[45]

In 1838, for instance, the Salpetriere's Jean Etienne Dominique Esquirol published *Des Malades mentales* (On Mental Illness), within which he distinguished the mentally deficient patient whose "mental faculties" had never developed, from the mentally deranged patient whose "faculties" became abnormal subsequent to development, such as through trauma or disease.[46] In the same year, American psychiatrist Isaac Ray published *A Treatise on the Medical Jurisprudence of Insanity*, in which he paralleled Esquirol by observing that the idiot and the imbecile possess a defective intelligence, whereas "mania" and "dementia" reflect postdevelopmental abnormality. In the 1850s, Benoit Augustin Morel declared that crime may be traced to the "physical, intellectual, and moral degeneration of the human species" and established what he termed morbid anthropology to study human degeneration.[47] In 1859, Paul Broca established the Societe d'Anthropologie de Paris to study the "natural history of man" by means of his zoological method.[48] In 1868, French psychiatrist Prosper Despine coined the term natural psychology for the study of abnormal intellectual and moral conditions among mental patients.[49] Influenced by Morel, Henry Maudsley published *The Physiology of Mind* and *The Pathology of Mind*, both in 1867, plus *Responsibility in Mental Disease* in 1874 and *Natural Causes and Supernatural Seemings* in 1886. Throughout Maudsley's works, he tried to bridge the distance between crime and insanity on the one hand and between hereditary and psychological causes of both crime and insanity on the other hand. Peter Scott reckoned that "Maudsley's acceptance of the criminal's motivation by forces of which he was not aware seems to anticipate the Freudian conccept of the Unconscious."[50] Scott has quoted Maudsley as having reasoned: "To say there is a criminal nature which is degenerated is one thing, a true thing; but to go on to say that all criminals are degenerate and bear on them the stigmata of degeneracy is another and quite false thing."[51] Mental degeneracy had been popularized throughout the nineteenth century as a primary cause of most crimes.[52]

By the end of the nineteenth century and the dawn of the Freudian age, of course, modern psychiatry and psychology had become more sophisticated and theories of simple "degeneracy" faded into oblivion. Nevertheless, the nineteenth century's concern for mental illness impacted greatly the Anglo-American criminal justice system, notwithstanding early misunderstandings about the true causes of and proper treatments for mental disorders. Foremost among all judicial reactions to the new tolerance of insanity is the example of the M'Naghten Rule decided by England's House of Lords in 1843. In *M'Naghten's Case* the House of Lords permitted a person who has been accused of a crime to raise in defense that he did not know the difference between right and wrong or that he did not know what he was doing because of *illness*:

[T]o establish a defense on the ground of insanity it must be clearly proved, that, at the time of the committing of the act, the party accused was labouring under such a defect of reason from disease of the mind as not to know the nature and quality of the act he was doing; or, if he did know it, that he did not know he was doing what was wrong.[53]

Prior to the M'Naghten Rule, England and most English-speaking jurisdictions permitted mental impairment to function as a defense to criminal responsibility only where the accused did not know the difference between right and wrong any more than a "wild beast."[54] In *M'Naghten*, therefore, the House of Lords allowed either "defect of reason" or "disease of the mind" to be introduced into evidence as the cause of the accused's failure to appreciate the distinction between what is right and what is wrong, in keeping with a growing popular recognition of mental defect and disease being the causes of insanity.

Most states of the United States have adopted the M'Naghten test of insanity as a defense to criminal responsibility and, in over one-half of these jurisdictions, the M'Naghten Rule is the only test for legal insanity the law will recognize. Many American jurisdictions have gone beyond the limits of the M'Naghten Rule, however, and have allowed persons accused of crimes to offer additional evidence supporting a claim of insanity. One such extension of M'Naghten is known as the Irresistible Impulse test and is the the outgrowth of Isaac Ray's book, *A Treatise on the Medical Jurisprudence of Insanity*, published first in 1838, in which he stated that there is an "immense mass of cases where people are irresistibly impelled to the commission of criminal acts while fully conscious of their nature and consequences."[55] Somewhat fewer than half of the American states that follow the M'Naghten Rule allow also the Irresistible Impulse test which permits a jury to acquit an accused by reason of insanity where the accused could not *control* his conduct at the time he committed a crime, usually one of a violent nature.[56]

In *State v. Jones* (1871),[57] New Hampshire rejected M'Naghten entirely, largely because of the esteem in which Chief Justice Charles Doe held Isaac Ray, who had written that insanity "is never established by a single diagnostic symptom, but by the whole body of symptoms, no particular one of which is present in every case."[58] The Supreme Court of New Hampshire reasoned in the *Jones* opinion, written by Justice Ladd, that a defendant must be acquitted by reason of insanity if his conduct "was the offspring or product of mental disease."[59] The course in *Jones* continued:

If the defendant had an insane impulse to kill his wife, which he could not control, then mental disease produced the act. If he could have controlled it, then his will must have assented to the act, and it was not caused by disease, but by the concurrence of his will, and was therefore a crime.[60]

Charles Doe's input into the *Jones* opinion is evident from the language used therein, reminiscent of Isaac Ray, and from correspondence between Doe and Ray,[61] as the late New Hampshire Chief Justice Frank R. Kenison acknowledged.[62] Through Doe, therefore, the input of Ray may be witnessed as it impacted the changing law of insanity across the United States for more than a hundred years between the middle of the nineteenth and the middle of the twentieth centuries.[63]

The notion of insanity intrigued many investigators during the latter part of the nineteenth century, and some tried to link it to heredity. Foremost among those researchers was Richard L. Dugdale who traced the "Jukes" family tree across several generations, finding among them a higher-than–anticipated proportion of alcoholics, criminals, paupers, prostitutes, and syphilitics. Dugdale published his findings in 1877,[64] one year after Cesare Lombroso had published his *L'Uomo delinquente* (see Chapter 5). Dugdale's study of the Jukes became a popular sensation throughout America, where members of the family were supposed to have resided since colonial times.;6[5] According to Dugdale, one Ada Jukes produced 1,200 descendants, among whom he discovered 280 paupers, 60 habitual thieves, and 140 other criminals that included 7 murderers and 50 prostitutes.[66] Subsequently, Arthur A. Estabrook found 715 additional descendants, of whom he documented 170 more paupers, 118 more criminals, 378 more prostitutes, and many additional deviants of different types.[67] Dugdale compared the "degenerate" Jukes family with the "blue-blooded" progeny of Puritan preacher Jonathan Edwards, some of whose offspring became American presidents and most of whom avoided collision with the law. In his introduction to a 1910 edition of Dugdale's book, sociologist Franklin Giddings said that Dugdale's first edition was "the best example of scientific method applied to a socio-logical investigation."[68] Dugdale did credit multiple factors as causing inferior offspring and criminal behavior, and, unlike Lombroso, Dugdale did not blame genetic defects exclusively for the birth of "degenerate" children but included the impact of the environment, also.[69] Thus, Dugdale's philosophy may be described as being naturalistic and not positivistic. Dugdale rejected the temptation to explain criminality in terms of any single factor.

In the aftermath of Dugdale's research, a number of similar attempts were made to trace family lineage to link crime to undesirable breeding.[70] Next to Dugdale's study of the Jukes, the most well-known of these was Henry H. Goddard's genealogy of the Kallikak family, which he published in 1925.[71] Goddard traced the offspring of one Martin Kallikak, Sr., through two separate families—through his illegitimate son, Martin, Jr., whom he fathered with a barmaid; and through other children Martin, Sr., fathered with his wife. Out of 1,046 heirs of Martin Kallikak, Jr., whom Goddard discovered, 262 were feebleminded and numerous others were alcoholics, epileptics, or prostitutes.[72] Feeblemindedness is inherited, criminality is not, Goddard had concluded earlier[73] and reaffirmed with his Kallikak study.

German psychiatrist Gustav Aschaffenburg reached a similar conclusion. "The one fact that we can establish with certainty is," he maintained, "that the inheritance of the children of drunkards, insane persons, and epileptics consists of physical and mental inferiority."[74] Aschaffenburg edited the prestigious *Monatschrift fur Kriminal-psychologie und Strafrechtreform* (Monthly for Criminal Psychology and Reform of the Criminal Law) between 1904 and 1935, when the Nazi regime removed him and he emigrated to America. The question left unanswered by Aschaffenburg's statement is why so?

William Healy pioneered in the use of the case study to trace a delinquent child's career back to its origin. As a psychiatrist who headed Chicago's Juvenile Psychopathic Institute early in the twentieth century, Healy had access to numerous delinquent case studies. In 1915, Healy published *The Individual Delinquent*, a book in which he accounted for biological, environmental, psychological, and social influences on predelinquent youth. His approach was truly naturalistic, and he recognized many factors as causing delinquency. Arthur E. Fink has argued that Healy, "like Lombroso more than a half century before, closed one era of criminology and opened the next."[75] Healy's research ended the notion that defective organisms alone cause criminal behavior.

In 1926, Healy and psychologist Augusta F. Bronner tested the intelligence of delinquent youth in Boston and Chicago, finding at least thirty-seven percent to be subnormal. Their conclusion: the delinquent male is five to ten times more likely than a normal boy to be mentally deficient.[76] Subsequently, they compared 105 delinquents with their 105 nondelinquent siblings, finding emotional disturbance in ninety-one percent of the delinquents compared to only thirteen percent of the nondelinquents.[77] In 1935, Healy and Franz Alexander published their *Roots of Crime*, in which they contended that crime is a substitute behavior for some other activity the offender wants but is unable to perform, such as sexual intercourse.[78] In that book, Alexander and Healy discuss seven case studies from their respective psychiatric practices, reaching the following conclusions:

[S]tealing is chiefly determined by irrational, emotional, and unconscious motives, and not so much by the rational motive of gain.

(1) His stealing is a reaction to a strong sense of inferiority giving him a feeling of bravado and toughness. This sense of inferiority is itself a reaction to a strong dependent, receptive wish expressed in the attitude of obtaining things without working for them. . . .

(2) His stealing also is a means of getting rid of guilt feelings which he has toward his brother. He helps his brother, exposes himself to danger for his sake, and even goes to jail for him, thereby relieving his guilt feelings.

(3) His stealing is also a spite reaction toward his mother, having the unconscious significance: "If you spend your interest and love on the brother and not on me, then I take revenge on you by disgracing you as a criminal. . . .

(4) Finally . . . criminality is also a means of getting into jail, where he can indulge in a carefree, vegetative existence, gratifying his infantile, parasitic wishes.[79]

Alexander and Healy summarized their "four unconscious motives" behind their thief's stealing: (1) overcompensation for a sense of inferiority; (2) attempt to relieve a sense of guilt; (3) spite reaction toward his mother; and (4) direct gratification of dependent tendencies in a carefree existence in prison.[80] Thus, Alexander and Healy analyze theft in terms of symbolic behavior, a ramification of the Freudian school of psychoanalysis.[81]

The notion that criminals have a lower intelligence than members of the general population was refuted by Clark University psychologist Carl Murchison in 1926,[82] who compared prisoners to draftees in the army and found the intelligence test performance had reached similar conclusions using less rigorous techniques.[83] However, more recently several criminologists have rethought this issue and obtained varying results. For instance, in 1969, Travis Hirschi published the results of his study in Contra Costa County, California, during the course of which he examined police records on more than 3,600 boys, both black and white. He found that, among both races, boys having high verbal achievement scores on the Differential Aptitude Test (DAT) tended to have fewer official offenses, indicating to some extent at least that academic competence may be an inverse predictor of delinquency.[84]

In 1976, Robert Gordon announced a direct correlation between the distribution of intelligence quotient (IQ) variations and prevalence of delinquency among juveniles whom he had studied, regardless of a community's density of population.[85] The next year, in 1977, Hirschi and statistician Michael J. Hindelang determined that a low IQ is a good predictor of "official" delinquency but an even better predictor of self-reported delinquency,[86] thus casting doubt upon the arguments advanced by some of Hirschi's earlier skeptics who warned that academic competence might help a delinquent to escape detection and punishment and, consequently, to disguise his delinquency. Hirschi and Hindelang suggested the concept of the IQ had been associated with criminologists such as Goring and Goddard who were physicians and that when sociologists became popular as criminologists between the two world wars, they intentionally understated the significance of IQ as a predictor of delinquency in order to draw attention away from the individual delinquent or offender and toward the social conditions they felt influenced criminal behavior more directly.

The critical question for criminologists with a naturalistic orientation remains whether IQ is innate or the product of the environment in which the child has been raised. The nature theorists argue that a high or a low IQ is inherited, while the nurture theorists contend that IQ results from how and where a child is raised. Contemporary nature theorists include Arthur Jensen and Richard Herrnstein, who have stated that genetic factors outweigh environmental factors in producing IQ.[87] Nurture theorists of the 1920s and 1950s offered evidence that intelligence tests could be culture-biased,[88] an argument advanced vehemently today by those who oppose misplaced reliance upon IQ.[89] What is more, some studies have indicated that a culturally deprived child's IQ will increase upon the child's entry into a nondeprived environment, such as a middle-class foster home.[90] The debate over the extent to which IQ influences delinquency and criminality, as well as the debate as to the extent to which heredity or social environment affects IQ, are naturalistic issues that will continue to provoke controversy for some time. What they reflect, however, is the ongoing dominance of the multiple-factor approach to understanding the causation of crime.

The naturalistic influence in criminology during the twentieth century has impacted the American judicial system on a number of occasions.

In 1924, for instance, Virginia enacted a statute permitting sterilization of patients confined in institutions for the feebleminded. Carrie Buck was the daughter of a feebleminded mother and herself the mother of a feebleminded child, but she resisted sterilization in the courts. Writing for a unanimous Supreme Court of the United States in *Buck v. Bell* (1927), Justice Oliver Wendell Holmes, Jr., upheld Virginia's right to sterilize Carrie Buck, explaining:

We have seen more than once that the public welfare may call upon the best citizens for their lives. It would be strange if it could not call upon those who already sap the strength of the state for these lesser sacrifices, often not felt to be such by those concerned, in order to prevent our being swamped with incompetence. It is better for all the world, if instead of waiting to execute degenerate offspring for crime, or to let them starve for their imbecility, society can prevent those persons who are manifestly unfit from continuing their kind. The principle that sustains cumpulsory vaccination is broad enough to cover cutting the Fallopian tubes. . . . Three generations of imbeciles is enough.[91]

Since it was handed down, *Buck v. Bell* has fallen into disgrace, but it does reflect quite fairly the reasoned and naturalistic viewpoint of Justice Holmes, typical of the naturalistic criminology emerging in contrast to positivism in the 1920s. In *The Common Law*, Holmes had written almost a half-century earlier, just before going on the bench of the Supreme Judicial Court of Massachusetts:

As to the violation of equal rights which is charged, it may be replied that the dogma of equality makes an equation between individuals only, not between an individual and the community. No society has ever admitted that it could not sacrifice individual welfare to its own existence. If conscripts are necessary for its army, it seizes them, and marches them, with bayonets in their rear, to death. It runs highways and railroads through old family places in spite of the owner's protest . . . sacrifices his will and his welfare to that of the rest.[92]

Although Holmes was fond of positivist criminologists such as Lombroso and Garofalo, whom he called "the Italians," clearly his own philosophy of criminology was much more naturalistic, more reminiscent of Dugdale and Goddard.

As society came to understand more about insanity and mental illness, courts of law became more eager to recognize low intelligence as a disease of the mind, allowing evidence of mental disorders such as senility,[93] feeblemindedness,[94] and paranoia[95] to alleviate criminal responsibility in proper cases. In 1954, moreover, the United States Court of Appeals for the District of Columbia Circuit announced a new test for insanity in *Durham v. United States*,[96] in which "an accused is not criminally responsible if his unlawful act was the product of mental disease or defect."[97] Following the doctrine set forth first by Isaac Ray and judicialized for New Hampshire through Charles Doe, Judge David L. Bazelon wrote in *Durham* the following suggested instruction for a jury on the question of a defendant's insanity:

If you the jury believe beyond a reasonable doubt that the accused was not suffering from a diseased or defective mental condition at the time he committed the criminal act charged, you may find him guilty. If you believe he was suffering from a diseased or defective mental condition when he committed the act, but believe beyond a reasonable doubt that the act was not the product of such mental abnormality, you may find him guilty. Unless you believe beyond a reasonable doubt either that he was not suffering from a diseased or defective mental condition, or that the act was not the product of such abnormality, you must find the accused not guilty by reason of insanity.[98]

Relying upon Isaac Ray, also, the District of Columbia Circuit held that the M'Naghten Rule "does not take sufficient account of psychic realities and scientific knowledge" and that "it is based upon one symptom and so cannot validly be applied in all circumstances."[99] In 1955, the American Law Institute's Model Penal Code project drafted what has become known as the "substantial capacity" test of insanity, which modernized the M'Naghten Rule's language without altering much of its substance. The text recites:

A person is not responsible for criminal conduct if at the time of such conduct as a result of mental disease or defect he lacks substantial capacity either to appreciate the criminality [wrongfulness] of his conduct or to conform his conduct to the requirements of law.[100]

The substantial capacity test was adopted by most United States courts of appeals[101] and by statute or case law in several states.[102]

NOTES

1. See B. Inglis, A HISTORY OF MEDICINE (1965), and C. Singer and E. Ashworth, A SHORT HISTORY OF MEDICINE (1962).

2. See W. Overholser, *An Historical Sketch of Psychiatry*, 10 J. CLIN. PSYCHOPATHOLOGY (1949).

3. See M. Prince, THE DISSOCIATION OF A PERSONALITY: A BIBLIOGRAPHICAL STUDY IN ABNORMAL PSYCHOLOGY (1906) and THE UNCONSCIOUS (1914).

4. See N. D. C. Lewis, A SHORT HISTORY OF PSYCHIATRIC ACHIEVEMENT 35 (1941).

5. *Id.* at 91.

6. E. Nagel, "Naturalism Reconsidered," 28 PROCEEDINGS OF THE AMERICAN PHILOSOPHICAL ASSOCIATION 7–10 (1954–55); reprinted in E. Nagel, LOGIC WITHOUT METAPHYSICS (1956). (Emphasis in the original.)

7. *Supra*, note 4 at 134.

8. Examples are projection, repression, substitute responses, and symbolic behavior—all documented by case "types." See J. Whitwell, HISTORICAL NOTES ON PSYCHIATRY (1936), and E. Mann, MANUAL OF PSYCHOLOGICAL MEDICINE AND ALLIED NERVOUS DISORDERS (1883).

9. See E. Nordenshiold, THE HISTORY OF BIOLOGY (1928), and S. Leek, PHRENOLOGY (1970).

10. See A. Fink, THE CAUSES OF CRIME: BIOLOGICAL THEORIES IN THE UNITED STATES, 1800–1915 (1938).

11. H. Lauvergne, *Les forcats consideres sous le rapport physique morale et intellectuel observes au bagne de Toulon* (1844).

12. *Id.* See C. Bernaldo de Quiros, MODERN THEORIES OF CRIMINALITY 3 (1912).

13. *Supra*, note 10 at 154–55, n.6.

14. Eastern State Penitentiary, *Twenty-seventh Annual Report* 42 (1856).

15. C. Caldwell, ELEMENTS OF PHRENOLOGY (1824).

16. *Supra*, note 10 at 8–9.

17. See C. Carus, GRUNDZUGE EINTER NEUEN UND WISSENSCHAFTLICHEN KRANIOSCOPIE (Principles of a New and Scientific Craniology; 1840).

18. See S. Schafer, THEORIES IN CRIMINOLOGY 165 (1969).

19. See O. Kinberg, BASIC PROBLEMS OF CRIMINOLOGY (1935).

20. E. Kretschmer, KORPERBAU UND CHARAKTER (26th ed., 1955).

21. *Id.* at 331–57. Kretschmer added to this edition a chapter that he entitled "Konstitution and Verbrachen" (Constitutional Types and Crime). In his 4x4x4 case studies, Kretschmer attempted to correlate physique, personality, and criminality according to four predictive variables.

22. E. Spranger, LEBENSFORMEN, GEISTESWISSENSCHAFTLICHE PSYCHOLOGIE UND ETHIK DER PERSONLICHKEIT (1914).

23. R. Mueller-Freinfels, PHILOSOPHIE DER INDIVIDUALITAT (1921).

24. See E. Jaensch, ZUR EIDETIK UND INTERGRATIONSPSYCHOLOGIE (1941).

25. W. Sheldon, VARIETIES OF DELINQUENT YOUTH: AN INTRODUCTION TO CONSTITUTIONAL PSYCHIATRY (1949).

26. *Supra*, note 18 at 167. The question is whether Hooton was a positivist or a materialist. However, Hooton concluded that criminals are both mentally and physically "inferior" due to heredity. See E. Hooton, THE AMERICAN CRIMINAL: AN ANTHROPOLOGICAL STUDY 229, 306 (1939).

27. Sheldon rated endomorphy first, followed by mesomorphy, then ecto-morphy last, in the order of embryonic skin development. See *supra*, note 25 at 96.

28. Vold concluded instead: "There is no present evidence at all of phys-ical type, as such, having any consistent relation to legal and sociologically de-fined crime." G. Vold, THEORETICAL CRIMINOLOGY 74 (1958).

29. E. Sutherland, *Critique of Sheldon's Varieties of Delinquent Youth*, 18 AM. SOC. REV. 142–48 (1951).

30. For a discussion of this methodology, see S. Glueck and E. Glueck, UNRAVELING JUVENILE DELINQUENCY 192–96 (1950).

31. S. Glueck and E. Glueck, PHYSIQUE AND DELINQUENCY 9 (1956).

32. *Id*. at 226.

33. *Id*. at 221.

34. *Id*. at 224.

35. J. Cortes, DELINQUENCY AND CRIME 19 (1972). (Emphasis in the original.)

36. For a review of these criticisms, see *id*. at 19–21.

37. *Id*. at 28.

38. *Id*. at 53.

39. *Id*. at 89.

40. *Id*.

41. J. Roebuck, CRIMINOLOGY TYPOLOGY 39 (1967).

42. See *supra*, note 18 at 116–17.

43. *Id*. at 116.

44. See D. Rothman, THE DISCOVERY OF THE ASYLUM: SOCIAL ORDER AND DISORDER IN THE NEW REPUBLIC 249 (1971).

45. K. Christiansen, *Kriminologie (Grundlagen)* in R. Sieverts, ed., HANDWORTHERBUCH DER KRIMINOLOGIE 191 (1968). See also, M. Foucault, MADNESS AND CIVILIZATION: A HISTORY OF INSANITY IN THE AGE OF REASON (1965).

46. The book was published in 1845 as MENTAL MALADIES (E. Hunt, tr.). Esquirol had published DES ILLUSIONS CHEZ LES ALIENES in 1832, republished in 1833 as OBSERVATIONS ON THE ILLUSIONS OF THE IN-SANE (Liddell, tr.).

47. See *supra*, note 18 at 117.

48. *Id*.

49. P. Despine, PSYCHOLOGIE NATURELLE, ESSAI SUR LES FA-CULTES INTELLECTUELLES ET MORALES DANS LEUR ÉTAT NOR-MAL ET DANS LEUR MANIFESTATIONS ANORMALES CHEZ LES AL-IENES ET CHEZ LES CRIMINELS (1868).

50. P. Scott, *Henry Maudsley*, in H.Mannheim, ed., PIONEERS IN CRI-MINOLOGY 152 (1960).

51. *Id*. at 147–67.

52. See, *inter alia*, C. Fere, DEGENERESCENCE ET CRIMINALITE (1888), and A. Corre, LES CRIMINELS (1889) plus L'ETHNOGRAPHIC

CRIMINELLE? (1895). See also M. de Montyel, *Contribution a l'etude clinique des rapports de la criminalite et de la degenerescence*, ARCHIVES D'ANTHROPOLOGIE CRIMINELLE (1892).

53. 10 Cl. & F.200, 8 ENG. REP. 718 (1843). Daniel M'Naghten had shot to death Edward Drummond, private secretary to Prime Minister Sir Robert Peel. M'Naghten believed that Peel was conspiring to kill him and shot Drummond mistaking him for Peel. The jury found M'Naghten "insane."

54. See S. Glueck, MENTAL DISORDER AND THE CRIMINAL LAW (1925), and Platt and Diamond, *The Origins of the "Right and Wrong" Test of Criminal Responsibility and Its Subsequent Development in the United States: An Historical Survey*, 54 CAL. L. REV. 1227 (1966).

55. I. Ray, A TREATISE ON THE MEDICAL JURISPRUDENCE OF INSANITY 263 (3rd ed., 1855). Ray buttressed this view subsequently in CONTRIBUTIONS TO MEDICAL PATHOLOGY (1873).

56. States that follow the "Irresistible Impulse" test include: Alabama (*Parsons v. State*, 81 Ala. 577, 2 So. 854 (1886)); Arkansas (*Downs v. State*, 231 Ark. 466, 330 S.W. 2d 281 (1959)); Indiana (*Flowers v. State*, 236 Ind. 151, 139 N.E. 2d 185 (1956)); Michigan (*People v. Sharac*, 209 Mich. 249, 176 N.W. 431 (1920)); New Mexico (*State v. White*, 58 N.M. 324, 270 P. 2d 727 (1954)); Ohio (*State v. Robinson*, 83 Ohio L. Abs. 259, 168 N.E. 2d 328 (Ct. App, 1958)); Utah *State v. Kirkham*, 7 Utah 2d 108, 319, P. 2d 859 (1958)); Virginia (*Thompson v. Commonwealth*, 193 Va. 704, 70 S.E. 2d 284 (1952)); and Wyoming (*State v. Riggle*, 76 Wyo. 1, 298 P. 2d 349 (1956)). This is the federal rule. See *Davis v. United States*, 165 U.S. 373 (1897).

57. 50 N.H. 369, A. (1871). See also *State v. Pike*, 49 N.H. 399, A. (1869).

58. *Supra*, note 55 at 39 (5th ed., 1871).

59. *Supra*, note 57 at 398.

60. *Id*. at 399. See also Weihofen, *The Flowering of New Hampshire*, 22 U. CHI. L. REV. 356, 357 (1955).

61. See Reik, *The Doe-Ray Correspondence: A Pioneer Collaboration in the Jurisprudence of Mental Disease*, 63 Yale L. J. 145 (1953).

62. F. Kenison, *Charles Doe*, in H. Mannheim, ed., PIONEERS IN CRIMINOLOGY 199 (1960). Chief Justice Kenison indicated that Chief Justice Doe had assigned the *Jones* opinion to Justice Ladd in order to share credit for its contents. *Id*. at 203–4.

63. See Doe's language, also reminiscent of Ray, in an earlier opinion: "If it is necessary that the law shoud entertain a single medical opinion concerning a single disease, it is not necessary that that opinion should be a cast-off theory of physicians of a former generation. That cannot be fact in law, which is not face in science[.]" *Boardman v. Woodman*, 47 N.H. 120, 140 (1866; dissenting opinion of Doe, C. J.).

64. R. Dugdale, THE JUKES: A STUDY IN CRIME, PAUPERISM, DISEASE, AND HEREDITY (1877).

65. Supposedly, a descendant of Dutch settlers named Max had two sons who married into the Jukes family of six sisters. *Supra*, note 18 at 205.

66. *Id*. at 205–6.

67. See A. Estabrook, THE JUKES IN 1915 (1916).

68. *Supra*, note 64 at iii (1910 ed.). Other critics have been less generous. See S. Adams, *The Juke's Myth*, 2 SAT. REV. 48 (1955).

69. *Supra*, note 64 at 118 (4th ed., 1942).

70. See, *inter alia*, P. Aubry, *La contagiiion du meurtre* (1894), tracing the Keromgal family; and C. Davenport, *Hereditary Crime*, 13 AM. J. SO. 402 (1907), tracing the Nam family. See also, Prosper Despine's CHRETIEN FAMILY; Blackmar's SMOKY PILGRIMS; Kite's PINEYS; McCulloch's TRIBE OF ISHMAEL; and Poelman's ZERO FAMILY. *Supra*, note 18 at 205.

71. H. Goddard, THE KALLIKAK FAMILY: A STUDY IN HEREDITY OF FEEBLEMINDEDNESS (1925).

72. *Id*. at 19.

73. H. Goddard, FEEBLEMINDEDNESS: ITS CAUSES AND CONSE-QUENCES 8–9 (1914).

74. G. Aschaffenburg, CRIME AND ITS REPRESSION 129 (1913). He had published this book as DAS VERBRECHEN UND SEINE BEKAEMP-FUNG in 1903.

75. *Supra*, note 10 at 178. Yet, other criminologists have questioned the validity of Healy's own research. For example, Sutherland and Cressey have argued that Healy showed a predisposition toward interpreting delinquency in terms of emotional disturbance. See E. Sutherland and D. Cressey, PRINCI-PLES OF CRIMINOLOGY 174 (7th ed., 1966).

76. W. Healy and A. Bronner, DELINQUENCY AND CRIMINALS: THEIR MAKING AND UNMAKING (1926).

77. W. Healy and A. Bronner, NEW LIGHT ON DELINQUENCY AND ITS TREATMENT (1936).

78. F. Alexander and W. Healy, ROOTS OF CRIME 33 (1935).

79. *Id*. at 67.

80. *Id*. at 68.

81. See S. Freud, *Criminals from a Sense of Guilt*, in 14 THE COM-PLETE PSYCHOLOGICAL WORKS OF SIGMUND FREUD 332–33 (1940).

82. C. Murchison, CRIMINAL INTELLIGENCE (1926).

83. See C. Stone, *A Comparative Study of the Intelligence of Three Hundred Fifty-three Men of the United States Army*, 12 J. CRIM. L. & CRIM. 238 (1921), and H. Adler and M. Worthington, *The Scope of the Problems of Delinquency and Crime as Related to Mental Deficiency*, 30 J. PSYCHO-ASTHETICS 47 (1925).

84. T. Hirschi, CAUSES OF DELINQUENCY 80 (1969). Note, however, that Hirschi studied police records, so that he tracked "official" law violations only. Thus, academic competence may predict how well a lad avoids getting caught as much as how law-abiding he remains.

85.   R. Gordon, *Prevalence: The Rare Datum in Delinquency Measurement and Its Implications for the Theory of Delinquency*, in M.Klein, ed., THE JUVENILE JUSTICE SYSTEM 201 (1976).

86.   T. Hirschi and M. Hindelang, *Intelligence and Delinquency: A Revisionist Review*, 42 AM. SOC. REV. 572 (1977).

87.   See A. Jensen, BIAS IN MENTAL TESTING (1979) and *How Much Can We Boost IQ and Scholastic Achievement?* 39 HARV. ED. REV. 1 (1969); and R. Herrnstein, *IQ*, 228 ATLANTIC 44 (1971).

88.   See J. Slawson, THE DELINQUENT BOYS (1926), and K. Eels, INTELLIGENCE AND CULTURAL DIFFERENCES (1951).

89.   See L.Kamin, *Burt's IQ Data*, 195 SCIENCE 246 (1977).

90.   See F. Palmer, *The Effects of Minimal Early Intervention on Subsequent IQ Scores and Reading Achievement* (1976 Report to the Education Commissions of the States); and S. Scarr and R. Weinberg, *IQ Test Performance of Black Children Adopted by White Families*, 31 AM. PSYCH. 726 (1976).

91.   274 U.S. 200, 207 (1927).

92.   O. Holmes, THE COMMON LAW 43 (1881).

93.   See *State v. Hadley*, 65 Utah 109, 234 P. 240 (1925).

94.   See *State v. Johnson*, 233 Wis. 668, 290 N.W. 159 (1940).

95.   See *State v. Elsea*, 251, S.W. 2d 650 (Mo. 1952).

96.   94 U.S. App. D.C. 228, 214 F. 2d 862 (D.C. Cir., 1954).

97.   *Id*, at 874–75.

98.   *Id*. at 875. The District of Columbia Circuit modified *Durham* on several occasions. *Carter v. United States*, 252 F. 2d 608 (D.C. Cir., 1957); *Blocker v. United States*, 274, F. 2d 572 (D.C. Cir., 1959); *McDonald v. United States*, 312 F. 2d 847 (D.C. Cir., 1962); and *Washington v. United States*, 390 F. 2d 444 (D.C. Cir., 1967). Eventually, it rejected the Durham Rule altogether in *United States v. Brawner*, 471 F. 2d 969 (D.C. Cir., 1972). See *The Durham Rule in the Real World*, in R. Simon, THE JURY AND THE DEFENSE OF INSANITY 202 (1967). Critics of the Durham Rule felt it opened the door to psychiatric testimony that was too broad and confusing to jurors. Also, the term "product" seemed not sufficiently specific to convey its meaning.

99.   *Id*. at 874.

100.   Model Penal Code 4.01. (Proposed Official Draft, 1962.)

101.   See e.g., *Wade v. United States*, 426 F. 2d 64 (9th Cir., 1970).

102.   See *Conn. Gen. Stats.* 53A–13; *Ill. Rev. Stats.* ch. 38, 6–2; *Md. Ann. Code*, art. 59, 9(a); *Mont. Rev. Code* 95–501; and *Vt. Stats.*, tit. 13, 4801. See *Terry v. Commonwealth*, 371 S.W. 2d 862 (Ky., 1963); *Commonwealth v. McHoul*, 352 Mass. 544, 226 N.E. 2d 556 (1967); *State v. Shoffner*, 31 Wis. 2d 412, 143 N.W. 2d 458 (1966).

7

Pragmatism and the Environmental Experience of People Interacting in Groups

Sometimes pragmatism has been labeled America's contribution to philosophy, a credit that is partially but not completely deserved. John Dewey, the most famous pragmatist philosopher, defined his philosophy in 1909 for the *Century Dictionary* as:

[t]he theory that the processes and the materials of knowledge are determined by practical or purposive considerations—that there is no such thing as knowledge determined by exclusively theoretical, speculative, or abstract intellectual considerations.

William James, who was the first person to mold pragmatism into a separate philosophy, remarked that "[i]t has no dogmas, and no doctrine save its methods."[1] Charles Sanders Peirce called pragmatism the "laboratory method," and James called Peirce the founder of pragmatism, although in time Peirce repudiated the philosophy advanced by James. Charles Darwin's theory of human evolution contributed significantly to the emergence of pragmatism, as it had to positivism and naturalism, also. Dewey wrote that the influence of Charles Darwin upon philosophy "resides in having conquered the phenomena of life for the principle of transition, and thereby freed the new logic for application to mind, life, and morals."[2] Expressed somewhat differently, Darwin stressed the importance of adaptation, which Dewey accepted as the inducement for studying environmental experience as an explanation of human conduct. Pragmatism is concerned with what is happening, rather than being contented with what has happened, in contrast to positivism. This dynamic element of pragmatism is found in the legal philosophy of Nicholas St. John Green and in the judicial philosophies of Oliver Wendell Holmes, Jr., and Roscoe Pound.

   The decade between 1894 and 1904 John Dewey spent teaching at the University of Chicago, establishing what became known as the Chicago School of Pragmatic Instrumentalism. In 1917, Dewey authored a chapter in the volume, *Creative Intelligence*, in which he wrote that "[p]hilosophy recovers itself when it ceases to be a device for dealing with the problems of philosophers and becomes a method, cultivated by philosophers, for dealing with the problems of men." To John Dewey and most pragmatist thinkers, human beings grow continuously as they proceed through their life experiences interacting with other people:

Continued psychological existence of the young is only one phase of interest in the consequences of association. Adults are equally concerned to act so that the immature learn to think, feel, desire and habitually conduct themselves in certain ways. Not the least of the consequences that are striven for is that the young shall learn to judge, purpose and choose from the standpoint of associated behavior and its consequences. . . . [W]*hat* they think and strive for, the content of their beliefs and intentions is a subject-matter provided by association. Thus, man is merely *de facto* associated, but he *becomes* a social animal in the makeup of his ideas, sentiments and deliberate behavior. *What* he believes, hopes for and aims at is the outcome of association and intercourse.[3]

Dewey asserted that people group themselves for political and nonpolitical forms of association such as scientific inquiry, religious worship, artistic pleasure, recreation, education, and commerce, with the reminder that:

[I]n each case some combined or conjoint action, which has grown up out of "natural," that is, biological, conditions and from local contiguity, results in producing distinctive consequences—that is, consequences which differ in kind from those of isolated behavior.[4]

Dewey warned, however, that some social interactions are viewed as being deleterious:

If the consequences of a friendship threaten the public, then it is treated as a conspiracy; usually it is not the state's business or concern. Men join each other in partnership as a matter of course to do a piece of work more profitably or for mutual defense. Let its operation exceed a certain limit, and others not participating in it find their security or prosperity menaced by it, and suddenly the gears of the state are in mesh.[5]

   Roscoe Pound reached the following conclusion, writing in his 1942 book, *Social Control through Law*:

[T]he sociological movement in jurisprudence is a movement for pragmatism as a philosophy of law; for the adjustment of principles and doctrines to the human conditions they are to govern rather than to assumed first principles; for putting the human factor in the central place and relegating logic to its true position as an instrument.[6]

Similarly, Pound went on to summarize the business and purpose of the law according to the pragmatist viewpoint:

Looked at *functionally*, the law is an attempt to satisfy, to reconcile, to harmonize, to adjust . . . overlapping and often conflicting claims and demands, either through securing them directly and immediately, or through securing them directly and immediately, or through securing certain individual interests, so as to give effect to the greatest total of interests or to the interests that weigh most in our civilization, with the least sacrifice of the scheme of interests as a whole.[7]

The functional approach of pragmatism is an outgrowth of utilitarianism that gained popularity steadily until it came to dominate the field of criminology by the 1940s.[8]

EARLY PRAGMATISM IN CRIMINOLOGY

The study of crime from a pragmatic viewpoint is not exactly new. Indeed, the pragmatist perspective in criminology has roots that anteceded the twentieth century by about one hundred years. The movement toward viewing crime for a social-concensus framework emerged in western Europe at the close of the eighteenth century following publication in 1798 by Thomas Robert Malthus of *Essay on the Principle of Population as It Affects the Future Improvement of Society*. An English economist, Malthus prophesized that the earth's population would multiply geometrically but that its food supply would increase only arithmetically, eventually causing famine, pestilence, war, and social conflict such as crime in the absence of what he urged should be "moral restraint." In addition to continence to delay the feared population expansion, Malthus warned that people would have to resist the temptation to commit depredations on each other. Immediately, investigators throughout Europe set out to gather what became known as "moral statistics" by means of cartography, or the systematic gathering of social information relative to a population's motivation, led by French statistician André Michel Guerry whose studies George B. Vold has called the "first work in 'scientific criminology' ".[9]

Guerry analyzed crime data by geographic districts across France, calculating per capita crime rates and charting regional variations on maps much as twentieth-century ecologists of the Chicago school of sociology were to do a century afterward. In 1829, Guerry published his preliminary data, which in 1833 became his famous *Essai sur la statistique morale* (Essay on Moral Statistics). A number of other researchers worked contemporaneously with Guerry, both individually and in groups, to compile what became known as "moral statistik." In England, where Malthus had enjoyed the greatest popularity, committees were established at various levels of government to trace the origins of juvenile delinquency.[10] In 1835, Adolphe Quetelet published his statistical analysis of crime rates in Belgium, France, Luxembourg, and Holland, entitled *Sur l'homme et la development de ses facultes; ou essai de physique sociale* (On Man and the Development of His Faculties; Or, an Essay on Social Structure). A Belgian astronomer and mathematician, Quetelet became known both as the "father of statistics" and as "the first social criminologist" because of his view that "[s]ociety prepares the crime and the guilty [person] is only the instrument by which it is accomplished."[11] Quetelet set forth what he called his "thermic law" of seasonal variation in morality, a thesis that provoked widespread debate.[12] Official crime reports were published, such as the *Compte generale* by France beginning in 1825 and the *Gazette* by London beginning in 1828.

Early pragmatist criminologists could not agree upon the chief causes of or reasons for crime, any more than modern ones have done. For instance, in 1847 Whitworth Russell viewed the crime wave of 1842 as having been triggered by "the general distress, commercial, manufacturing, and agricultural, which prevailed throughout the country during that year."[13] After analyzing crime rate data for England over the thirty-seven-year period between 1810 and 1847, Joseph Fletcher argued there was "an immediate connection . . . between the price of food [wheat] and the amount of commitments, every access to the former being followed by an access in the latter."[14] John Clay investigated commitments to the Preston House of Corrections for the years 1835–1854 and concluded that although "hard times . . . may add a few cases" convictions for summary offenses increased much more substantially during "good times,"[15] a claim that provoked an ongoing polemic with Richard Hussey Walsh, who took the opposing point of view.[16] Many of the debates were published in the *Journal of the Statistical Society of London*.

Thereafter, for more than half a century, various economists purported to find significant correlations between the cost of essential crops, notably rye, and the crime rates of different nations. Among these was a study by Georg von Mayr in which he found that the theft rates would increase by one theft per 100,000 inhabitants of Bavaria between 1836 and 1861, whenever the price of rye increased there by one half-penny, but that a comparable fall in the price of rye would be accompanied by a commensurate reduction in the rate of theft.[17] More recent investigations have yielded opposite results, that in times of economic prosperity crime seems to soar at a rate higher than it does during times of economic depression.[18] Concern for economic causes of crime departs from the pragmatist perspective and enters the arena of analytic thought discussed in Chapter 8.

As early as 1843, English demographer G. C. Holland observed an association between a poverty environment and crime:

Among the numerous causes which appear inseparable from manufactories, producing crime and immorality, the following deserve particular notice. The crowding together of the working classes in narrow streets, filthy lanes, alleys and yards, is a serious evil and one which has hitherto increased in all manufacturing towns. The poor are not resident in these places from choice, but from necessity. Families are not huddled together into dark, ill ventilated rooms, from any peculiar pleasure it affords. They may, indeed, have become insensible of the inconvenience and wretchedness of such situations, but slender and uncertain means do not enable them to command more comfortable abodes. They are fixed by circumstances.[19]

George B. Vold has noted that Holland's observation is an early application of the idea that " 'we learn by association' in criminality as in life otherwise."[20]

The feeling that criminal behavior may be learned by interaction with others who have acquired criminal skills beforehand emerged in the publications of Gabriel Tarde: *La Criminalite comparee* (Comparative Criminality), 1886; *Les lois de L'imitation* (The Laws of Imitation), 1890; and *La philosophie penale* (Penal Philosophy), 1890. In a rapid-fire sequence, Tarde published these books and various related articles in which he argued that criminal behavior is learned from environmental influences rather than having been inherited or stumbled upon accidently. He concluded that conduct becomes viewed as being criminal when the majority of the people within a given geographic area perceive the conduct with "alarm and indignation."[21] On the origin of criminal behavior, Tarde suggested:

The majority of murderers and notorious thieves began as children who have been abandoned, and the true seminary of crime must be sought for upon each public square or each crossroad of our towns, whether they be small or large, in those flocks of pillaging street urchins, who, like bands of sparrows, associate together, at first for marauding, and then for theft, because of a lack of education and food in their homes.[22]

Tarde defied the positivist trend of the late nineteenth century, so popular on the European continent in the wake of Cesare Lombroso's *L'Uomo delinquente*, published in 1876 (see Chapter 5), and Tarde denied that biological or physical factors play anything but a miniscule role in the breeding of juvenile delinquents and adult criminal offenders. Instead, Tarde went on to add in his *Penal Philosophy*:

One could . . . write a treatise on the art of becoming an assassin. Keep bad company; allow pride, vanity, envy and hatred to grow in you out of all proportions; close your heart to tender feelings, and open it only to keen sensations; suffer also—harden yourself from childhood to blows, to intemperances, to physical torments, grow hardened to evil, and insensible, and you will not be long in becoming devoid of pity; become irrascible and vengeful, and you will be lucky if you do not kill anyone during the course of your life.[23]

Noting three types of repetitive patterns, Tarde formulated his three laws of imitation: (1) human beings imitate each other in proportion to the extent they live in close contact; (2) as a rule, the inferior person imitates the superior person; and (3) when two mutually exclusive "fashions" come together, one will be substituted for the other, so that while the older method declines, the newer one advances. Tarde called this third law his law of insertion, exemplified by the decline in the number of assaults and homicides caused by knives and a corresponding increase in the number proportion resulting from firearms.

Before becoming head of the French Justice Department's Bureau of Statistics, Tarde had served as a small-town magistrate for fifteen years, a background that appears to have influenced his judicial reform proposals. A social psychologist by training, Tarde was influenced by the nineteenth-century naturalistic concern for treating mental illness, epitomized in France. As Robert H. Gault noted, the central theme of Gabriel Tarde's *Penal Philosophy* was his concept of moral responsibility,[24] particularly his notions of personal identity and social similarity. By individual identity, Tarde referred to a person's self-concept, or his ability to remember his moral training and social obligations. When someone suffers from an epileptic fit, has been hynotized, or loses his memory due to disease or trauma, Tarde reasoned, then he cannot be responsible for his conduct even though it may violate the criminal laws. By social similarity, Tarde referred to anyone's familiarity with the customs and norms of the culture within which he lives. Therefore, Tarde went on, an immigrant who has but just arrived in a new country cannot bear criminal responsibility for violating that nation's criminal laws.[25]

Tarde contended that the judicial process should be limited to making a determination whether a person accused of a crime is innocent or guilty as charged and that punishment should be determined by experts in medicine and psychology on the basis of their subsequent evaluation of the offender's personality. He shared Raffaele Garofalo's distrust of juries, a view each of them may have acquired during the course of their lengthy magisterial service. Unlike Garofalo, Tarde did not think much more highly of judges, either, and declared that no judge is competent to sit on both a civil and a criminal bench at the same point in time. Tarde's skepticism of jurors and of judges who pretend to wear multiple hats played a vital role in the development of the modern juvenile justice system, particuarly within the United States early in the twentieth century, where specialized judges came to adjudicate delinquency without juries,[26] a practice that has continued down to the present time. His emphasis on the social origins of crime has been deemed to be "a cornerstone of present American criminological theories,"[27] and his conception of a criminal being a professional inspired the important subsequent research and theories of sociologists such as Frederic M. Thrasher, Clifford R. Shaw, Henry D. McKay, and Edwin H. Sutherland.[28]

Within a few months after publication of Tarde's *La philosophie penale* in France, William Douglas Morrison published *Crime and Its Causes* in England during 1891, paralleling much of what Tarde argued. Morrison agreed with Tarde that crime originates from the interface of two factors: what Morrison termed the "organism" (corresponding to the "personal identity" of Tarde) and the environment (corresponding to the "social similarity" of Tarde).[29] However, Morrison, an Anglican priest, suggested that it is more convenient to analyze that causation of crime in terms of three rather than two categories: (1) cosmical origins, including climate and temperature variations; (2) individual origins such as age, sex, and mental characteristics; (3) social origins, comprising the economic, moral and political conditions of society.[30] In this respect, Morrison paralleled Enrico Ferri, whose book, *Criminal Sociology*, Morrison translated from Italian into English in 1895.[31]

As the editor of Fisher Unwin's Criminological Series, Morrison wrote an introduction to his translation of Ferri's book and another introduction to *The Female Offender* (1895), authored in Italian by Cesare Lombroso and Lombroso's son-in-law, Guglielmo Ferrero. In his introduction to the latter, Morrison mentioned that Lombroso's theory of atavistic degeneracy was insufficient to explain crime.[32] Only when society copes with environmental conditions that produce criminals can it reduce criminality, Morrison argued.[33] Thus, clearly, he was not a positivist, as is buttressed by Morrison's passage in his own book:

The closeness of the connection between degeneracy and crime is, to a considerable extent, determined by social conditions. A degenerate person, who has to earn his own livelihood, is much more likely to become a criminal than another degenerate person who has not. Almost all forms of degeneracy render a man more or less unsuited for the common work of life; it is not easy for such a man to obtain employment. . . . A person in this unfortunate position often becomes a criminal, not because he has strong anti-social instincts, but because he cannot get work. Physically, he is unfit for work, and he takes to crime as an alternative.[34]

Morrison believed, with Sir Francis Galton, that social statistics can be used to ascertain many causes of criminal behavior, and he advocated a life-history data collection technique for use to achieve this aim.[35] Morrison had assembled many case histories during his service as a prison chaplain for fifteen years ending in 1898.

Father Morrison's contribution to criminology is marked more by the publication of his second book, *Juvenile Offenders*, in 1900, because it became the standard work in its field until World War II.[36] Morrison's statistical evidence supported an inference that illegitimate children are more likely to become delinquents than are legitimate ones, other factors being equal.[37] However, Morrison explained that the cause of delinquency is not the bastardy status itself, any more than it is that delinquency rates are higher for children whose parents have been convicted of a crime because of their conviction status. Instead, he reasoned that parents of illegitimate children and parents who have been convicted of crimes lack the sound moral character necessary to direct their children toward nondelinquent careers.[38] In addition, Morrison noted that a child's economic condition derives from his parents', and he observed a close association between the economic position of parents and their moral character.

In *Juvenile Offenders*, Morrison identified three varieties of "repression" useful in curbing delinquency:[39] (1) admonitory, where an offender is warned of future misbehavior consequences or placed under supervision; (2) educational, where an offender is sent to a reform school to learn a trade; and (3) punitive, where an offender is subjected to corporal punishment, fined, or imprisoned. He favored warnings and fines and opposed imprisonment except as a measure of last resort because he felt imprisonment transforms a naive juvenile offender into a hardened criminal.[40] Morrison viewed traditional prisons as being ineffective because the prison environment stands in obvious contrast to life in the free world outside, and he argued that imprisonment could be made more effective if institutional conditions were similar to ordinary life styles.[41] In this sense, Morrison seems to have anticipated Earnest A. Hooton, or Hooton patterned his recommendation after Morrison (see Chapter 5).

When reform schools emerged in England and America throughout the nineteenth and early twentieth centuries, they were viewed as being respectable alternatives to prisons for wayward youth. Morrison supported the objectives of reform schools and offered empirical evidence of their success as measured by low recidivism rates.[42] On the other hand, Morrison worried over the psychological harm imprisonment caused inmates in confinement:

Imprisonment so far from serving the purpose of protecting society adds considerably to its dangers. The casual offender is the person to whom crime is merely an isolated incident in an otherwise law-abiding life. The habitual criminal is a person to whom crime has become a trade; he is a person who makes his living by preying on the community. The prison is the breeding ground of the habitual criminal. The habitual offender is the causal offender to begin with. But the prison deteriorates him, debases him mentally and morally, reduces him to a condition of apathy, unfit and indisposed of life; and when liberated he is infinitely more dangerous to society than when he entered it. It is not sufficiently recognized that punishment may be of a character which defeats the ends of justice.[43]

Similarly, Morrison explained the burgeoning cost of imprisonment by suggesting that prison sentences increase the size of the habitual criminal class. Contrary to Jeremy Bentham, Morrison accused municipalities of "adding to the dimensions of the police force for the mere pleasure of seeing a larger proportion of the adult male population walking around in blue uniforms[.]"[44] Though Bentham fostered growth of the professional police force and Morrison remained skeptical of a society that enlarges the size of its police force, both Bentham and Morrison played significant roles in stimulating the systematic collection of data pertaining to crime, although they were separated in time by almost a century. Morrison focused the attention of the Royal Statistical Society onto crime data,[45] urging the ongoing collection of information pertaining not only to crimes reported to the police but also to activities of the courts and of prisons. Although many American prisons published annual reports from the middle of the nineteenth century, Morrison's influence inspired them to contain more precise statistical references to support the evaluation of their performance.

THE ECOLOGISTS

William Douglas Morrison's book *Juvenile Delinquency* inspired in a number of Americans the desire to control delinquency by regulating the social groups within which potential delinquents interact. First, they had to learn where delinquency was most likely to occur and what patterns evidenced its occurrence. In the first two decades of this century, Edith Abbott and Sophonisba Breckenridge studied "delinquent neighborhoods" in and around Chicago, examining the significance of boarding houses, canals and rivers, and railroad tracks as these and other factors appeared to make neighborhoods produce delinquents, which led to their publication in 1912 of a book entitled *The Delinquent Child and the Home*. Studying the ecology of crime became popular upon the publication in 1925 of *The City: The Ecological Approach to the Study of the Human Community* by Robert E. Park, Ernest W. Burgess, and Roderick D. McKenzie, all professors at the University of Chicago's Department of Sociology.

In the book *The City*, Ernest W. Burgess suggested that one organic unit replaces another through a process of invasion, dominance, and succession, beginning from the central business district and expanding outward in "concentric zones."[46] Burgess drew upon the theories of his colleague, Robert E. Park, whose experience as a newspaper reporter studying Chicago social conditions for a quarter-century had helped him develop a theory of human ecology derived from the ecology of nature typified by animals and plants living in the wild.[47] Together, Burgess and Park divided Chicago into a set of five major concentric circles and some subcircles, calling each geographic area within a particular circle a zone. Their first zone they referred to as the central business district, known in Chicago then and now as The Loop, containing major department stores, governmental headquarters, hotels, and office buildings. Their second zone they called a "zone in transition," containing a "factory zone" nearest to the central business district, and beyond that buildings that had begun to deteriorate on account of their age, inhabited by the city's poorest residents, at the time mostly immigrants. Next, in their third zone, Burgess and Park witnessed a maze of "workingmen's homes," beyond which in a fourth zone they saw single-family dwellings being built for the middle class, and beyond which in turn was a fifth zone encompassing suburbs which they labeled they "commuters' zone."[48] According to their theory of human ecology, each zone of Chicago or any major city expands outward so as to envelop and eventually displace the next zone outwardly contiguous to it. This is the process of invasion, dominance, and succession. The displacement is not limited to merely an alteration in the usage of buildings, however, but entails a change in customs and values of those who inhabit the displaced zones. Thus, what had been "natural areas" where ethnic people lived and shared homogenous cultures became occupied by people emigrating from their own "natural areas," causing the emergence of "interstitial areas" replete with social problems as one group of people moved in and another moved out. The cycle flourished, Clifford Shaw witnessed, as periodically a new group came to displace an old group in a manner resembling the drive of the red Native American (Indian) westward by the white European settlers.

Clifford R. Shaw utilized Robert E. Park's theory of human ecology as the basis for his study of delinquency in Chicago during a turbulent period when Prohibition induced widespread alcohol smuggling by the Chicago mob then dominated by Al Capone. Working at Chicago's Institute for Juvenile Research, Shaw endeavored to investigate how juveniles became detached for their conventional associations and involved in illegal activities. In 1929, he published some preliminary findings in a book he entitled *Delinquent Areas*. Afterward, he teamed up with Henry D. McKay, with whom he published *Social Factors in Juvenile Delinquency* in 1931. Early on, Shaw had found that, even in the worst of the neighborhoods he had studied, no more than one-fifth of the youngsters who lived there had been charged with a crime or an act of delinquency in court. He set forth, therefore, to compile the life histories from youth who had been labeled delinquent by the judicial process, in order to unravel the significance, if any, of their environment on their unlawful behavior.

Shaw and McKay constructed "spot maps" on which they interfaced the residences of adolescents known to be delinquent as well as those known to be truants from school, the incidence of diseases such as tuberculosis associated with substandard housing, and the locations of demolished dwellings suggesting zoning transitions from residential to commercial or industrial. Their data pointed to the following conclusions:

1. Neighborhoods with the highest rates of delinquency were located within or nearby areas of heavy industry, the same areas where residential population was decreasing and dwellings were being demolished to make space for new factories; these areas Burgess and Park had called "zones in transition."

2. Neighborhoods with the highest rates of delinquency had the lowest economic status, the lowest percentage of families owning their own homes, but the highest percentage of families on welfare, plus the highest rates of infant deaths, insanity, and tuberculosis.

   3. Neighborhoods with the highest rates of delinquency had the highest con-
   centrations of black or foreign-born heads of family households.[49]

However, Shaw and McKay cautioned that economic conditions did not
cause delinquency. Moreover, they found that as one set of immigrant
groups moved into the transitional zones and another set moved away,
delinquency rates remained the highest within the transitional zones but
failed to increase within outer zones into which former residents of the
transitional zones had moved. Finally, they discovered that delinquency
rates for various ethnic and racial groups living within a transitional area
were proportional to the overall delinquency rate of the area, regardless
of where the immigrant group came from or when, prompting Shaw and
McKay to remark:

In the face of these facts it is difficult to sustain the contention that, by themselves, the factors of race, nativity, and nationality are vitally related to the
problem of juvenile delinquency. It seems necessary to conclude, rather, that
the significantly higher rates of delinquents found among the children of Negroes, the foreign born, and more recent immigrants are closely related to existing differences in their respective patterns of geographical distribution within
the city. If these groups were found in the same proportion in all local areas,
existing differences in the relative number of boys brought into court from the
various groups might be expected to be greatly reduced or to disappear entirely.[50]

Thus, Shaw and McKay determined with substantial empirical evidence
that delinquency is associated with social conditions under which a child
lives during his formative years, rather than the biological characteristics of his parents. Shaw and McKay replicated their own research in
such other cities as Birmingham, Cleveland, Denver, Philadelphia,
Richmond, and Seattle, where additional data supported the conclusions
drawn from their earlier Chicago research, as they indicated in the Hoo-
ver Administration's *Report on the Causes of Crime* assembled in 1931
by the National Commission on Law Observance and Enforcement.[51]
Shaw and McKay returned to Chicago and replicated the initial studies
they had conducted there, using more sophisticated techniques and larger
samples of the population, whereupon they confirmed most of their earlier findings in a 1942 book, *Juvenile Delinquency and Urban Areas*.[52]
Other investigators have replicated much of the methodology used by
Shaw and McKay, largely confirming their results in numerous other
cities,[53] notwithstanding some criticism of their methods.[54]
   Despite criticism, the Shaw-McKay theory of delinquency has with-

stood the test of time and has done so well.[55] In 1932, Clifford R. Shaw founded twenty-two neighborhood delinquency crisis intervention centers in six Chicago districts, which have become known collectively as the Chicago Area Project. Participants in that project were encouraged to prevent their own delinquency by expressing antidelinquency behavior as a means of achieving status, such as by intervening to divert other predelinquent youth from violating the law.[56] Despite some criticism of this project,[57] it continued to operate until Shaw's death in 1957 and has become the model for a number of similar neighborhood centers in other American cities,[58] such as the Anti-Crime Crusade of Indianapolis, the St. Paul Community Service Project, and the Back of the Yards Project founded and run by Saul D. Alinsky,[59] which set out to reduce unemployment and diseases plus substandard housing in high-risk delinquency areas.

Clifford R. Shaw compiled numerous life histories on individual delinquents of different types, which he published in various books during the 1930s, beginning with *The Jackroller* in 1930. The next year, in 1931, he observed in *The Natural History of a Delinquent Career* that, in urban areas having high delinquency rates, "the conventional traditions, neighborhood institutions, public opinion, through which neighborhoods usually effect a control over the behavior of the child, were largely disintegrated."[60] In his 1938 book, *Brothers in Crime*, Shaw noted that delinquents "are not different from large numbers of persons in conventional society with respect to intelligence, physical condition, and personality traits"[61] but that, because parents and neighbors of delinquent youth tend to show approval of unlawful behavior, the typical delinquent has grown up "in a social world in which [delinquency has been] an accepted and appropriate form of conduct" but where there has been a "lack of preparation, training, opportunity, and proper encouragement for successful employment in private industry."[62] That thesis, developed to a slightly different and greater extent, became Edwin H. Sutherland's famous theory of differential association the next year in 1939.

Since Shaw, various ecologists have attempted to hone in on the precise factors prevalent within a neighborhood that cause its delinquency rate to rise.[63] After studying delinquency rates in Baltimore, Bernard Lander concluded that the lack of stability, rather than a physical deterioration, of neighborhoods causes the rate of delinquency to rise:

The delinquency rate in a *stable* community will be low in spite of its being characterized by bad housing, poverty, and propinquity to the city center. On the other hand, one would expect a high delinquency rate in the area characterized by normlessness and social instability.[64]

Lois B. DeFleur studied some five thousand juvenile court records in Argentina between 1958 and 1961, finding that ecological patterns of delinquency there differed significantly from those in the United States, which triggered her warning that more ecological studies of delinquency outside of America may be necessary before cross-cultural data may be relied upon to explain delinquency here.[65] Nevertheless, she credited the American ecologists of the 1920s with having provided an important background for subsequent culture conflict and subcultural theories of delinquency, a credit that others have disputed in part, at least.[66]

THE INTERACTIONISTS

The Philadelphia publishing house, J. B. Lippincott Company, asked Indiana University sociologist Edwin Hardin Sutherland in 1921 to write a textbook on criminology, then emerging as a popular academic discipline in the wake of Prohibition. Initially, Sutherland wanted to pursue the lingering debate, then at its height, over whether crime results from environmental conditions or heredity, and in doing so he resolved to utilize some embryonic sociological concepts. The first edition of Sutherland's *Criminology* appeared on the market in 1924. Sutherland set out to examine the various "concrete" conditions that might explain the causation of criminal behavior, but, as his research progressed, he came to reject all concrete conditions as having any validity in predicting criminal conduct. He witnessed sex as being the "concrete" condition most associated with crime, inasmuch as most persons who were targeted as being criminal offenders, then as now, belonged to the male gender. Yet, Sutherland reasoned that a person's sex alone is not a sufficient explanation of why he or she commits a crime. That prompted Sutherland toward abstract explanations of crime, such as the role communication plays during a child's learning experiences.[67] Sutherland's viewpoint on the etiology of crime remained somewhat vague through the second edition of his book, published a decade after the first in 1934, this time entitled *Principles of Criminology*.

The deleterious impact that a "corrupt atmosphere" might exert upon young persons during their formative period of life had been projected by a number of theorists such as J. A. E. Lacassagne[68] in France and Adolf Baer[69] in Germany at the end of the nineteenth century. Nevertheless, the notion of criminal associations among predelinquent and delinquent youth remained overlooked or at least underexamined until 1927 when Frederic M. Thrasher published *The Gang*. Thrasher had studied 1,313 gangs in Chicago, resolving that gangs come in four types: (1) the diffuse gang, having loose leadership and transient solidarity; (2) the solidified gang, having a high degree of loyalty and little internal friction, the product of longer association; (3) the conventionalized gang, sort of like an athletic club; and (4) the criminal gang, whose members are most likely to become career offenders.[70] Thrasher observed that a group of predelinquent youth becomes a gang only upon fulfillment of certain conditions:

It does not become a gang, however, until it begins to excite disapproval and opposition, and thus acquires a more definite group-consciousness. It discovers a rival or an enemy in the gang in the next block; its baseball or football team is pitted against some other team; parents or neighbors look upon it with suspicion or hostility; "the old man around the corner," the storekeepers, or the "cops" begin to give it "shags" (chase it away); or some representative of the community steps in and tries to break it up. This is the real beginning of the gang, for now it starts to draw itself more closely together.[71]

Thus, Thrasher noted that a gang chooses whether to become delinquent as well as in what way(s) it will do so because of the beliefs, norms, and values available to it at the time its members make their critical choice. In that way, Thrasher germinated the association concept that Clifford R. Shaw would expand upon a decade later in his 1938 book, *Brothers in Crime*. Moreover, Thrasher germinated the beginning of labeling theory, also, or the process Frank Tannenbaum would call the "dramatization of evil" in his 1938 book, *Crime and the Community*:

The first dramatization of "evil" which separates the child out of his group for specialized treatment plays a greater role in making the criminal than perhaps any other experience. It cannot be too often emphasized that for the child the whole situation has become different. He now lives in a different world. He has been tagged. A new and hitherto nonexistent environment has been precipitated out for him.

The process of making the criminal, therefore, is a process of tagging, defining, identifying, segregating, describing, emphasizing, making conscious and self-conscious; it becomes a way of stimulating, suggesting, emphasizing, and evolving the very traits that are complained of.[72]

The year 1938 became a momentous year for interaction theories in criminology, topped only, perhaps, by the following year, 1939.

In 1939, Sutherland published a new edition of his *Principles of Criminology*, in which he set forth a theory of differential association which he feared might be "an hypothesis which might quickly be murdered or commit suicide."[73] At that time, Sutherland limited his theory of differential association to career criminals,[74] such as those he had described in some detail the preceding year within his book, *The Professional Thief*. In the 1939 book, Sutherland restated certain propositions he had advanced earlier in its 1934 edition,[75] to which he added new hypotheses, arriving at seven propositions:

1. The processes which result in systematic criminal behavior are fundamentally the same form as the processes which result in systematic lawful behavior.

2. Systematic criminal behavior is determined in a process of association with those who commit crimes, just as systematic lawful behavior is determined in a process of association with those who are law abiding.

3. Differential association is the specific causal process in the development of systematic criminal behavior.

4. The chance that a person will participate in systematic criminal behavior is determined roughly by the frequency and consistency of his contacts with the patterns of criminal behavior.

5. Individual differences among people in respect to personal characteristics or social situations cause crime only as they affect differential association or frequency and consistency of contacts with criminal patterns.

6. Cultural conflict is the underlying cause of differential association and therefore of systematic criminal behavior.

7. Social disorganization is the basic cause of systematic criminal behavior.[76]

Sutherland's 1939 version of the differential association theory explained only "systematic criminal behavior," however, such as a card shark, a circus grifter, or a professional thief. When the fourth edition of *Principles of Criminology* appeared in 1949, Sutherland revised the theory of differential association, then applied the revised version to all crime generally, but to white–collar crime specifically in his 1949 book by that title.[77]

Since 1947, Sutherland's revised theory of differential association has remained unchanged, as Donald R. Cressey has pointed out in later editions of Sutherland's criminology book.[78] The final version of Sutherland's differential association theory embodies nine points, *verbatim* as follows:

1. Criminal behavior is learned.

2. Criminal behavior is learned in interaction with other persons in a process of communication.

3. The principal part of the learning of criminal behavior occurs within intimate personal groups.

4. When criminal behavior is learned, the learning includes (a) techniques of committing the crime, which are sometimes very complicated, sometimes very simple; (b) the specific direction of motives, drives, rationalizations, and attitudes.

5. The specific direction of motives and drives is learned from definitions of the legal codes as favorable or unfavorable.

6. A person becomes delinquent because of an excess of definitions favorable to violation of law over definitions unfavorable to violation of law.

7. Differential association may vary in frequency, duration, priority, and intensity.

8. The process of learning criminal behavior by association with criminal and anticriminal patterns involves all of the mechanisms that are involved in any other learning.

9. While criminal behavior is an expression of general needs and values, it is not explained by those general needs and values, since noncriminal behavior is an expression of the same needs and values.[79]

Sutherland's theory of differential association provoked considerable criticism, particularly from naturalists such as Sheldon Glueck.[80] In 1944, Sutherland drafted a private paper entitled "The Swan Song of Differential Association" in which he acknowledged that some criticisms of his theory were valid because "it is improper to view criminal behavior as a closed system, and participation in criminal behavior is not to be regarded as something that is determined exclusively by association with criminal patterns[.]"[81]

Sir Leon Radzinowicz has remarked that "[i]t was only because of Sutherland's high standing and solid reputation that this thesis evoked as much interest as it did."[82] That statement and similar ones demean differential association unreasonably, however, and deny its significance within certain limitations, such as in explaining criminal careers, which Sutherland intended it to explain originally. Sutherland expanded Gabriel Tarde's theory of imitation, using the language developed by twentieth-century American sociologists. Certainly Sutherland enjoyed a solid reputation, and deservedly so, but the popularity of differential association has been a consequence not of Sutherland's professional reputation but of the mass appeal pragmatism has had in America since the time of John Dewey's Chicago School of Pragmatic Instructionalism and the Chicago School of Human Ecology founded by Robert E. Park and Ernest W. Burgess but popularized by Clifford R. Shaw. Pragmatism's appeal spread to Europe, particularly after World War II,[83] when it reached its zenith in the United States.

Despite his many critics, little doubt exists but that Edwin H. Sutherland was the most popular criminologist of the twentieth century and the most popular American criminologist of all time, truly a "pioneer" in the field, not in spite of his differential association theory but because of it. Since his death in 1950, to be sure, the popularity of differential association has waned as an explanation of individual criminal behavior, largely because it has left questions unanswered. As George B. Vold noted in 1958:

Its shortcomings appear not to be due to any probability that the associations-complex of the delinquent is any less important now than it seemed twenty years ago, but rather to the fact that the theory outran the capacity of either psychology or social psychology to give adequate, scientific answers to the question of why there are such qualitative differences in human association.[84]

Donald R. Cressey has said Sutherland failed to state his theory clearly,[85] having devoted but two pages to the nine propositions he advanced. Be that as it may, numerous pragmatic-oriented criminologists have tried to refine the basic differential association theory in the years since the death of Sutherland in 1950, beginning with Edward M. Lemert's *Social Pathology* in 1951. Perhaps, among all these theories, the judicial process has felt the impact most of the theory of differential opportunity set forth by Richard A. Cloward and Lloyd E. Ohlin in their 1960 book, *Delinquency and Opportunity*.

Lemert distinguished two forms of "deviancy," or public perception of wrongdoing: primary deviancy and secondary deviancy.[86] He theorized that a primary deviant violates the law on account of social circumstances and situations that render deviancy necessary, such as poverty or racial bigotry, without actually wanting to become a deviant. As societal reaction places the "deviant" label on this individual, however, Lemert projected he would become a secondary deviant upon readjusting his self-image to accommodate the deviancy label. Upon adopting some form of a deviant image, according to Lemert, this secondary deviant makes a commitment to a career in deviancy that consists also, ordinarily, of a criminal career. Lemert described the "labeling process," or process of stigmatization,[87] which Lemert called "a product of differentiating and isolating processes."[88] Many "subcultural" theories emanate from Lemert, as did Cloward and Ohlin's differential opportunity theory, also, although they have not credited Lemert to any marked extent.[89]

Richard A. Cloward and Lloyd Ohlin have given ample credit to Robert K. Merton, who, in that criminologically eventful year 1938, published an article in which he argued that crime and deviancy result from the inability of everyone to achieve equal success and, consequently, can be culturally induced.[90] University of Wisconsin sociologist Marshall B. Clinard called that article by Merton "possibly the most frequently quoted single paper in modern sociology."[91] In 1958, moreover, Merton published *Social Theory and Social Structure*, in which he argued that the "culture" within which a person has been raised from childhood approves certain goals, or social objectives, but disapproves others; and approves certain norms that may be followed in the pursuit of goals, but disapproves of others. Merton described norms sanctioned by a culture as its "institutionalized means," such as education, deferred gratification, hard work, and honesty, in contrast to the use of force or fraud,[92] which could be used to achieve "legitimate" goals such as accumulated wealth, prestige, and social status.[93] However, Merton noted that "institutionalized means" such as hard work generate little reward unless the hard worker achieves wealth, also, causing a "strain" on lower-class individuals whose ability to achieve wealth is limited by their inferior skills and a social structure hostile to their upward mobility. Therefore, Merton concluded, "[i]t's not how you play the game, it's whether you win,"[94] at least in the minds of lower-class Americans who are willing to commit crimes in order to gain the wealth necessary to any success in life. He suggested that individuals will "adapt" to the interface of goals and means, in five different ways: through (1) conformity (accept culture goals and institutionalized means); (2) innovation (accept culture goals but reject institutionalized means); (3) ritualism (reject culture goals but accept institutionalized means); (4) retreatism (reject culture goals and institutionalized means); and (5) rebellion (accept culture goals and institutionalized means sometimes; reject them at other times).[95] Thus, "right-thinking" people become "conformists" while many criminals become interested in "innovation," particularly white-collar offenders such as businessmen. The priest becomes a "ritualist," the drug addict a "retreatist."

Cloward and Ohlin published *Delinquency and Opportunity* in 1960, in which they revised slightly Merton's modes of adaptation into a typology they referred to as the "orientation of lower-class youth."[96] Instead of focusing upon the lower-class youth's struggle to accumulate monetary wealth, as Merton had done, Cloward and Ohlin segregated this youth's effort to improve his economic condition from what they saw as his dual preoccupation with entering into the middle class.[97] They divided lower-class youth into four "types" that, they postulated, could predict delinquency. Their Type I youth, they said, desires to improve his economic position and to enter the middle class; their Type II youth desires to enter the middle class but not to improve his economic circumstances. Because both of these youth types share values consistent with the middle class, according to Cloward and Ohlin, they do not pose much of a delinquency threat. On the other hand, these theorists saw their Type III youth committing most delinquent acts, because this group desires wealth without desiring entry into the middle class. Consequently, they want "fast cars, fancy clothes, and swell dames"[98] without being willing to work hard, and so they steal. The Type IV category of youth corresponded to Merton's "retreatism," made up of alcoholics and drug addicts.

When he was attorney general of the United States, Robert F. Kennedy read *Delinquency and Opportunity*, after which he involved the authors in revising federal policy toward delinquency.[99] The efforts of Ohlin, particularly, led to the Juvenile Delinquency Prevention and Control Act of 1961. It strove to improve education and job opportunities for predelinquents and to organize lower-class neighborhoods into community action groups similar to Clifford R. Shaw's Chicago Area Project. Ultimately, the 1961 Juvenile Act was expanded to include all people from the lower-socioeconomic spheres of society, delinquent or not, as a part of President Lyndon B. Johnson's "War on Poverty." Several investigators have conducted research to test differential opportunity theory since Cloward and Ohlin, on both delinquents[100] and nondelinquents.[101] To date, none has exerted the same amount of influence on governmental policy at any level compared to that enjoyed by Cloward and Ohlin in relation to the federal policies formulated during the decade of the 1960s.

Efforts have been made in recent years to combine Sutherland's theory of differential association with the learning theory expounded by B. F. Skinner in his 1938 book, *The Behavior of Organisms*.[102] For instance, Albert Bandura has attempted to trace the mechanics of aggression to social learning experiences in several of his works.[103] As a result, Robert Burgess and Ronald Akers set forth their "differential association—reinforcement theory of criminal behavior"[104] in 1966, suggesting that people learn social as well as antisocial behavior by the process of operant conditioning whereby behavior is reinforced when rewarded (positive reinforcement) or when punishment is avoided (negative reinforcement), but behavior is weakened by stimuli such as punishment or the loss of a reward (negative punishment). According to Akers' more recent works, referring simply to differential reinforcement,[105] "deviant behavior can be expected to the extent that it has been differentially reinforced over alternative behavior . . . and is defined as desirable or justified."[106] Definitions are acquired through interaction in peer groups and the family.

Similarly, various "control" theories have emerged in recent years, suggesting implicitly that most people would violate the law if only they dared to do so or thought they could avoid detection. One such theory was Travis Hirschi's social bond theory, advanced in his 1969 book, *Causes of Delinquency*, in which he argued that people maintain a social bond with society on account of attachment, commitment, involvement and belief. Because of their attachment to their parents, teachers, and right-thinking peers, Hirschi's theory goes, nondelinquent youth become committed to conventional norms and values such as going to college and saving money for the future. The time and effort they expend toward conventional activities, or their involvement, keep their right-thinking beliefs from being weakened or shattered.[107]

A similar approach was taken by Ohio State University criminologist Walter C. Reckless, who has suggested that both internal and external containments help insulate some youth from becoming delinquent.[108] Internal containments would include a person's strong self-concept and a high tolerance for frustration. External containments would include social norms and values, as well as effective supervision. Reckless has argued that containments work to help a person resist the temptations of internal "pushes" such as restlessness; external "pulls' such as the lure of deviant subcultures; and external "pressures" such as minority status and unemployment.[109]

Another spin-off from Sutherland's differential association theory is Daniel Glaser's differential anticipation theory, suggesting that "[a] person's crime or restraint from crime is determined by the consequences he anticipates from it" in terms of the "social bonds"; differential learning by which we acquire tastes, skills, and rationalizations"; and the "perceived opportunities" of both "prospects" and "risks" from conforming to or violating the law.[110] Whenever the expectation of gain exceeds the expectation of loss, people are likely to commit crimes, Glaser has warned.

A good example of how efforts have been made recently to improve "social bonds" among juveniles is Project New Pride"[111] begun during the decade of the 1970s in Denver County, Colorado. By 1979, according to Law Enforcement Assistance Administration statistics, a noticeable success had been achieved among some 160 people who completed the New Pride program: the recidivism rate among these individuals during their first twelve months following program completion was 27 percent, compared with 32 percent for the control group. Cost of New Pride is said to have been approximately four thousand dollars per year, compared with a cost of some twelve thousand dollars per year for institutional placement.

THE SUBCULTURALISTS

A third group of pragmatists emerged during the 1940s and 1950s, beginning with William Foote Whyte's classic 1943 book, *Street Corner Society*, where he showed that a slum resident could achieve upward mobility faster by excelling in a racket, such as bookmaking, than by conventional means. Whyte opened the door to what has become known as subcultural theory, although he was influenced in substance by *The Gang*, published in 1927 by Frederic M. Thrasher, and by Robert K. Merton's famous 1938 paper. Whyte utilized portions of Sutherland's initial (1939) differential association theory and examined the extent to which members of Chicago's forty-two gangs formed attachments with law violators compared to law abiders such as school teachers and other positive role models.[112] He found that predelinquent youth who avoided significant attachments with the latter formed them with the former, the implication being that a violent subculture offers its own role models.

University of Connecticut sociologist Albert K. Cohen took the Whyte model further in his 1955 book, *Delinquent Boys*, within which he suggested that the middle-class measuring rod may be the talisman of delinquency. According to Cohen, a lower-class child is expected to function within middle-class institutions, at least from the moment when he enters the American public school system, an unreasonable expectation in view of this child's lack of preparation for conformity to middle-class standards. When this child is rebuffed by middle-class teachers because he fails to meet middle-class standards such as neatness and politeness, Cohen found, a lower-class child becomes "negativistic" toward middle-class values and may enter a subculture that espouses contradictory values. In this way, Cohen proposed, a lower-class child comes to resort to dishonesty and violence to gain status in a delinquent subculture. Harvard University criminologist Walter B. Miller developed a similar theory of delinquent subcultures arising from what, in 1958, he called lower-class focal concerns such as "trouble, toughness, smartness, excitement, fate, and autonomy," shared by children who have been reared primarily by a single female parent.[113] Critics of Cohen and Miller have questioned whether lower-class children really want to be middle class.[114] Critics of Miller have stressed that his theory pertains only to delinquent residents of inner-city areas[115] and then, possibly, only to black delinquent residents there.[116]

NOTES

1. W. James, PRAGMATISM: A NEW NAME FOR SOME OLD WAYS OF THINKING, Lecture II (1907).

2. See R. Beck, PERSPECTIVES IN SOCIAL PHILOSOPHY 321 (1967) quoting from J. Dewey. THE INFLUENCE OF DARWIN ON PHILOSOPHY AND OTHER ESSAYS IN CONTEMPORARY THOUGHT (1910).

3. See R. Beck, PERSPECTIVES IN SOCIAL PHILOSOPHY 324–325 (1967), quoting from J. Dewey, THE PUBLIC AND ITS PROBLEMS (1927).

4. Id. at 325.

5. Id. at 326.

6. Id. at 323, quoting R. Pound, SOCIAL CONTROL THROUGH LAW (1942).

7. R. Pound, *A Survey of Social Interests*, 57 HARVARD L. REV. 39 (1943). (Emphasis added.)

8. See W. Chambliss, FUNCTIONAL AND CONFLICT THEORIES OF CRIME 1–23 (1974).

9. G. Vold, THEORETICAL CRIMINOLOGY 164–65 (1958). See also T. Morris, *Some Ecological Studies of the 19th Century*, in H. Voss and D. Petersen, eds., ECOLOGY, CRIME AND DELINQUENCY 65–76 (1971), and Y. Levin and A. Lindesmith, *English Ecology and Criminology of the Past Century*, id. at 47–64.

10. For instance, in 1800 the Borough of Birmingham received the report of the Committee of Justices Appointed to Consider the Treatment of Juvenile Offenders. Sixteen years afterward the City of London appointed a Committee for the Investigation of the Causes of the Alarming Increase of Juvenile Delinquency in the Metropolis. See A. Lindesmith and Y. Levin, *The Lombrosian Myth in Criminology*, 42 AM. J. SOC. 653, 658 (1937).

11. See C. Bernaldo de Quiros, MODERN THEORIES OF CRIMINALITY 10 (A. DeSalvio, tr., 1911).

12. M. Drobisch studied the potential connection between moral statistics and freedom of the will, in DIE MORALISCHE STATISTIK UND DIE WILLENSFREIHEIT (1867). Alexander von Oettingen examined the relationship of moral statistics and social ethics, in DIE MORALSTATISTIK IN IHRER BEDEUTUNG FUR EINE SOZIALETHIK (1874). Moral statistics were compared with criminal data by Georg von Mayr in MORALSTATISTIK MIT EINSCHLUSS DER KRIMINALSTATISTIK (1917).

13. W. Russell, *Abstract of the "Statistics of Crime in England and Wales from 1839–1843,"* 10 J. STATIS. SOC. LONDON 38 (1847). See also H. Mayhew and J. Binney, THE CRIMINAL PRISONS OF LONDON (1862).

14. J. Fletcher, *Moral and Educational Statistics of England and Wales*, 12 J. STATIS. SOC. LONDON 151, 176 (1849).

15. J. Clay, *On the Effect of Good or Bad times on Commitals to Prison*, 18 J. STATIS. SOC. LONDON 74, 79 (1855).

16. R. Walsh, *A Deduction from the Statistics of Crime for the Last Ten Years*, 20 J. STATIS. SOC. LONDON 23 (1857), to which Clay retorted in 20 J. STATIS. SOC. LONDON 384 (1857).

17. See T. Sellin, RESEARCH MEMORANDUM ON CRIME IN THE DEPRESSION 22 (1937).

18. See P. Wiers, *Wartime Increase in Michigan Delinquency*, 10 AM.

SOC. REV. 515 (1945). See also D. Bogen, *Juvenile Delinquency and Economic Trends*, 9 AM. SOC. REV. 178 (1944), and J. Reinemann, *Juvenile Delinquency in Philadelphia and Economic Trends*, 20 TEMPLE L. Q. 576 (1947). Delinquency seems to be associated *inversely* with unemployment, also. See D. Glaser and K. Rice, *Crime, Age, and Employment*, 24 AM. SOC. REV. 679 (1959), and M. Guttentag, *The Relationship of Unemployment to Crime and Delinquency*, 24 J. SOC. ISSUES 105 (1968).

19. G. Holland, VITAL STATISTICS OF SHEFFIELD 138 (1843).

20. G. Vold, THEORETICAL CRIMINOLOGY 233 (2nd ed., 1979).

21. G. Tarde, *Misere et criminalite*, 29 REVUE PHILOSOPHIQUE (1890). He published numerous of his articles as a collection in ÉTUDES PENALES ET SOCIALES (1891).

22. G. Tarde, PENAL PHILOSOPHY 252 (R. Howell, tr., 1912).

23. *Id.* at 256.

24. *Supra*, note 21 at ix (introduction to the English edition by Robert H. Gault).

25. Gault found the limits of individual identity and social similarity difficult to measure, and moral responsibility problematical as a result. *Id.* at ix–xviii.

26. See M. Wilson Vine, *Gabriel Tarde*, in H. Mannheim, ed., PIONEERS IN CRIMINOLOGY 228, 238 (1960).

27. *Id.* at 228.

28. *Id.* at 292, 294 (2nd ed.; 1972).

29. See G. Rodin, *Willian Douglas Morrison*, in H. Mannheim, ed., PIONEERS IN CRIMINOLOGY 341, 345 (2nd ed., 1972).

30. W. Morrison, CRIME AND ITS CAUSES 21 (1891).

31. Morrison omitted the entirety of Ferri's first section because he saw it as being too heterodox. T. Sellin, *Enrico Ferri*, in H. Manneheim, ed., PIONEERS IN CRIMINOLOGY 371, n. 19 (2nd ed., 1972).

32. C. Lombroso and G. Ferrero, THE FEMALE OFFENDER v–vi (introduction by William D. Morrison, 1895).

33. *Id.* at viii–xi, xviii, and xx.

34. *Supra*, note 29 at 199.

35. *Id.* at 3–4.

36. See A. Saunders, *et al.*, YOUNG OFFENDERS: AN ENQUIRY INTO JUVENILE DELINQUENCY 9 (1942).

37. W. Morrison, JUVENILE OFFENDERS 129 (1900).

38. *Id.* at 145–48.

39. *Id.* at 180–81.

40. *Id.* at 220.

41. *Id.* at 234.

42. *Id.*, chap. 13.

43. W. Morrison, *Prison Reform: Prisons and Prisoners*, 69 FORTNIGHTLY REV. 782 (1898). Father Morrison devoted much of his later life to lobbying for changes in sentencing patterns, in his role as the rector of Saint

Marylebone Church in London. See W. Morrison, *Excessive Sentences*, THE TIMES (London) 12 (February 2, 1892). He became rector in 1908 and served in that capacity until his death in 1942 at the age of ninety-one.

44. W. Morrison, *Are Our Prisons a Failure?* 61 FORTNIGHTLY REV. 467 (1894).

45. See W. Morrison, *The Interpretation of Criminal Statistics*, 60 J. ROYAL STATIS. SOC. 1 (1897).

46. E. Burgess, *The Growth of the City*, in R. Park, E. Burgess, and R. McKenzie, ed., THE CITY: THE ECOLOGICAL APPROACH TO THE STUDY OF THE HUMAN COMMUNITY 51 (1928 ed.).

47. For a discussion of how animals and plants function in their natural habitats to maintain the balance of nature (ecology), see P. Colinvaux, INTRODUCTION TO ECOLOGY 61–90 (1973); C. Elton, THE ECOLOGY OF INVASIONS BY ANIMALS AND PLANTS (1958); R. Ricklefs, ECOLOGY 751–55 (1973).

48. *Supra*, note 46 at 55.

49. C. Shaw and H. McKay, JUVENILE DELINQUENCY AND URBAN AREAS 147–52 (1969 ed.).

50. *Id.* at 162–63.

51. C. Shaw and H. McKay, *Social Factors in Juvenile Delinquency*, in REPORT ON THE CAUSES OF CRIME (1931).

52. C. Shaw and H. McKay, JUVENILE DELINQUENCY AND URBAN AREAS: A STUDY OF RATES OF DELINQUENTS IN RELATION TO DIFFERENT CHARACTERISTICS OF LOCAL COMMUNITIES IN AMERICAN CITIES (1942).

53. See C. Schmid, SOCIAL SAGA OF TWO CITIES: AN ECOLOGICAL AND STATISTICAL STUDY OF THE SOCIAL TRENDS IN MINNEAPOLIS AND ST. PAUL (1937); S. Lottier, *Distribution of Criminal Offenses in Metropolitan Regions*, 29 J. CRIM. L. CRIM. & POL. SCI. (1939); N. Hayner, *Delinquency Areas in the Puget Sound Region*, AM. J. SOC. 314–28 (1933).

54. See C. Jonassen, *A Reevaluation and Critique of the Logic and Some Methods of Shaw and McKay*, in H. Voss and D. Petersen, eds., ECOLOGY, CRIME AND DELINQUENCY 133–45 (1971); and S. Kobrin, *The Formal Logical Properties of the Shaw-McKay Delinquency Theory*, *Id.* at 101–31.

55. See *supra*, note 49 at xlvii (introduction to the 1969 ed. by James F. Short, Jr.).

56. See E. Burgess, J. Lohman, and C. Shaw, *The Chicago Area Project*, NAT'L. PROB. ASSOC. YRBK. 8–28 (1937); F. Romano, *Organizing a Community for Delinquency Prevention*, NAT'L. PROB. ASSOC. YRBK. 1–12 (1940); C. Shaw and J. Jacobs, *The Chicago Area Project*, PROC. AM. PRIS. ASSOC. 40–53 (1939).

57. See S. Kobrin, *The Chicago-Area Project—A 25-Year Assessment*, ANN. AM. SOC. POL. & SOC. SCI. 19–20 (1959), and A. Sorrentino, *The Chicago Area Project After 25 Years*, FED. PROB. 40–45 (1959).

58. See W. Miller, *The Impact of a "Total-Community" Delinquency Control Project*, 10 SOC. PROBS. 168–91 (1962).

59. See S. Alinsky, REVEILLE FOR RADICALS 81–82 (1946).

60. C. Shaw, THE NATURAL HISTORY OF A DELINQUENT CAREER 229 (1931).

61. C. Shaw, BROTHERS IN CRIME 350 (1938).

62. *Id.* at 356.

63. See, *inter alia*, R. Chilton, *Continuity in Delinquency Area Research: A Comparison of Studies for Baltimore, Detroit, and Indianapolis*, 29 AM. SOC. REV. 71–83 (1946).

64. B. Lander, TOWARDS AN UNDERSTANDING OF JUVENILE DELINQUENCY 89 (1954). (Emphasis in the original.).

65. L. DeFleur, *Ecological Variables in the Cross-Cultural Study of Delinquency*, 45 SOC. FORCES 556–70 (1967).

66. See K. Polk, *Urban Social Areas and Delinquency*, 14 SOC. PROBS. 320, 322 (1967).

67. A. Cohen, A. Lindesmith, and K. Schuessler, THE SUTHERLAND PAPERS 2 (1956).

68. J.Lacassagne, *Marche de la criminalite en France de 1825 à 1880*, REVUE SCIENTIFIQUE 674–84 (1881).

69. A. Baer, DER VERBRECHER IN ANTHROPOLOGISCHER BEZIEHUNG 410–11 (1893).

70. F. Thrasher, THE GANG 47–67 (1927).

71. *Id.* at 30.

72. F. Tannenbaum, CRIME AND THE COMMUNITY 19–20 (1938).

73. *Supra*, note 66 at 18. Sutherland said he stated his theory "openly in the expectation that it will be criticized and will thus lead to the development of a more satisfactory theory of criminal behavior." E. Sutherland, PRINCIPLES OF CRIMINOLOGY v (4th ed., 1947).

74. E. Sutherland, PRINCIPLES OF CRIMINOLOGY 4–9 (3rd ed., 1939).

75. Sutherland remarked later that this theory had been contained in "scattered passages and was not developed" in earlier editions. E. Sutherland, PRINCIPLES OF CRIMINOLOGY v (4th ed., 1947).

76. *Supra*, note 74.

77. E. Sutherland, WHITE COLLAR CRIME 234–56 (1949).

78. See E. Sutherland and D. Cressey, CRIMINOLOGY 78 (9th ed., 1974). Commencing with the fifth edition in 1954 after Sutherland's death in 1950, Lippincott reverted to the original title, CRIMINOLOGY, and commissioned Donald R. Cressey to update it periodically.

79. E. Sutherland and D. Cressey, CRIMINOLOGY 75–77 (9th ed., 1974).

80. See S. Glueck, *Theory and Fact in Criminology: A Criticism of Differential Association*, 7 BRIT. J. CRIM. 92–109 (1956). For an example of more recent criticisms, see J. Cortes with F. Gatti, DELINQUENCY AND CRIME: A BIOPSYCHOSOCIAL APPROACH 166–67 (1972).

81. *Supra*, note 74 at 37.

82. L. Radzinowicz, IDEALOGY AND CRIME 82 (1966).

83. Note, for instance, Edmund Mezger's notion of "responsibility for the life conduct," or *Lebensfuhrungsschuld*, described in E. Mezger, STRAF-RECHT (1948), and Ernst Seelig's "forms of life," or *Lebensformen*, described in E. Seelig, *Die Gliederung der Vebrecher*, in E. Seelig and K. Weindler, eds., DIE TYPEN DER KRIMINELLEN (1949).

84. *Supra*, note 20 at 198.

85. *Supra*, note 78 at 78. Cressey said Sutherland's "statement gives the impression that there is little concern for explaining variations in crime and delinquency rates," which he implies is an erroneous impression. *Id*.

86. See E. Lemert, SOCIAL PATHOLOGY 75–76 (1951). See also E. Lemert, HUMAN DEVIANCE, SOCIAL PROBLEMS, AND SOCIAL CONTROL 40–64 (1967).

87. See E. Goffman, STIGMA: NOTES ON THE MANAGEMENT OF SPOILED IDENTITY (1963).

88. *Supra*, note 85 at 73.

89. Instead, they have credited French sociologist Emile Durkheim (see Chapter 9), Robert K. Merton, and Edwin H. Sutherland. See R. Cloward and L. Ohlin, DELINQUENCY AND OPPORTUNITY *passim* (1960).

90. R. Merton, *Social Structure and Anomie*, 3 AM. SOC. REV. 672–82 (1938). See also, R. Merton, SOCIAL THEORY AND SOCIAL STRUCTURE (1957).

91. M. Clinard, ANOMIE AND DEVIANT BEHAVIOR 10 (1964).

92. R. Merton, SOCIAL THEORY AND SOCIAL STRUCTURE 187 (1957).

93. *Id*. at 193.

94. *Id*. at 190.

95. *Id*.

96. R. Cloward and L. Ohlin, DELINQUENCY AND OPPORTUNITY 97 (1960).

97. Cloward and Ohlin have been criticized severely for assuming that a typical lower-class American youth wants to become middle class. On this point, see J. Douglas, *Deviance and Order in a Pluralistic Society*, in J. McKinney and E. Tiryakian, eds., THEORETICAL SOCIOLOGY: PERSPECTIVES AND DEVELOPMENTS 368–401 (1970). See also W. Miller, *Lower Class Culture as a Generating Milieu of Gang Delinquency*, 14 J. SOC. ISSUES 5–19 (1958).

98. *Supra*, note 96.

99. See L. Empey, AMERICAN DELINQUENCY 294–300 (1978).

100. See S. Kobrin, J. Puntil, and E. Peluso, *Criteria of Status among Street Groups*, 4 J. RES. CRIME & DELIN. 98–118 (1967); R. Rivera and J. Short, *Significant Adults, Caretakers, and Structures of Opportunity: An Exploratory Study*, in J. Short, ed., GANG DELINQUENCY 242 (1968).

101. See D. Elliott and H. Voss, DELINQUENCY AND DROPOUT (1974).

102. B. Skinner, THE BEHAVIOR OF ORGANISMS: AN EXPERIMENTAL ANALYSIS (1938).

103. A. Bandura, AGGRESSION: A SOCIAL LEARNING ANALYSIS (1973), SOCIAL LEARNING THEORY (1977), and *The Social Learning Perspective: Mechanisms of Aggression*, in H. Toch, ed., PSYCHOLOGY OF CRIME AND CRIMINAL JUSTICE 198–236 (1979).

104. R. Burgess and R. Akers, *A Differential Association-Reinforcement Theory of Criminal Behavior*, 14 SOC. PROBS. 128–47 (1966).

105. See R. Akers, DEVIANT BEHAVIOR: A SOCIAL LEARNING APPROACH (1977).

106. R. Akers, M. Krohn, L. Lonza-Kaduce, and M. Radosevich, *Social Learning and Deviant Behavior: A Specific Test of a General Theory*, 44 AM. SOC. REV. 636, 638 (1979).

107. T. Hirschi, CAUSES OF DELINQUENCY 231 (1969).

108. See W. Reckless, THE CRIME PROBLEM (1955).

109. See W. Reckless, *Containment Theory*, in M. Wolfgang, L. Savitz, and N. Johnston, eds., THE SOCIOLOGY OF CRIME AND DELINQUENCY 402 (2nd ed., 1970).

110. D. Glazer, CRIME IN OUR CHANGING SOCIETY 126 (1978).

111. See Law Enforcement Assistance Administration, EXEMPLARY PROJECTS (1979), for descriptions for Project New Pride and similar programs designed to enhance "social bonds."

112. W. Whyte, STREET CORNER SOCIETY 104–8 (1943).

113. *Supra*, note 96.

114. W. Miller, *Lower Class Culture as a Generating Milieu of Gang Delinquency*, 14 J. SOC. ISSUES 5–19 (1958).

115. J. Clark and E. Wenninger, *Socio-Economic Class and Area Correlates of Illegal Behavior among Juveniles*, in M. Wolfgang, *et al.*, eds., THE SOCIOLOGY OF CRIME AND DELINQUENCY 451–52 (2nd ed., 1970).

116. K. Polk, *Urban Social Areas and Delinquency*, 14 SOC. PROBS. 320–25 (1967).

8

Analytic Criminology: Rejecting the Language of the Law

As the scientific method took root throughout the eighteenth and nineteenth centuries, greater reliance came to be placed upon logic, or the correctness of reasoning premised upon relationships between propositions. Late in the nineteenth century, a new philosophical school known as logical positivism emerged, and it transformed during the twentieth century into what has become known as analytic philosophy. Logical positivists expressed concern about the truth of any given statement. They argued that no statement can be meaningful without the circumstances under which it would be true or false first being examined. They concluded that meaning depends upon verification.

Logical positivists distinguished three types of propositions: analytic, synthetic, and emotive. Analytic propositions, such as 2 + 2 = 4, are necessarily true or false, but they yield no knowledge of reality. Synthetic propositions give knowledge, but they become meaningful only when verified in sensory experience, and unless they are verified they are nonsense. Emotive propositions declare value judgments, such as "sin is bad," but have no cognitive function. Logical positivists believed that, among all logical propositions, some may be found to be mistakes or misunderstandings in the use of language, while others will turn out to be valid scientific questions.

Twentieth-century analytic philosophers have continued in the direction pointed out by logical positivists. They have rejected the harmonious designs set forth by earlier philosophers that cannot be proven true. They have remained contented to conduct piecemeal explorations of traditional logical expressions in search of evidence to confirm or refute their accuracy. One early twentieth-century analytic philosopher was George Edward Moore, who declared in his *Principia Ethica* (1902) that: "To search for 'unity' and 'system,' at the expense of truth, is not . . .

the proper business of philosophers.'' Some years later, in 1922, Moore published *The Refutation of Idealism* in which he favored the revival of classical realism, particularly that from Plato.

Another pioneer in analytic philosophy was Ludwig Wittgenstein, who observed in his 1922 work, *Logisch-philosophische Abhandlung* (published in English as *Tractatus Logico-Philosophicus*) that all propositions are ''pictures'' of reality, which may be true or false images. Years later, in 1953, Wittgenstein's posthumous *Philosophische Untersuchungen* (Philosophical Investigations) abandoned the ''picture'' theory and tried to show by means of what he called ''language games'' that there is no essence of language at all.

A third analytic philosopher, John Langshaw Austin, explored various usages of common words such as ''appears,'' ''looks,'' and ''seems,'' concluding in *Sense and Sensibilia* (1962) that this use of language makes nonsense. Another of Austin's posthumous books, *How To Do Things with Words* (1962), fairly summarizes the argument of most analysts, who remain skeptical of the way we say things.

Justice Oliver Wendell Holmes, Jr., known widely as a pragmatist, expressed some doubt about the authenticity of the law's language in an address delivered on January 8, 1897:

At present, in very many cases, if we want to know why a rule of law has taken its particular shape, and more or less if we want to know why it exists at all, we go to tradition. We follow it into the Year Books, and perhaps beyond them to the customs of the Salian Franks, and somewhere in the past, in the German forests, in the needs of Norman kings, in the assumptions of a *dominant class*, in the absence of generalized ideas, we find out the practical motive for what now best is justified by the mere fact of its acceptance and that men are accustomed to it.[1]

Class consciousness has been at the root of most analytic thought in criminology for some time, particularly since 1916 when Dutch criminologist Willem Adriaan Bonger wrote in his famous book, *Criminality and Economic Conditions*, that crime is ''an immoral act'' which is ''harmful to the interests of a group of persons united by the same interests.''[2] Yet of course, analytic thought does not have to be marxist, in criminology or elsewhere.

What analytic thought is concerned with across its spectrum, generally, are different types of morality, as analytic philosopher W. B. Gallie has observed:

One Morality or many? Liberal morality and Socialist morality; bourgeois morality and Georges Sorel's ''morality of producers''; Protestant morality and

Catholic; Greek morality and Christian; "aristocratic" morality and "slave" morality; "open" morality and "closed" morality—what, if any, is the relevance of such distinctions as these to moral philosophy?

Looked at from one angle, they suggest something obvious enough; the fact that in different times and places different systems or aggregates of moral belief have prevailed, and the fact that sometimes in one and the same community different groups of people have adhered to different, in some cases to violently conflicting, moral beliefs.[3]

Gallie went on to posit four lines of interpretation as to why people disagree over moral philosophy. One explanation, he said, is the monarchic view, holding that "in every moral situation there is only one right judgment to be made or action to be chosen," while another explanation, "the idealist interpretation[,] . . . represents morality as essentially one and absolute and eternal, and yet such that it inevitably differentiates itself into radically conflicting forms or phases."[4] A third explanation, Gallie continued, is a polyarchic view, reminiscent of Aristotle and Hume, "maintaining that, far from there being one single set of valid moral standards, there are an indefinite number of these, embodied in different moralities whose cardinal principles are not mutually corrigible."[5] A fourth explanation, Gallie concluded, is ethical relativism, which "maintains that different moralities are always relative to other and more basic differences between groups, communities, civilizations: . . . differences in . . . experimental and historical knowledge, forms and traditions of tribal and national life, methods of organizing production and distribution of goods, and so on."[6] This latter explanation is analytic thought.

ANALYTIC CRIMINOLOGY: CLASS CONSCIOUSNESS AND THE EARLY PHILOSOPHY

In 1892, Emile Durkheim received the first doctorate in sociology ever awarded by the University of Paris, and, the next year, he published his dissertation as *De la division du travail social* (The Division of Labor in Society). Therein, Durkheim rejected Herbert Spencer's notion of modern society being a system through which selfish individuals agree to exchange commodities solely for personal gain. Instead, Durkheim distinguished two forms of society: a more primitive mechanical form where there is a high degree of social homogeneity and a low division of labor; and a more sophisticated organic form where there is much greater heterogeneity of values and a higher division of labor.

In the mechanical form of society, Durkehim argued, laws repress most individuals from deviating from the group norms, but a small amount of crime keeps such a society from becoming too pathologically controlled. In the organic form of society, however, Durkheim reckoned, a demand is made for some degree of uniformity among its members because no society is totally "organic," and he called this uniformity *le conscience*, or the collective conscience, meaning the "totality of social like-nesses."[7] However, Durkheim conceded that "[t]here cannot be a so-ciety in which the individuals do not differ more or less from the col-lective type."[8] As a society becomes organic, Durkheim warned, it will experience some lawlessness, or *anomie*, to a pathological extent.[9]

Durkheim wrote *Les regles de la methode sociologigue* (The Rules of Sociological Method) in 1895, followed in 1897 by *Le suicide: Étude de sociologie* (Suicide: A Study in Sociology) .[10] In *Les Regles*, Dur-kheim declared that crime is inevitable:

Imagine a society of saints, a perfect cloister of exemplary individuals. Crimes, properly so called, will there be unknown; but faults which appear venial to the layman will create there the same scandal that the ordinary offense does in or-dinary consciousnesses. If, then, this society has the power to judge and pun-ish, it will define these acts as criminal and will treat them as such. For the same reason, the perfect and upright man judges his smallest failings with a severity that the majority reserve for acts more truly in the nature of an of-fense.[11]

In that way, Durkheim defined crime in terms of whether or not mem-bers of a group are willing to punish one of their own for engaging in some given form of conduct. He said "the immediate physical milieu in which each of us is placed, the hereditary antecedents, and the social influences vary from one individual to the next, and consequently diver-sify consciousness."[12] Durkheim went on to warn that:

Nothing is good indefinitely and to an unlimited extent. . . . To make pro-gress, individual originality must be able to express itself. In order that the originality of the idealist whose dreams transcend his century may find expres-sion, it is necessary that the originality of the criminal, who is below the level of his time, shall also be possible. One does not occur without the other.[13]

Finally, Durkheim reached the following conclusion:

Let us make no mistake. To classify crime among the phenomena of normal sociology, is not merely to say that it is an inevitable, although regrettable, phenomenon, due to the incorrigible wickedness of men; it is to affirm that it is a factor in public health, an integral part of all societies.[14]

Against this context, one may understand the relativity with which Durkheim viewed crime:

From this point of view, the fundamental facts of criminality present themselves to us in an entirely new light. Contrary to our current ideas, the criminal no longer seems to be a totally unsociable being, a sort of parasitic element, a strange and unassimilable body, introduced into the midst of society. On the contrary, he plays a definite role in social life. Crime, for its part, must no longer be conceived as an evil that cannot be too much suppressed. There is no occasion for self-congratulation when the crime rate drops noticeably below the average level, for we may be certin that this apparent progress is associated with some social disorder.[15]

According to Durkheim, therefore, some amount of crime is natural in society, without which society would become unhealthy.

As any society becomes more and more "organic," Durkheim prophesized, individuals living in that society can expect to feel alienated, a feeling that is likely to be accompanied by anomie. Durkheim wrote about the emergence of anomie in Le suicide:

a. No living being can be happy or even exist unless his needs are sufficiently proportioned to his means. In other words, if his needs require more than can be granted, or even merely something of a different sort, they will be under continual friction and can only function painfully.

b. In the animal, at least in a normal condition, this equilibrium is established with automatic spontaneity because the animal depends on purely material conditions.

c. This is not the case with man, because most of his needs are not dependent on his body. . . . A more awakened reflection suggests better conditions, seemingly desirable ends craving fulfillment. . . . Nothing appears in man's organic nor his psychological constitution which sets a limit to such tendencies. . . . Thus, the more one has, the more one wants, since satisfactions received only stimulate instead of filling needs.

d. A regulative force must play the same role for moral needs which the organism plays for physical needs. . . . [S]ociety alone can play this moderating role; for it is the only moral power superior to the individual, the authority of which he accepts. . . .

e. [A]t every moment of history there is a dim perception, in the moral consciousness of societies, of the respective value of differential social services, the relative reward due each, and the consequent degree of comfort appropriate on the average to workers in each occupation. . . . Under this pressure, each in his sphere vaguely realizes the extreme limit set to his ambitions and aspires to nothing beyond. . . . Thus, an end and goal are set to the passions.

f. But when society is disturbed by some painful crisis or by beneficient but abrupt transitions, it is momentarily incapable of exercising this influence; there come the sudden rises in the curve of suicides. . . .

g. In the case of economic disasters, indeed, something like a declassification occurs which suddenly casts certain individuals into a lower state than their previous one. Then they must reduce their requirements, restrain their needs, learn greater self-control . . . [s]o they are not adjusted to the condition forced on them, and its very prospect is intolerable. . . .

h. It is the same if the source of crisis is an abrupt growth of power and wealth. Then, truly, as the conditions of life are changed, the standard according to which needs were regulated can no longer remain the same; for it varies with social resources. . . . The scale is upset; but a new scale cannot be immediately improvised. Time is required for the public conscience to reclassify men and things. So long as the social forces thus freed have not regained equilibrium, their respective values are unknown and so all regulation is lacking for a time. The limits are unknown between the possible and the impossible, what is just and what is unjust, legitimate claims and hopes and those which are immoderate. Consequently, there is no restraint upon aspirations. . . . Appetites, not being controlled by a public opinion become disoriented, no longer recognize the limits proper to them. Besides, they are at the same time seized by a sort of natural erethism simply by the greater intensity of public life. With increased prosperity desires increase. At the very moment when traditional rules have lost their authority, the richer prize offered these appetites stimulates them and makes more exigent and impatient of control. The state of deregulation or anomy is thus further heightened by passions being less disciplined, precisely when they need more disciplining.[16]

Durkheim concluded that, during the nineteenth century, institutions such as the church, government, and guilds that once had regulated man's appetites ceased to function in that respect in France. Thus, the same freedom of appetites that had inspired the French Revolution created anomie and an accompanying high suicide rate.[17]

Durkheim reflected somewhat of a marxian posture on crime, even though few of Karl Marx's views on crime are known. One statement by Marx is sufficient to establish his position:

A philosopher produces ideas, a poet poems, a clergyman sermons, a professor compendia and so on. A criminal produces crimes. If we look a little closer at the connection between this latter branch of production and society as a whole, we shall rid ourselves of many prejudices. The criminal produces not only crime but also criminal law, and with this also the professor who gives lectures on criminal law and in addition to this the inevitable compendium in which this same professor throws his lectures onto the general market as "commodities". . . .

The criminal moreover produces the whole of the police and of criminal justice, constables, judges, hangmen, juries, etc.; and all these different lines of businesses, which form equally many categories of the social division of labour, develop different capacities of the human spirit, create new needs and new ways of satisfying them. Torture alone has given rise to the most ingenious mechanical inventions, and employed many honourable craftsmen in the production of instruments.[18]

In *Die Lage der Arbeitenden Klasse in England* (The Condition of the Working Class in England), Friedrich Engels noted that the number of crimes increased by a factor of six between 1815 and 1842 and that crime rates were higher in agricultural compared with industrial areas.[19] Engels attempted to trace crime to a demoralization of the masses characteristic of a capitalistic society devoid of humanity. Nevertheless, the Italian Filippo Turati was the first person to set forth a marxist theory of criminology in his 1883 book, *Il delitto e la questione sociale*, in which he declared that crime is the "monopoly" of the poor.[20] In the same year, 1883, Enrico Ferri asserted his belief that Darwin, Marx, and Spencer formed "the great scientific trinity" of the nineteenth century.[21]

The last quarter of the nineteenth century was replete with a number of marxist thinkers who expounded their views on the causes of crime. Bruno Battaglia, writing on *La dinamica del delitto* (The Dynamics of Crime) in 1886, said that criminal character is "affirmed or denied" by one's social relations and that workers cannot avoid criminality unless the fruits of their labor are distributed among them equally without profits going to the burgeoisie. Antonio Marro declared that the "desperate" financial condition of the proletariat induces the nervous system to fail in some workers, leading to their deviancy. In his 1886 book, *I caratteri dei delinquenti* (Some Characteristics of Criminals), Marro prophesized that crime cannot be eliminated until the capitalist system is destroyed. Paul Lafargue found in his book, *Der wirtschaftliche Materialismus*, published also in 1886, that an increase in the crime rate coincided with an increase in French production of commodities. Achille Loria, writing *Les bases economiques de la constitution sociale* (The Economic Bases of the Social System) published in 1894, blamed the capitalist structure of Western society for crimes, as had Napoleone Colajanni in his 1889 book, *Sociologia Criminale*, and as did August Bebel in his 1899 book, *Die Frau und der Sozialismus* (The Woman and Socialism). Colajanni exerted perhaps the most influence of these late nineteenth-century marxists, in part at least because he based his theory on comparative statistics from England, Ireland, Italy and Scotland. Political handbooks of the period, such as Lux's *Sozialpolitisches Handbuch* of 1892, held that crime is a normal by-product of capitalism's degeneracy. Except for Colajanni's studies, however, nineteenth-century marxist criminology consisted primarily of rhetoric.

In 1905, Willem Adriaan Bonger published his doctoral thesis in law at the University of Amsterdam, entitled *Criminalite et conditions economiques*, which was translated into English in 1916 and published in the United States as part of the Modern Criminal Science Series under the title, *Criminality and Economic Conditions*. In his introduction to the 1969 edition of this book, Austin Turk indicated that Bonger felt no conduct could be "naturally" moral or immoral, because he thought morality reflected current but changing sentiments of any given society.[22] Bonger clarified that view in a 1913 article, "Galoof en Misdaad" (Faith and Crime),[23] in which he disputed the religious basis for morality inherent within the *moralstatistik* fabric of pragmatistic criminologists such as Alexander von Oettingen.[24] Bonger did note the likelihood that mankind would experience an "evolution of morality":

The process of growth most clearly points to the continual progress of organization in society. Through this organization, the evolution of morality must come into action. To say it with the words of Manouvrier: "We must act in such a way that every man continually gets more and more interested in being useful to his equals and less and less in damaging them. That is the formula which we have to apply.[25]

In 1932, Bonger published *An Introduction to Criminology*.[26] His third book, *Race and Crime*,[27] wherein he endeavored to show that economic deprivation rather than heredity has caused high proportions of any culture's minority populations to commit crimes, appeared in the Dutch language in 1939 immediately before Bonger committed suicide as Germany commenced to occupy The Netherlands in 1940.

ANALYTIC CRIMINOLOGY: TWENTIETH-CENTURY TRENDS

Robert K. Merton's famous 1938 paper, "Social Structure and Anomie,"[28] while largely a pragmatist work itself, opened the door to a surge of analytic criminology in America. Merton argued that anomie affects the lower socioeconomic classes disproportionately and permanently because of a social structure that discriminates against them:

It is only when a system of cultural values extols, virtually above all else, certain common success-goals for the population at large while the social structure rigorously restricts or completely closes access to approved modes of reaching these goals for a considerable part of the same population, that deviant behavior ensues on a large scale.[29]

In this sense, therefore, Merton applied Durkheim's theory to what he witnessed in the pre- and post-war American society.[30] It is of critical significance to remember, however, as Donald R. Cressey has reminded us, that Merton "slips into a theory of deviant behavior, rather than limiting himself to a theory of the origin of deviant subcultures. Deviant behavior on a large scale can arise only *after* invention of deviant subcultures."[31] Since the 1950s, analytic criminology has taken on at least three distinguishing shapes: "conflict" theory, "critical" or "new criminology," and "radical" or marxist criminology. Each of these forms a different analytic perspective.

"Conflict Theory" Perspective

The year 1958 signaled the emergence of conflict theory into full swing within criminology. That year, Ralf Dahrendorf published an article he scolded as being unrealistic pragmatistic "consensus" models that purported to explain causation of crime and in which he urged the adoption of a conflict model.[32] That year, also, George B. Vold published the first edition of *Theoretical Criminology*, the first criminology textbook "to use the general conditions and principles of a sociology of conflict as the basis for an explanation of crime."[33] The next year, in 1959, Dahrendorf published his book *Class and Class Conflict in Industrialized Society*.

Dahrendorf viewed society as being compared to two distinctive groups: those who possess authority and use it to dominate, and those who lack authority and consequently become the subjects of domination. To Dahrendorf, these two groups are in conflict with one another. However, Dahrendorf rejected basic marxist principles of a simple bifurcation between the bourgeoisie and the proletariat as being "old-fashioned" and inapplicable to today's technological age because: "The working class of today, far from being a homogeneous group of equally unskilled and impoverished people, is in fact a stratum differentiated by numerous subtle and not so subtle distinctions."[34] For instance, Dahrendorf noticed that the needs and objectives of the unskilled and semiskilled laborers may conflict with those of skilled laborers just as they may conflict with the needs and objectives of classes who perform no physical labor at all, such as the owners or managers of industry. Dahrendorf explained conflict:

As with change, we have grown accustomed to look for special causes or circumstances whenever we encounter conflict; but, again, a complete turn is necessary in our thinking. Not the presence but the absence of conflict is surprising and abnormal, and we have good reason to be suspicious if we find a society or social organization that displays no evidence of conflict. To be sure, we do not have to assume that conflict is always violent and uncontrolled. There is probably a continuum from civil war to parliamentary debate, from strikes and lockouts to joint consultation. . . . [W]e must never lose sight of the underlying assumption that conflict can be temporarily suppressed, regulated, channeled, and controlled but that neither a philosopher-king nor a modern dictator can abolish it once and for all.[35]

Thus, Dahrendorf departed from Marx's vision of a peaceful "dictatorship of the proletariat," but his departure from Marx functioned to underscore the amount of the conflict within Dahrendorf's arguments. He stressed that, in every society, both social changes and social conflicts are "everywhere"; that in all societies some people coerce others; and that every group of people living within any society contributes not only to change within that group and society but also to their eventual "disintegration."[36] Dahrendorf posited the source of this conflict as being what he termed a set of "imperatively co-ordinated associations": "There is a large number of imperatively co-ordinated associations in any given society. Within every one of them we can distinguish the aggregates of those who dominate and those who are subjected."[37] Thus, Dahrendorf abandoned Marx's notion of "class" and substituted for it "authority" as being the fundamental reason for conflict in society.[38]

Conflict criminology did not begin in 1958, nor was George B. Vold the first conflict criminologist. Roots of conflict criminology are traceable as far back as 1924 when Charles H. Cooley published *Social Organization*. During a momentous year for criminology, 1938, Thorsten Sellin published *Culture, Conflict and Crime*,[39] and Sellin's conflict approach became even more evident the next year with his publication of an article in which he witnessed the black American as being relegated to an inferior social caste accompanied by economic deprivation.[40] Vold himself admitted that he was influenced by conflict-oriented sociologists such as Georg Simmel[41] and Lewis A. Coser[42] in addition to Cooley.[43] Vold admitted, also, to having been influenced by the political-conflict model advanced by Harold D. Lasswell in his 1936 book, *Politics: Who Gets What, When, How*.[44] Vold made the following observation:

The struggle between those who support the law and those who violate it existed in the community before there was legislative action. It was the basis for the battle in the legislature; it is then continued through the judicial proceedings of prosecution and trial; and it culminates eventually in the prison treatment of the violators by those who wish to have the law enforced. The principle of compromise from positions of strength operates at every stage of this conflict process.[45]

Moreover, Vold indicated that he drew his conflict theory from research on political corruption, particularly in large American cities,[46] and from "the clash of interests of company management and labor unions."[47] Clearly, therefore, Dahrendorf and Vold popularized conflict theory in 1958 by drawing upon research and theories that had been in progress some two decades or more earlier.

What George B. Vold saw in the decade of the 1950s, however, was an escalation in the rate of occurrence of "political" crimes, ranging from black civil rights activists committing civil disobedience toward laws they felt discriminated against their civil rights, to white reactionaries trying to maintain an apartheid system. Vold observed "many situations in which criminality is the normal, natural response of normal, natural human beings struggling in understandably normal and natural situations for the maintenance of the way of life to which they stand committed."[48] Therefore, Vold observed that "[t]o the dominant white, the Negro is acceptable and desirable only "in his place," a place of obvious social inferiority . . . as cheap laborer . . . recognizably subordinate to . . . the white majority."[49] Vold felt such "political" crimes stood in marked contrast to traditional conventional crimes, such as theft for private gain. Political crimes, Vold thought, could not be explained by the then-popular theories of criminology. However, he cautioned that his conflict theory cannot explain every form of criminal behavior and warned that this theory "should not be stretched too far."[50]

Vold's conflict theory has been stretched considerably, however, particularly by Austin T. Turk and Richard Quinney, before Quinney abandoned conflict theory for a conceptual framework that is more marxist. Quinney entered the arena of conflict theory almost tangentially by taking into account "societal reaction" as an exacerbation of criminal behavior within a 1967 book, *Criminal Behavior Systems: A Typology*, which he co-authored with Marshall B. Clinard. Clinard and Quinney identified a type of political criminal consisting of such seemingly diverse offenders as the traitor and the spy, Nazi war collaborators and American draft resisters, Ku Klux Klansmen and Weathermen.[51] In effect, Clinard and Quinney updated George B. Vold, but they did more than that. They provided an evident intellectual linkage between the pragmatist labeling theories advanced in the early 1950s by Edwin M. Lemert and others[52] and the Dahrendorf-Vold conflict theory, because a "societal reaction" to crime functions as a labeling process that entangles the "political" offender, according to conflict theory.

In his 1970 book, *The Social Reality of Crime*, Richard Quinney went on to recite six conflict-oriented propositions concerning the nature and etiology of crime:

1. Crime is a definition of human conduct that is created by authorized agents in a politically organized society.
2. Criminal definitions describe behaviors that conflict with the interests of the segments of society that have the power to shape public policy.
3. Criminal definitions are applied by the segments of society that have the power to shape the enforcement and administration of criminal law.
4. Behavior patterns are structured in segmentally organized society in relation to criminal definitions and within this context persons engage in actions that have relative probabilities of being defined as criminal.
5. Conceptions of crime are constructed and diffused in the segments of society by various means of communication.
6. The social reality of crime is constructed by the formulation and application of criminal definitions, the development of behavior patterns related to criminal definitions, and the construction of criminal conceptions.[53]

Quinney drew upon several earlier criminological theories in formulating his six propositions. His first proposition, for instance, has origins in the pragmatic perspective of the "interactionists," particularly labeling theorists,[54] while his second proposition stems in large measure from Vold,[55] as does his third, and his fourth proposition comes from Sutherland's differential association theory. The last two of Quinney's propositions seem to flow at least partially from a 1966 book by sociologists Peter L. Berger and Thomas Luckmann, *The Social Construction of Reality*, wherein they observed the subjectivity of society and its dependency upon both individual perception and ideology.

Austin T. Turk expanded Quinney's six propositions into ten of his own by 1978,[56] where he seemed to return to Ralf Dahrendorf's assumption that authority, which Turk calls "power," is at the root of conflict theory:

1. Individuals differ in their perceptions, understanding of social phenomena, and commitment to conventional or unconventional lines of action.
2. Divergence and disagreement lead people to be in conflict with one another.
3. Each conflicting party or person tries to promote his or her way of thinking or acting as the most appropriate one.

4. The result is a conscious struggle over the distribution of available resources and the opportunity to succeed in life goals.

5. People with similar understanding, beliefs, and commitments tend to join forces; people who join forces tend to develop and strengthen their mutual beliefs and understandings.

6. Continuing conflicts tend to become institutionalized in the form of stratification systems. Conflict groups tend to become a fixed, independent part of the social structure.

7. Such systems are characterized by economic exploitation sustained by political domination in all forms—from the most clearly violent to the most subtle forms of political persuasion.

8. Power is the single most important attribute in determining a group's position in the social structure. Changes in the position a social group manifests in society reflect only changes in the distribution of power.

9. Group members share experiences in dealing with group members, group antagonists, and the environment in which people live.

10. Human interrelationships are essentially dynamic and subject to constant changes. Hence, the basic social process is one of conflict.

In Turk's first major book, *Criminality and Legal Order* published in 1969, he prophesized the significance of conflict theory upon criminal justice policy:

There are indications that some authorities are beginning to understand that such norm violations as juvenile misconduct, family disorganization, indifference to hygiene, personality disorder, and lack of usable work skills constitute insoluble problems until and unless a total, determined attempt is made to destroy the structures of values and social relationships—the cultural and social structures—creating and perpetuating the unwanted patterns of language and behavior, and to force people into the structures that lead to "good."[57]

Turk went on in his 1969 book to indicate how the criminalization process works. He said the initial factor is the meaning any given violation of the law has for "first-line enforcers" such as the police, which is followed by the degree of agreement or disagreement shared by those whom he called "high-level enforcers" such as judges and prosecutors.[58] If law enforcers at all levels find a particular form of conduct very offensive, Turk warned, there are likely to be high rates of arrest, conviction, and prison sentences. Moreover, Turk admonished that the relative power of law resisters in relation to law enforcers affects the extent of conflict, because if the two groups share equal power, enforcers become cautious in making arrests, but when resisters acquire greater power than enforcers, laws are repealed or otherwise amended.[59] Finally, Turk suggested that both enforcers and resisters could minimize conflict with each other by avoiding "conflict moves" to any "unrealistic" extent, meaning, by minimizing interaction with each other,[60] at least in any formal sense.

Various research has been undertaken in an effort to evaluate empirically different conflict theory tenets. For example, one group tested the assertion of conflict theory that convicted offenders who are from the lowest socioeconomic strata of society receive the most severe criminal sanctions, such as capital punishment and long terms of imprisonment, but found that this "hypothesis will have to be abandoned, or at least modified."[61] In other words, they failed to uncover an empirical basis for the underlying assumptions set forth by conflict theorists. Few aspects of conflict theory have withstood empirical testing, even using the least rigorous methodological techniques. One reason for this may be that comparatively few empirical tests of conflict theory have been conducted, perhaps because it has lost much of its popular appeal. Many of its former supporters have either returned to pragmatism or moved on to marxism, as Richard Quinney seems to have done during the late 1970s.

"Critical Criminology" Perspective

A new criminological thought emerged in 1973 when Ian Taylor, Paul Walton, and Jock Young published *The New Criminology*, thereby at once coining as a concept the title to their book, whether or not the word "new" was used accurately in that context. Thereafter, much of the debate over the conflict approach lost its fervor, and criminologists who had once fought for the conflict perspective began to adopt the critical perspective. In a sense, actually, what has turned into the critical perspective epitomizes analytic thought, as is evident from a description entitled "Toward a New Criminology" written by Eugene Doleschal and Nora Klapmuts:

The new criminology concentrates not on the officially designated criminal but on (1) the definition of crime—the decision to make, for instance, intoxication by marijuana or other drugs criminal while intoxication by alcohol (the drug of those who make the laws) is noncriminal; and (2) the selection of certain lawbreakers for identification as criminals—for example, the decision to arrest, prosecute, and imprison the lower-class man who steals a hundred dollars and to deal informally with the upper-class embezzler of thousands of dollars by quiet settlement to avoid damaging his reputation.

The new criminology views crime as an integral part of society—a normal, not a pathological, kind of human behavior. It assumes that crime cannot be eliminated—although its structure and form might be affected by changes in crime control policy, and that crime in some form serves useful purposes by integrating what is known as law-abiding society and in defining its boundaries. Most of all, it points out that deviance is a relative concept, that what we call "crime" and "criminals" are more or less arbitrarily defined as classes of acts and actors rather than clear-cut distinctions implied by the labels "criminal" and "noncriminal". . . . Criminal labels are usually dispensed in ways that uphold the established order and do not threaten the lives and life styles of the classes or groups with power and influence.[62]

Gresham M. Sykes has commented further on "The Rise of Critical Criminology":

[A]t the heart of this orientation lies the perspective of a stratified society in which the operation of the criminal law is a means of controlling the poor (and members of minority groups) by those in power who use the legal apparatus to (1) impose their particular morality and standards of good behavior on the entire society; (2) protect their property and physical safety from the depredations of the have-nots, even though the cost may be high in terms of the legal rights of those it perceives as a threat; and (3) to extend the definition of illegal or criminal behavior to encompass those who might threaten the status quo. The middle classes or the lower middle classes are drawn into this pattern of domination either because (1) they are led to believe they too have a stake in maintaining the status quo; or (2) they are made a part of agencies of social control and the rewards of organizational careers provide inducements for keeping the poor in their place.[63]

Marvin Wolfgang has described critical criminology as a school of thought that tries to maintain an alliance with the power system at the same time as it criticizes or even attacks that system for its failure to promote social justice.[64]

Richard Quinney appears to have moved into critical criminology as early as 1973 with publication of his book, *Critique of Legal Order*, in which he outlined a critical theory of criminal law in a way that epitomizes analytic thought:

1. American society is based on an advanced capitalist economy.
2. The state is organized to serve the interests of the dominant economic class, the capitalist ruling class.
3. Criminal law is an instrument that the state and dominant ruling class use to maintain and perpetuate the social and economic order.
4. Crime control in capitalist society is accomplished by a governmental elite, representing dominant ruling class interests, to establish domestic order.

5. The contradiction of advanced capitalism—the disjunction between existence and essence—requires that the subordinate classes remain by whatever means necessary, especially by the legal system's coercion and violence.

6. Only with the collapse of capitalist society based on socialist principles, will there be a solution to the crime problem.[65]

Quinney went further in his 1973 book, noting that "[t]he law in capitalist society gives political recognition to powerful interests";[67] that, in addition to legislative bodies at all levels, criminal justice advisory bodies and agencies "operate to preserve domestic order for the ruling class";[66] and that "[t]he rates of crime in any state are an indication of the extent to which the ruling class, through its machinery of criminal law, must coerce the rest of the population, thereby preventing any threat to its ability to rule and possess."[68]

In their 1973 book, *The New Criminology*, authors Ian Taylor, Paul Walton, and Jock Young characterized Emile Durkheim as having been "unambiguously radical in his approach to social order,"[69] and they credited him as being the one who pioneered the inception of a "radical politicality" in the study of deviancy.[70] These writers declared, referring to critical criminologists:

They have broken with the tendency to reduce what is in reality a number of overlapping and sometimes contradictory systems of social relations . . . to a monolithic culture where deviants are seen as pathological blemishes on the otherwise perfectible and integrated whole. This has opened up the possibility of a theory which can encompass change, conflict, and struggle.[71]

Taylor, Walton, and Young offered their evaluation of what they called "the new conflict theorists," including Dahrendorf, Vold, Turk, and Quinney, and concluded that these conflict theorists were "not especially new"[72] and that they continue to regard criminal behavior as being both deterministic and pathological.[73] On the contrary, the authors of *The New Criminology* set forth their alternative social theory of deviancy in seven propositions:

1. *A Political Economy of Crime.* An acceptable social theory must be able to place the deviant act in terms of its wider structure.

2. *A Social Psychology of Crime.* An acceptable social theory must be able to explain the different events, experiences, or structural developments that precipitate the deviant act.

3. *The Social Dynamics of the Act.* An acceptable social theory must be able to explain the relationship between beliefs and action, between the optimum

"rationality" that men have chosen and the behaviors they actually carry through.

4. *A Social Psychology of Social Reaction*. The theory must offer an explanation of the immediate reaction of the social audience in terms of the range of choices available to that audience.

5. *A Political Economy of Social Reaction*. An acceptable social theory must present an effective model of the political and economic imperatives that underpin "lay ideologies" as well as the "crusades" which emerge to control or alter the amount and level of deviance.

6. *The Outcome of the Social Reaction on Deviant's Further Action*. A social explanation of deviance would be one in which the deviant actor is always endowed with some degree of consciousness about the likelihood and consequences of reaction against him, and his subsequent decisions are developed from that initial degree of consciousness.

7. *The Scope of Theoretical Analysis*. A social theory of deviance must present all of these formal requirements as they appear in the real world, that is, in a complex, dialectical relationship to one another.[74]

In this way, these authors contended, it might be possible to "move criminology out of its own imprisonment in artificially segregated specifics, and bring the parts together again in order to form the whole."[75] Apparently, what Taylor, Walton, and Young are saying is that criminologists have failed to see the forest by staring at its trees.

In 1976, William Chambliss recited concisely the meaning of crime from an analytic framework:

Crime is a political phenomenon. What gets defined as criminal or delinquent behavior is the result of a political process within which rules are formed which prohibit or require people to behave in certain ways. . . . Thus, to ask "why is it that some acts get defined as criminal while others do not" is the starting point for all systematic study of crime and criminal behavior. Nothing is inherently criminal; it is only the response that makes it so.[76]

Critical criminology moves toward a marxist perspective through the theories of Chambliss and Richard Quinney. In his 1977 book, *Class, State, and Crime*, Quinney observed that "Criminal Justice has emerged as a principal feature of modern, advanced capitalist society. When a society cannot solve the social problems of its own creation, policies for the control of the population must be devised and implemented."[77] Moreover, Quinney warned that "[t]he final development of capitalism' is also the initial development of socialism. Thus, as criminal justice falters with the development of capitalism, new socialist forms of justice emerge"[78] "to project and solidify the working class against internal and external enemies, as well as against elitist bureaucratic tendencies in the state apparatus."[79] Adding to this, Chambliss has argued that "[t]he criminal law creation process organizes into it the views of those classes who control the economic resources as a result of the entire matrix of recruitment, socialization, and situational pressures upon those who create the laws."[80] Finally, Chambliss has concluded that "the heart of a capitalist economic system is the protection of private property. . . . It is not surprising, then, to find that the criminal law reflects this basic concern."[81]

Sometimes, it may be difficult to distinguish "critical" from a truly marxist criminology. One basis, advanced by Marvin Wolfgang, is that "critical" criminology is "more reactive than proactive,"[82] meaning that "critical" criminology does not aim to overthrow the "ruling class" much as it may criticize the way it feels such a group dominates society. On the other hand, clearly, marxism in criminology is no different from marxism generally. It is truly proactive instead of being reactive.

The Marxist Perspective

Marxist criminology overlaps considerably with "critical" criminology on a number of theoretical viewpoints. The fundamental difference rests in the commitment of true marxists to activism as a means of changing society. Marxists refer to this change as *praxis*, which rests at the core of radical criminology because "in the Marxian view social science should subordinate theory to practice,"[83] as marxist sociologists stress. Be that as it may, most marxist criminologists have been academicians whose theories have yet to be tested in practice, as radical criminologists Herman Schwendinger noted back in 1974 by observing that this form of criminology has been limited to a "small number of outspoken students and a smaller number of determined faculty."[84] Most radical criminologists operated out of the University of California at Berkeley's School of Criminology during the decade of the 1960s. When Ronald Reagan, as governor of California, hurled them out of academia, however, few availed themselves of the ensuing opportunity for *praxis*! Radical ex-Berkeley criminologist Anthony Platt wrote in 1974 of the "Prospects for a Radical Criminology in the United States" by urging fellow radical criminologists to participate more in social activism "by organizing educational conferences, supporting defendants in political trials, participating in campus protests, and helping to develop programs such as community control of the police[.]"[85]

Tony Platt had outlined the etiology of radical criminology as follows:

The roots of this radicalism are to be found in political struggles—the civil rights movement, the anti-war movement, the student movement, third world liberation struggles inside as well as outside the United States, and anti-imperalist movements—and in the writings of participants in these struggles—George Jackson (1970), Angela Davis (1971), Eldridge Cleaver (1968), Tom Hayden (1970), Sam Melville (1971), Bobby Seale (1968), Huey Newton (1973), Malcom X (1964) and Rucheu Magee, to name a few.[86]

In 1975, Herman and Julia Schwendinger asserted that crime should be studied as a violation of "human rights":

Criminologists must be able to identify those forms of individuals' behavior and social institutions which should be engaged in order to defend human rights. To defend human rights, criminologists must be able to sufficiently identify the violations of these rights—by whom and against whom; and how and why.[87]

The Schwendingers have alleged, also, that rape is the product of a capitalist "strain" that also makes a female rape victim feel guilty that she has been "let down" by men on whom she has been conditioned since childhood to depend for protection.[88] The Schwendingers have authored a "radical perspective" on delinquency within which a marxian position is evident: (1) the American legal system is designed to protect the capitalist mode of production by safeguarding property owned by the bourgeoisie; (2) the American public school system secures a steady labor force; (3) both rural and urban proletariats challenge the bourgeoisie; (4) even the foundation of American constitutional law is aimed at perpetuating a class system where the worker continues to be exploited; (5) laws appearing to protect the proletariat, such as collective bargaining rights, are deceptive and intended to strengthen management; (6) all laws in a capitalistic system contradict their stated purpose and perpetuate a system characterized by anarchy, crime, and oppression.[89]

Stephen Spitzer has illuminated ways he says our capitalist society regulates deviants, according to his marxist perspective. For example, capitalist society may "normalize" those who used to be "deviant" by decriminalizing their conduct, such as when the Supreme Court halted states from prohibiting abortions; or society may "convert" a "deviant" and absorb him or her into the system, such as Clifford Shaw did in his Chicago Area Project by recruiting gang leaders to divert younger juveniles from delinquency; or it may "contain" potential "deviants" by herding them into ghetto areas where they can be controlled; and, in some instances, society may support criminal enterprises, such as organized crime, that provide a livelihood for people whom otherwise the state might have to support on welfare.[90]

The analytic thought inherent even within marxist criminology is evident from statements made by Tony Platt concerning the definitions of crime:

In the past we have been constrained by a legal definition of crime which restricts us to studying and ultimately helping to control only legally defined "criminals." We need a more humanistic definition of crime, one which reflects the reality of a legal system based on power and privilege. To accept the legal definition of crime is to accept the fiction of neutral law. A human rights definition of crime frees us to examine imperialism, racism, sexism, capitalism, exploitation and other political or economic systems which contribute to human misery and deprive people of their potentialities.[91]

Platt has noted, moreover, that "the liberal emphasis on pragmatism, short-range solutions and amelioration reveals an attitude of cynicism and defeatism concerning human potentiality and the possibility of far-reaching changes in society":

This focus serves to exclude or underestimate the possibility of a radically different society in which cooperation replaces competition, where human values take precedence over property values, where exploitation, racism and sexism are eliminated, and where basic human needs are fulfilled.[92]

The difference between radical and nonradical views of crime becomes apparent from Spitzer's marxist declaration that:

[P]opulations become generally eligible for management as deviant when they disturb, hinder or call into question any of the following:

1. The capitalist modes of appropriating the product of human labor (e.g., when the poor "steal" from the rich)
2. The social conditions under which capitalist production takes place (e.g., those who refuse or are unable to perform wage labor)
3. Patterns of distribution and consumption in capitalist society (e.g., those who use drugs for escape and transcendence rather than sociability and adjustment)
4. The process of socialization for productive and nonproductive roles (e.g., youth who refuse to be schooled or those who deny the validity of "family life")
5. The ideology which supports the functioning of capitalist society (e.g., proponents of alternative forms of social organization).[93]

The analytic thought of marxism focuses, ordinarily, upon "production" and, consequently, marxist criminology views changes in crime patterns as being linked inextricably to alterations in the capitalist economic system. As economist David M. Gordon observed more than a decade ago, radicals "argue that nearly all crimes in capitalist societies represent perfectly rational responses to . . . the organization of capitalist institutions, for those crimes help provide a means to survival in a society within which survival is never assured."[94]

NOTES

1. O. Holmes, *The Path of the Law*, 10 HARVARD L. REV. (1897). (Emphasis added.)

2. W. Bonger, CRIMINALITY AND ECONOMIC CONDITIONS 379 (H. Horton, tr., 1916).

3. W. Gallie, *Liberal Morality and Socialist Morality*, PHILOSOPHY 24 (1949).

4. *Id.* at 25.

5. *Id.*

6. *Id.*

7. E. Durkheim, DE LA DIVISION DU TRAVAIL SOCIAL 80, n. 10 (1893).

8. E. Durkheim, LES REGLES DE LA METHODE SOCIOLOGIQUE 70 (1895).

9. *Anomie* is a Greek word, loosely translated as lawlessness.

10. Durkheim was descended from several rabbinical scholars and published works on the sociology of religion, also, such as LES FORMES ELEMENTAIRE DE LA VIE RELIGIEUSES (The Elementary Forms of Religious Life) in 1912. Finally, in 1924, he published SOCIOLOGIE ET PHILOSOPHIE.

11. E. Durkheim, THE RULES OF SOCIOLOGICAL METHOD 68–69 (1965 ed., S. Solovay and J. Mueller, trs.).

12. *Id.* at 69.

13. *Id.* at 71.

14. *Id.* at 67.

15. *Id.* at 72.

16. E. Durkheim, SUICIDE 246–53 (J. Spaulding, tr.,). Durkheim seems to have predicated some of this on L. M. Moreau-Christopher, DU PROBLEME DE LA MISERE ET DE LA SOLUTION CHEZ LES PEUPLES ANCIENS ET MODERNES (1851).

17. *Id.* at 254–58. Durkheim sounded not unlike some positivists, as Ferri must have sensed when he called Durkheim "the most original and the most genuine positivist" among French sociologists. See S. Schafer, THEORIES IN CRIMINOLOGY 77 (1969).

18. K. Marx, THEORIES OF SURPLUS VALUE 287–88 (R. Simpson, tr., 1969).

19. He blamed this condition on the "blocked" mobility of the working classes. F. Engels, THE CONDITION OF THE WORKING CLASS IN ENGLAND IN 1844 (1845).

20. F. Turati, CRIME AND SOCIAL QUESTION (1883).

21. E. Ferri, SOCIALISMO E CRIMINALITA (1883). See C. Bernaldo de Quiros, MODERN THEORIES OF CRIMINALITY 67 (A. deSalvo, tr., 1967).

22. W. Bonger, CRIMINALITY AND ECONOMIC CONDITIONS (intro. to the 1969 ed. by A. Turk).

23. See J. van Bemmelen, *William Adriaan Bonger*, in H. Mannheim, ed., PIONEERS IN CRIMINOLOGY 429, 445 (2nd ed., 1972).

24. See Chapter 7, note 11.

25. *Supra*, note 21 at 450. Bonger was fond of quoting French anthropologist Leonce Manouvrier, an environmentalist, whose works on crime Bonger praised in CRIMINALITY AND ECONOMIC CONDITIONS at 175.

26. Published in English (E. van Loo, tr.) in 1936.

27. Published in English (E. van Loo, tr.), posthumously in 1943, with a preface by Northwestern University law professor John W. Wigmore.

28. AM. SOC. REV. 672–82. See Chapter 7, note 11.

29. R. Merton, SOCIAL THEORY AND SOCIAL STRUCTURE 146 (1957).

30. For a comparison of Merton with Durkheim, see J. Horton, *The Dehumanization of Anomie and Alienation: A Problem of the Ideology of Sociology*, 15 BRIT. J. SOC. 294–295 (1964).

31. E. Sutherland and D. Cressey, CRIMINOLOGY 99, n. 14 (9th ed., 1974).

32. R. Dahrendorf, *Out of Utopia: Toward a Reorientation of Sociological Analysis*, 64 AM. J. SOC. 115–27 (1958).

33. G. Vold, THEORETICAL CRIMINOLOGY 282 (2nd ed., 1979).

34. R. Dahrendorf, CLASS AND CONFLICT IN INDUSTRIALIZED SOCIETY 6 (1958).

35. *Supra*, note 32 at 126–27.

36. *Supra*, note 34 at 48.

37. *Id.* at 171. Earlier, Dahrendorf had written of "imperatively coordinated groups." See R. Dahrendorf, *Toward a Theory of Social Conflict*, 2 J. CONFLICT RES. 170–83 (1958).

38. See I. Taylor, P. Walton, and J. Young, THE NEW CRIMINOLOGY 238 (1973). They said Vold was the first criminologist to "accord a significant place to crime as a product of social conflict." *Id.*

39. Published by the Social Science Research Council of New York.

40. T. Sellin, *The Negro and the Problem of Law Observance and Administration in the Light of Social Research*, in C. Johnson, ed., THE NEGRO IN AMERICAN CIVILIZATION 451 (1939).

41. *Supra*, note 33 at 282, n. 1; 283, n. 3; 284, n. 6 and n. 7; 285, n. 11; and 286, n. 14. See G. Simmel, CONFLICT (K. Wolff, tr., 1955) and THE WEB OF GROUP AFFILIATIONS (R. Bendix, tr., 1955) plus K. Wolff, THE SOCIOLOGY OF GEORG SIMMEL (1950).

42. *Supra*, note 33 at 282, n. 1; 284, n. 6 and n. 8; 285, n. 11; and 286, n. 13. See L. Coser, THE FUNCTIONS OF SOCIAL CONFLICT (1956).

43. *Supra*, note 33 at 284, n. 8 and 285, n. 9.

44. *Supra*, note 33 at 287, n. 15. See also H. Lasswell and A. Kaplan, POWER AND SOCIETY (1950); E. Latham, THE GROUP BASIS FOR POLITICS (1952).

45. *Supra*, note 33 at 288.

46. *Supra*, note 33 at 293. See L. Steffens, THE SHAME OF THE CITIES (1904).

47. *Supra*, note 33 at 293–94. See C. Walker, AMERICAN CITY: A RANK AND FILE HISTORY (1937), and M. Vorse, LABOR'S NEW MILLIONS (1938).

48. G. Vold, THEORETICAL CRIMINOLOGY 218–19 (1958).

49. *Supra*, note 33 at 295.

50. *Supra*, note 48.

51. M. Clinard and R. Quinney, CRIMINAL BEHAVIOR SYSTEMS: A TYPOLOGY 14–19 (1967).

52. See Chapter 7, note 85.

53. R. Quinney, THE SOCIAL REALITY OF CRIME 15–23 (1970).

54. See Chapter 7, note 85.

55. Quinney acknowledged Vold for his second and third propositions. *Supra*, note 53 at 17, n. 42; and 18, n. 44. Quinney revised his propositions in 1975 without significantly affecting their substance. See R. Quinney, CRIMINOLOGY: ANALYSIS AND CRITIQUE OF CRIME IN AMERICA 37–39 (1975).

56. A. Turk, *Analyzing Official Deviance: For Nonpartisan Conflict Analyses in Criminology*, in J. Inciardi, ed., RADICAL CRIMINOLOGY: THE COMING CRISIS 78–91 (1980).

57. A. Turk, CRIMINALITY AND LEGAL ORDER 58 (1969).

58. *Id*. at 65–67.

59. *Id*. at 67–70.

60. *Id*. at 70.

61. See T. Chiricos and G. Waldo, *Socioeconomic Status and Criminal Sentencing: An Empirical Assessment of a Conflict Proposition*, 40 AM. SOC. REV. 768 (1975).

62. E. Doleschal and N. Klapmuts, *Toward a New Criminology*, 5 CRIME & DELIN. 607, 623 (1973).

63. G. Sykes, *The Rise of Critical Criminology*, 65 J. CRIM. L. & CRIM. 206 (1974).

64. M. Wolfgang, "Developments in Criminology in the United States with Some Comments on the Future." Paper presented at the Fifth National Conference, Institute of Criminology, University of Cambridge (1973).

65. R. Quinney, CRITIQUE OF LEGAL ORDER 16 (1973).

66. *Id*. at 52.

67. *Id*. at 59.

68. *Id*. at 52.

69. I. Taylor, P. Walton, and J. Young, THE NEW CRIMINOLOGY 87 (1973).

70. *Id.* at 89.

71. *Id.* at 118–19.

72. *Id.* at 266–67.

73. *Id.* at 267.

74. *Id.* at 270–78.

75. *Id.* at 279.

76. W. Chambliss, *The State and Criminal Law*, in W. Chambliss, ed., WHOSE LAW? WHAT ORDER? 66, 101 (1976). See also B. Krisberg, CRIME AND PRIVILEGE: TOWARD A NEW CRIMINOLOGY (1975).

77. R. Quinney, CLASS, STATE AND CRIME v (1977).

78. *Id.* at 145.

79. *Id.* at 163.

80. *Supra*, note 76 at 80.

81. *Id.* at 85.

82. *Supra*, note 64 at 18.

83. D. Hodges, *Marxism as Social Science*, in M. Curtis, ed., MARXISM 91 (1970).

84. H. Schwendinger, CRIME AND SOCIAL JUSTICE 1 (1974). He went on to warn that "the number involved, however, should not minimize the qualitative significance of the development of a Radical Criminology." *Id.*

85. A. Platt, *Prospects for a Radical Criminology in the United States*, 1 CRIME & SOC. JUST. 2, 7 (1974).

86. *Id.* at 2.

87. H. Schwendinger and J. Schwendinger, *Defenders of Order or Guardians of Human Rights?*, in I. Taylor, P. Walton, and J. Young, eds., CRITICAL CRIMINOLOGY 134 (1975).

88. H. Schwendinger and J. Schwendinger, *Rape Victims and the False Sense of Guilt*, 13 CRIME & SOC. JUST. 4–17 (1980).

89. H. Schwendinger and J. Schwendinger, *Delinquency and Social Reform: A Radical Perspective*, in L. Empey, eds., JUVENILE JUSTICE 246–90 (1979).

90. S. Spitzer, *Toward a Marxian Construct of Deviance*, 22 SOC. PROBS. 638–51 (1975).

91. E. Currie, *A Dialogue with Anthony M. Platt*, 8 ISSUES IN CRIM. 28, 29 (1973).

92. *Supra*, note 85 at 3.

93. *Supra*, note 90 at 642.

94. D. Gordon, *Class and the Economics of Crime*, 3 REV. RAD. POL. ECON. 51, (1971). See also D. Gordon, *Capitalism, Class, and Crime in America*, 19 CRIME & DELIN. 163–86 (1973).

9

The Existential Condition of Criminology: Beyond Right and Wrong

Existentialism is an enigmatic term used loosely to describe a philosophy that emphasizes the limits of reason plus the insignificance of experience and that is preoccupied with human existence, particularly in its tragic aspects such as uncertainty and despair. Taken in its broadest sense, existentialism is apt to apply historically to biblical philosophies such as those evident in the Book of Job, to the philosophy of St. Augustine, and to that of seventeenth-century French mathematician Blaise Pascal. One could argue that existentialism is a spin-off from idealism, particularly from some thoughts expressed by Immanuel Kant in his three critiques[1] and in his *Fundamental Principles of the Metaphysics of Ethics*, published in 1785, wherein Kant set forth his philosophy of law. Existentialism may encompass some works by Fyodor M. Dostoevsky, such as *Crime and Punishment* (1866–67) and *The Brothers Karamazov* (1879–80); and by Franz Kafka, particularly *"Das Urteil"* (The Judgment), 1913, *"In der Strafkolonie"* (In the Penal Colony), 1919, and *Der Prozess* (The Trial), 1925. Perhaps existential thought was weaned in theistic works of Soren Kierkegaard, such as *Fear and Trembling* (1843), *The Concept of Dread* (1844), and *Thoughts on Crucial Situations* (1845). Perhaps existential thought reached adolescence in atheistic works of Friedrich Nietzsche, particularly *Thus Spake Zarathustra* (1883–92), *Beyond Good and Evil* (1886), and *The Will to Power* which Nietzsche left unfinished upon becoming insane in 1889.

Taken most narrowly, existentialism could pertain exclusively to the gloomy philosophies expressed by four twentieth-century continental Europeans: Martin Heidegger, Karl Jaspers, Gabriel Marcel, and Jean Paul Sartre, with or without Kierkegaard and Nietzsche.[2] As existentialism became the household word we think of it as being today, Sartre declared in 1947 that it "is now so loosely applied to so many things that it no longer means anything at all."[3]

An existentialist views the individual as being radically free to elect among an array of choices that confront him or her throughout life, being unfettered by limitations such as heredity, historical or social conditions, or even mortality. This exhilarating prospect is accompanied, however, by the anguish a person senses in knowing that he is entirely responsible for his own destiny, having been condemned to an absurd degree of freedom inherent in the human condition, and that he will never be able to achieve any real harmony with other things in the world around him, including other people, social institutions, or even his own "facticity." The mass culture of the modern technological age, some existentialists believe, has caused the phenomenal world to decompose so that the meaning of rational concepts, objects, time and history have withered away to the point where all coherence has vanished, leaving man in a state of nothingness where he faces despair all alone. Upon comprehending this absurdity, insecurity, and the meaninglessness of his situation together with that of the world around him, an existentialist may argue, man can accept his destiny without any illusions and triumph over it.

Illusions, precisely, have been the traditional concepts used in explaining the causation of crime, from the existential viewpoint. To the existentialist, for instance, it seems as much of an illusion to blame crime on capitalist society, as the analysts have done, as to blame it on man's having fallen from God's Grace, as some realists used to do, or to blame crime on the offender's heredity, as positivist criminologists suggested. In fact, speaking existentially, any formula for identifying the causation of crime has to be an illusion because crime itself can be nothing more than a mere illusion. It is part of man's existence, part of his torment. As Nietzsche reasoned, "[a] *species* comes to be, a type becomes fixed and strong, through the long fight with essentially constant *unfavorable* conditions."[4] Among such unfavorable conditions is crime. Therefore, crime can be a beneficial and invigorating experience for human beings.

In 1886, Nietzsche published *Jenseits von Gut and Bose* (Beyond Good and Evil), in which he argued that "exploitation" is normal in society:

Life itself is *essentially* appropriation, injury, overpowering of what is alien and weaker; suppression, hardness, imposition of one's own forms, incorporation and at least, at its mildest, exploitation. . . . . "Exploitation" does not belong to a corrupt or imperfect society; it belongs to the *essence* of what lives, as a basic organic function; it is a consequence of the will to power, which is after all the will to life. . . . . If this should be an innovation as a theory—as a reality it is the *primordial* fact of all history; people ought to be honest with themselves at least that far.[5]

Moreover, Nietzsche asserted that "[l]ife itself is will to power":

[W]e succeed in explaining our entire instinctive life as the development and ramification of *one* basic form of the will—namely of the will to power, as *my* proposition has it; suppose all organic functions could be traced back to this will to power and one could also find it in the solution to the problem of procreation and nourishment . . . —then one could have gained the right to determine *all* efficient force univocally as—*will to power*. The world viewed from inside, the world defined and determined according to its "intelligible character"—it would be "will to power" and nothing else.[6]

Subsequently, Nietzsche expanded on this view by saying that "[i]n the case of an animal, it is possible to trace all its drives to the will to power; likewise all the functions of organic life to this one source."[7] Ultimately, Nietzsche strove for his ideal in human existence, which he termed "Dionysian" affirmation of the world as it is "without subtraction, exception, or selection"[8]:

The word "Dionysian" means . . . a reaching out beyond personality, the everyday, society, reality, across the abyss of transitoriness: a passionate-painful overflowing into the darker, fuller, more floating states; an ecstatic affirmation of the total characcter of life . . . the great pantheistic sharing of joy and sorrow that sanctifies and calls good even the most terrible and questionable qualities of life; the eternal will to procreation, to fruitfulness, to recurrence; the feeling of the necessary unity of creation and destruction.[9]

"Dionysus is a *judge*!—Have I been understood?", Nietzsche proclaimed.[10] He concluded that "there are no moral phenomena at all, but only a moral interpretation of phenomena."[11] Instead, he explained his own view that "morality" is "a system of evaluations that partially coincides with the conditions of a creator's life,"[12] which he called "rank" and which precipitated his statement that "[m]oralities must be forced to bow first of all before the *order of rank*."[13] Thus spake Zarathustra through Nietzsche,[14] setting forth his basic premise that ethics and morality are relative.

Dostoevsky carried forth this existential thought within *Crime and Punishment*, such as when student-murderer Rodion Romanovitch Raskolnikoff explains that he killed to advance his ambitions:

The fact is, that one day, I asked myself the following question: "Supposing Napoleon to have been in my place, supposing that to commence his career he had neither had Toulon, nor Egypt, nor the crossing of Mont Blanc, in lieu of all these brilliant exploits, he was on the point of commiting a murder with a view to secure his future, would he have recoiled at the idea of killing an old woman, and of robbing her of three thousand roubles? Would he have agreed that such a deed was too much wanting in prestige and much too—criminal a one?'' For a long time, I have split my head on that question, and could not help experiencing a feeling of shame when I finally came to the conclusion that he not only would not have hesitated, but that he would not have understood the possibility of such a thing. Every other expedient being out of his reach, he would not have flinched, he would have done so without the smallest scruple. Hence, I ought not to hesitate—being justified on the authority of Napoleon!'' [15]

Raskolnikoff's syllogism is a *non-sequitur*, of course, since whatever Napoleon might have done does not justify subsequent conduct to any logical extent. Yet, a major premise of existentialism is that life does not follow any logical order. As Raskolnikoff admitted shortly after the above passage, speaking again to his friend Sonia Semenovna: "Why, the very fact of asking myself: 'Would Napolean have murdered this woman?' was sufficient proof that I was no Napoleon.'' [16]

Nietzsche's existentialism is similar, at least superficially, to analytic thought in that both recognize the impact of class distinction on the making of laws and morality. What most analysts have considered to be bad, however, Nietzsche deemed beyond good and evil.[17] He deemed it "the will to truth" and considered it to be part of the existential condition:

There is *master-morality* and *slave-morality*;—I would at once add, however, that in all higher and mixed civilizations, there are also attempts at the reconciliation of the two moralities; but one finds still oftener the confusion and mutual misunderstanding of them, indeed, sometimes their close juxtaposition— even in the same man, within one soul. The distinctions of moral values have either originated in a ruling caste, pleasantly conscious of being different from the ruled—or among the ruled class, the slaves and dependents of all sorts. In the first class, when it is the rulers who determine the conception of "good," it is the exalted, proud disposition which is regarded as the distinguishing feature, and that which determines the order of rank. The noble type of man separates from himself the beings in whom the opposite of this exalted, proud disposition displays itself: he despises them. Let it at once be noted that in this first kind of morality the antithesis "good" and "bad" means practically the same as "noble" and "despicable";—the antithesis "good" and "*evil*" is of a different origin. The cowardly, the timid, the insignificant, and those thinking merely of narrow utility are despised; moreover, also, the distrustful, with their constrained glances, the self-abasing, the doglike kind of men who let themselves be abused, the mendicant flatterers, and above all the liars:—it is a fundamental belief of all aristocrats that the common people are untruthful. "We truthful ones"—the nobility in ancient Greece called themselves. It is obvious the designations of moral value were at first applied to *men*, and were only derivatively and at a later period applied to *actions*; it is a gross mistake, therefore, when historians of morals start with questions like, "Why have sympathetic actions been praised?" The noble type of man regards *himself* as a determiner of values; he does not require to be approved of; he passes the judgment: "What is injurious to me is injurious in itself; he knows that it is he himself only who confers honor on things; he is a *creator of values*." [18]

Nietzsche noted the negative societal reaction to what he termed the "morality of the ruling class":

A morality of the ruling class, however, is more especially foreign and irritating to present-day taste in the sternness of its principle that one has duties only to one's equals; that one may act towards beings of a lower rank, towards all that is foreign, just as seems good to one, or "as the heart desires," and in any case "beyond good and evil": it is here that sympathy and similar sentiments can have a place. The ability and obligation to exercise prolonged gratitude and prolonged revenge—both only within the circle of equals—artfulness in retaliation, *refinement* of the idea in friendship a certain necessity to have enemies (as outlets for the emotions of envy, quarrelsomeness, arrogance—in fact, in order to be a good *friend*): all these are typical characteristics of the noble morality, which, as has been pointed out, is not the morality of "modern ideas," and is therefore at present difficult to realize, and also to unearth and disclose.—It is otherwise with the second type of morality, *slave-morality*. Supposing that the abused, the oppressed, the suffering, the unemancipated, the weary, and those uncertain of themselves, should moralize, what will be the common element in their moral estimates? Probably a pessimistic suspicion with regard to the entire situation of man will find expression, perhaps a condemnation of man, together with his situation. The slave has an unfavorable eye for the virtues of the powerful; he has a skepticism and distrust, a *refinement* of distrust of everything "good" that is there honored—he would fain persuade himself that the very happiness there is not genuine. . . . Slave-morality is essentially the morality of utility. . . . Everywhere that slave-morality gains the ascendency, language shows a tendency to approximate the significations of the words "good" and "stupid." [19]

So Nietzsche anticipated the response of marxist criminologists to the purpose of the laws.

The fact is, as Nietzsche alluded but stopped short of saying directly, that most criminals are leaders or at least ardent individuals rather than followers. This the marxist criminologists cannot understand because, of course, they are the sheep. Criminals possess the "morality of the ruling class" although, to be sure, and perhaps paradoxically in one sense, they are not rulers. They resist what they are told to do, even when the power of the law orders them to conform their behavior or be punished. Perhaps therein rests their misfortune, perhaps not, since the criminal attends to doing that which he desires to do during those moments of freedom, however fleeting such moments may be between prison terms. The career offender adheres closely to a code of ethics, however, that pervades his conduct with his peers, other criminals. Hence goes the old adage that there is "honor among thieves."

Similarly, the criminal is reluctant to interfere with another person's criminal activity, preferring instead to abide *omerta* or silence. Yet, he acquires enemies and prolongs his revenge until he can realize an artful retaliation. The criminal shares Nietzsche's master-morality: "The noble man honors in himself the powerful one, him also who has power over himself, who knows how to speak and how to keep silence, who takes pleasure in subjecting himself to severity and hardness, and has reverence for all that is severe and hard."[20] So, of course, can and does the criminal tolerate the hardship of imprisonment which becomes a futile remedy for his wrongdoing.

The criminal lives dangerously, giving credence to Nietzsche's observation that "the world is swarming with 'dangerous individuals'!"[21] Contrary to the prevailing view that this evidences a "sick" society, Nietzsche argued that danger is healthful:

I welcome all signs that a more manly, warlike age is about to begin. . . . For this there is now needed many pioneering valorous men, who cannot spring up out of nothing—any more than out of the sand and filth of our present civilization and its metropolitanism: men who understand how to be silent, solitary, resolute, content and steadfast in imperceptible activity: men who then with inner inclination seek after that which is to be *overcome* in them: . . . men in greater danger, more fruitful men, happier men. For, believe me!—the secret of the greatest fruitfulness and the greatest enjoyment of being is: *to live dangerously!* . . . Live at war with your peers and with yourselves. Be robbers and conquerors, as long as you cannot be rulers and owners[.][22]

So does today's criminal offender live dangerously indeed, but on his own terms. He has become his own Dionysus. He has to please himself, or please no one, even at the expense of facing protracted prison confinement. It is no answer that today's criminal offender is atavistic, as Lombroso postulated, just as it is an incomplete answer that he has enjoyed differential association with other criminals or a differential opportunity to become right thinking. Nor is it a valid answer that today's criminal is the product of capitalism in the sense that marxists contend, that the offender has been tormented into crime by an exploiting society.

CRITICAL LEGAL STUDIES OR NIHILISM?

Over the past decade, more or less, some existential coherence has emerged among American legal scholars, but largely outside of the domain of criminology. Led at least partially by Harvard law professor Roberto Managabeira Unger, a native of Brazil, these scholars have founded an intellectual movement known as "critical legal studies,"[23] the primary thesis of which seems to be that law, traditionally viewed as being autonomous, is in fact relative to social theory and social practice.[24] Unger and his colleagues have expressed a "moral skepticism"[25] that, in turn, has provoked a clamorous condemnation from some traditional legal scholars,[26] largely on account of their inference, accurate or not, from the collective "critical legal studies" that the viewpoint of Unger and his colleagues amounts to "nihilism."

Many existentialists including and since Nietzsche have been portrayed as being nihilists, once again accurately or not. Nihilism involves the repudiation of the very possibility of "truth" and "knowledge" expect as conduits for the survival of some person(s)' power and the increase of that power. Thus, a true nihilist rejects the possibility that man can achieve genuine understanding of himself or reality.[27] A number of philosophers have argued that Nietzsche was not a nihilist,[28] but Danto and others have contended that he was.[29] Among others, Duke University Law School Deal Paul D. Carrington has labeled Unger and other "critical legal studies" scholars as nihilists and demanded their resignation or removal from law school faculties.[30] Whether Nietzsche, Unger, or other scholars, past or present, represent "nihilism" is less important by far than an examination of the merits of the critical legal studies movement.

Unger's "moral skepticism" emerged in his 1975 book, *Knowledge and Politics*,[31] and became concretized more so in his next book, *Law in Modern Society*,[32] that he published the following year. In 1975, Unger compared two moralities: the morality of *desire* and the morality of *reason*, accusing both, in a truly existential fashion, of failing to provide real guidance for distinguishing right from wrong. Unger wrote that "the morality of desire provides no standards for preferring some desires to others" and that, consequently, "it fails to serve as a basis for the justification of criticism of choice."[33] In a subchapter to his 1975 book entitled "The Antinomy of Reason and Desire," Unger assumed that all desires "are random with respect to any given understanding of the world."[34] Unger concluded:

We are not entitled to assume that there exists an order among our choices and inclinations, an order reason might discover or impose on the will. A pattern among an individual's desires would only be possible if he were able to ask what the system of his ends committed him to in a particular case.[35]

Thus, according to Unger, the "morality of desire" provides no "standards" to be used as justification for anyone's personal preferences, notwithstanding that reason may enjoy "a subsidiary role in planning the satisfaction of appetites."[36] Because it provides no standards, the morality of desire, according to Unger, has to be "condemned" as "an ethic that is no ethic at all" but, at best, "an inadequate descriptive psychology."[37] Going further yet, Unger has urged that the "morality of desire" is inadequate even as a descriptive psychology because of "its failure to account for how in fact we praise and blame and for how our practices of moral judgment are connected with the development of our appetites and aversions"; the morality of desire "cannonizes contentment as the good, and defines contentment as the satisfaction of desire. But contentment cannot be achieved so long as we lack criteria with which to judge and order our ends. Once a desire is satisfied, another must come to take its place. . . . "[38] Without contentment, therefore, Unger has argued there can be no good; without the satisfaction of desire there is no contentment; desire cannot be satisfied. Insatiable as it is, the "pursuit of pleasure" is "forever condemned to remain a step short of its destination" because the "self" cannot "understand its own moral vocation as distinct from the sum of its particular desires," inasmuch as "it is impossible in the acquisition of knowledge to see a whole as different from the sum of its parts."[39]

Nor, according to Unger, is the "morality of reason" any more tenable than its "rival," the "morality of desire," because of two arguments: "My first objection is directed at the capacity of the morality of reason to serve as the foundation of moral judgments of any kind, and my second argument is concerned with the inadequacy of the way the moralist of reason conceives the moral life."[40] Because of this dilemma, Unger has concluded that "morality must be either workable and incoherent or coherent and unworkable, but it cannot be coherent and workable at the same time. It will always say either too much to be coherent or too little to be workable."[41] Against these criticisms, Unger has postulated that "the antinomy of reason and desire" consists of two "equally untenable and mutually contradictory moral doctrines":

If the morality of desire fails to provide guidance, abandoning us to our random and changing appetites, the morality of reason disregards or suppresses our existence as subjective beings with individual ends. The former prohibits us from bringing our striving to a conclusion; the other does not allow us to strive at all. One never concludes; the other never begins.[42]

In this fashion, Unger has rearticulated the existentialist's predicament of loneliness without guidance or direction in a world where choices bring about a "catch 22." In his 1976 book, Unger expanded significantly on his view of "the predicament of social theory" and offered an incisive regression analysis of the rise and fall of the rule of law in Western societies ("Law and Modernity"), based upon his apprehension that "bureaucratic law and a legal order emerge as alternative responses to the crisis of order that the weakening of custom represents."[43]

Within *Law in Modern Society*, Unger identified three concepts of law: (1) custom, (2) regulatory (bureaucratic) law, and (3) the legal order or legal system: apparently in an increasing order of "autonomy."[44] Unger argued in his 1976 book that law is "autonomous . . . when the rules formulated and enforced by government cannot be persuasively analyzed as a mere restatement of any identifiable set of nonlegal beliefs or norms, be they economic, political, or religious":

More specifically, an autonomous legal system does not codify a particular theology. As a body of profane rules, it stands apart from the precepts that govern man's relationship to God and from any single religion's view of social relations. . . . [L]egal reasoning has a method or style to differentiate it from scientific explanation and from moral, political, and economic discourse. . . . A special group, the legal profession, . . . manipulates the rules, staffs the legal institutions, and engages in the practice of legal argument.[45]

Unger noticed that in the liberal state "there is a separate body of legal norms, a system of specialized legal institutions, a well-defined tradition of legal doctrine, and a legal profession with its own relatively unique outlook, interests, and ideals," but, nevertheless, regulatory law persists "in the form of policy decisions or administrative commands" and customary law persists "in the patterns of interactional expectations and usages on which the legal order relies and which it influences."[46] Thus, nihilist or not, Unger succeeded in challenging the "autonomy" not only of the legal system but of its bureaucrats that include lawyers, judges, law school professors, and deans.[47]

Unger indicated almost a decade later in his monumental 1983 *Harvard Law Review* article, "The Critical Legal Studies Movement," that this movement has had split roots:

Two main tendencies can be distinguished in the critical legal studies movement. One tendency sees past or contemporary doctrine as the expression of a particular vision of society while emphasizing the contradictory and manipulable character of doctrinal argument. Its immediate antecedents lie in antiformalist legal theories and structuralist approaches to cultural history. . . . Another tendency grows out of the social theories of Marx and Weber and the mode of social and historical analysis that combines functionalist methods with radical aims. Its point of departure has been the thesis that law and legal doctrine reflect, confirm, and reshape the social divisions and hierarchies inherent in a type or stage of social organization such as "capitalism."[48]

Unger observed that both "tendencies" do several things:

1. Criticize the dominant style of legal doctrine and the legal theories that try to refine and preserve this style.

2. Repudiate in the course of this critique the attempt to impute current social arrangements to the requirements of industrial society, human nature, or moral orders.

3. Have yet to take a clear position on the method, the content, and even the possibility of prescriptive and programmatic thought, perhaps because some of the assumptions inherited from the radical tradition make it hard to turn constructive proposals into more than statements of commitment or anticipations of history.[49]

In this fashion, clearly, Unger obviated the basic differences between the existential tenets of the critical legal studies movement and the analytic philosophy of "critical criminology" discussed in Chapter 8, although some overlap is evident, particularly between analytic and existential marxists.[50] Even marxian existentialists do not deny but that factors other than economics shape the law.

Critical legal studies scholars have yet to write extensively within the area of criminal law but have done so mainly within civil law areas such as contracts and torts. Yet, civil law is not so different from the criminal law but that inferences may be drawn as to how these thinkers would evaluate the criminal law evolution. In a major article, Professor Duncan Kennedy identified three overlapping periods within which he found different phases of an ongoing conflict between "altriusm" and "individualism."[51] Professor Peter Gabel concretized such periods, again as to civil law, by comparing two landmark contract cases, one decided by the Supreme Court of the United State in 1885,[52] and the other by the New York Court of Appeals in 1918.[53] In the 1885 case, Gabel argued, the court accepted the premise that a contract imposes *absolute* liability, whereas twenty-five years later the New York court recognized *relative* liability.[54] Moreover, the earlier case treated contracts as raising primarily questions of *law*, but the latter case realized that contracts may raise questions of *fact*.[55] As part of the law's development from a "harsh" to a "fair" rule, Gabel discerned that social norms, such as "trade usage and custom," became considered by the 1918 court, unlike the 1885 court.[56] Thus, by 1918, "good faith" became a factor that could mitigate the letter of the contract law.[57] "Taken together," Gabel argued, "these movements in legal consciousness make up what is usually called the decline of formalism." [58] Is there not a parallel, partial if not complete, between this "decline of formalism" and the rise of the "exclusionary rule" with the Supreme Court's 1914 decision in *Weeks v. United States*?[59] Similarly, is there not a parallel with the "selective incorporation" of some portions of the Bill of Rights, *seriatim*, before and during the "criminal law revolution" of the 1960s?[60]

The critical legal studies movement has inspired some limited analysis of the substantive, if not the procedural, criminal law. One such effort was made by Professor Mark Kelman, in which he has argued that interpretive constructs of the substantive criminal law, such as absolute intentionalism and dogmatic rules, are legal fictions.[61] Kelman has identified both "broad and narrow" usage of different constructs, whichever functions better at the moment.[62] Thus, for example, a "narrow time frame focus obliterates the difficulties of deciding what constitutes a reasonable belief" that a girl has reached the age of consent in a statutory rape case,[63] an example of strict criminal liability; but "[b]road time-framing is used in the abandonment area because the general rule-oriented nature of the criminal law has already stumbled in the less rule-like attempt area."[64] Similarly, according to Kelman, the "shift between broad and narrow views of the defendant occurs in concurrence doctrine, which requires a union between actus reus and mens rea. . . . Except for felony-murder, we [purportedly] do not transfer or impute the mens rea of one crime to another one. . . . "[65] Yet, Kelman argues, the Model Penal Code definition of negligence "requires that the risk taken must be one that would be avoided by a reasonable person '*in the actor's* situation.' "[66] Thus, a defendant's view could vary according to his "class"—i.e., whether, as a gas meter thief, he deals with gas meters in general or poisonous substances in general.[67] Similarly, Kelman criticizes the "imperfect self-defense" (where a defendant reasonably believes his attacker is using imminent deadly force but a reasonable person would not)[68] and "impossible attempts" (such as where the goods the defendant thought he would receive had already been recovered by the police, and consequently, were no longer stolen).[69]

THE WILL TO POWER

The criminal is the exploiter! He is the capitalist *par excellence*. He is the one who is willing to take property forcibly away from other people, perhaps even their lives. He does so because of his wish to do so, and he wants to do so because he must pursue his "will to power," that being part of man's innate drive to dominate others. The will to power is the same force that compels the survival of the species and that establishes each creature's position within the wolfpack. Of course, the will to power manifests itself differently from one person to the next. We are all criminals! However, our criminality we pursue in different ways. Some of it the law overlooks. Some of it we succeed in keeping hidden. The actual variety of criminal behavior in which a person engages is a function, in part at least, of his varying life experiences and those of his ancestors accumulated within his collective unconscious. Thus, one person's will to power impels him to steal, while another's impels him to sell drugs, and yet another's impels him to kill.

Animals, including people, possess differential levels of ferocity, or propensities toward violence. The lion roars, the wolf howls, the coyote screeches, each giving the impression of being willing to do impending predations. Ferocity is but one product of the will of power. However, ferocity is a negative predictor of powerfulness because a truly powerful man or beast does not need to be ferocious. He takes what food he needs to eat and does so as silently as possible, without further ado. The man or beast who screams or acts as a predator beyond the force necessary to survive attempts to disguise his powerlessness by pretending to be powerful. Bluffing is one way of communicating one's will to power.

People learn various methods of maneuvering their will to power, often through differential association with other people, as Sutherland and others have noted, or through differential opportunities, as Cloward and Ohlin have observed. Thus, the predelinquent learns the skills and techniques necessary for a criminal career. But at the root of his desire for a criminal career in the first place is the will to power which each person harbors notwithstanding his social interaction or opportunity.

Just as some people learn how to temper their will to power—to displace it, to sublimate it, or otherwise to curtail their criminal propensities—others learn to propel it as they proceed vigorously into criminal careers. As people proceed on through life, as they grow, they become committed to specific outlets for fulfilling their will to power.

A fundamental outlet for this fulfillment is procreation, the desire to enlarge one's sphere of influence exponentially through bearing or siring children. Another outlet is spiritualism, where the priest leads his flock in search of eternal grace. The "good parent" and the "poor priest" resist temptations to steal or to rape, for instance, because getting caught at these socially scorned activities would render them powerless to continue raising their children or leading their flock, who would lose faith in them. A third outlet for the fulfillment of the will to power is in the military, where on account of a rigid caste system almost everyone exercises some individual power over someone else by virtue of rank. Collectively, marching armies, sailing navies, and flying air forces exercise power over allied and enemy warriors and civilians alike by force or threat of force, much as does the roaring lion in the wild jungle. A fourth outlet is business, a generally nonviolent arena of combat, where competition in the marketplace for economic profit and career advancement fulfills the will to power among the successful. A fifth outlet is politics, where private individuals are invested with public authority. Jurists sit in judgment to decide the innocence or guilt of accused criminal offenders. Police officers have discretion to make arrests or avoid them, of directing traffic, of forcibly entering people's homes. Correctional officers exercise dominion and control over prisoners, regulating the daily lives of their charges. The executioner, acting under power of law, exercises the ultimate will to power when he kills with impunity pursuant to a death warrant.

The law condones these manifestations of the will to power, even encourages them and sometimes commands them. These socially powerful people resist the temptations to exceed the scope of their sanctioned power bases, ordinarily, because getting caught means getting fired. However, *because* the *officially powerful* have vested interests in the maintenance of their official power bases and the appearances of legitimacy, they must forbear crime, notwithstanding their latent wish to become criminals and increase the scope of their power thereby. Due to their secret longing for criminal careers, they come to despise the criminals and, consequently, to deal harshly with convicted offenders.

LATENT AND BLATANT CRIME

When a person becomes thwarted in the exercise of his will to power, on the other hand, his first and ultimate task must be to restore it, no matter what the means or what the consequences. Thus, when the parent loses the respect of his or her children, when the priest is exposed as a hypocrite, when the soldier or sailor is court-martialed, when the businessperson is accused of unfair practices, or when the public official is exposed as being corrupt, it becomes gradually less important and finally unimportant whether he must resort to open criminal actions to restore his will to power. Thus, for instance, a police officer who has been exposed as being corrupt and has been fired may provide muscle for the mob; the narcotics detective who has been demoted may become a drug dealer; the vice detective a pimp. We are all latent criminals but, if exposed, we become blatant offenders. Even if not exposed as a criminal, ex-public officials tend to display their will to power by attacking their successors in public office. For example, the prosecutor who steps down ''to earn more money'' or is voted out of office is likely to publicize his demand as a defense lawyer by letting it be known, or at least supposed, that his inside knowledge of the courthouse can be used as easily to defeat the ''system'' as to maintain it.

CHANNELS AND LOCKS

Upon entering what may best be described as the channel separating latent from blatant crime, when the potential offender knowingly and intentionally violates the criminal law, he becomes confronted with locks through which he must pass continously to maintain his will to power. These locks separate degrees of criminality, and by passing through each lock the offender becomes elevated progressively into activities that entail ''higher'' levels of risk, more severe crime, greater perpetration of harm to victims, but concomitantly greater subcultural ''respect'' among other blatant criminal offenders. While one may begin criminal activity to fulfill conventional ambitions as part of a noncriminal will to power, the need to replicate crimes becomes paramount as the blatant criminal witnesses his growing powerlessness in the face of authority once his criminality becomes exposed.

Thus, one who stole originally to start a business, upon being exposed as a thief may not be able to maintain the business. Instead, he finds that he must continue to steal. Stealing becomes his business, the only means to fullfill his will to power. Ultimately, perpetration of criminal episodes itself, rather than value derived therefrom, may come to fulfill the blatant criminal's will to power. As he witnesses the powerlessness into which society relegates him on account of his being exposed as a blatant criminal, such an offender may incur a pathological desire to confound society. The will to power then drives this person to kill for the thrill of killing.

NOTES

1. CRITIQUE OF PURE REASON (1781), CRITIQUE OF PRACTICAL REASON (1788), and CRITIQUE OF JUDGMENT (1790). See R. von Kroner, KANT BIS HEGEL (1921–1924); S. Korner, KANT (1955); and J. Kemp, THE PHILOSOPHY OF KANT (1968).

2. See H. Blackham, SIX EXISTENTIALIST THINKERS (1959).

3. J. Sartre, *Existentialism Is a Humanism*, in W. Kaufmann, ed., EXISTENTIALISM FROM DOSTOEVSKY TO SARTRE 289 (1956).

4. F. Nietzsche, BEYOND GOOD AND EVIL 262 (W. Kaufmann, tr., 1966).

5. *Id.* at 259. (Emphasis in the original.)

6. *Id.* at 36. (Emphasis in the original.)

7. F. Nietzsche, THE WILL TO POWER 619 (W. Kaufmann and R. Hollingdale, trs., 1967). See also 658.

8. *Id.* at 1041.

9. *Id.* at 1050.

10. *Id.* at 1051. (Emphasis in the original.)

11. *Supra*, note 4 at 108.

12. *Supra*, note 7 at 256.

13. *Supra*, note 4 at 221. (Emphasis in the original.)

14. Nietzsche's most famous book, and perhaps his best, was ALSO SPRACH ZARATHUSTRA (Thus Spake Zarathustra), published in four parts between 1883 and 1892.

15. F. Dostoevsky, CRIME AND PUNISHMENT Part V, chap. 4 (1866–67).

16. *Id.*

17. Nietzsche felt ethical values can and should be "willed" by people with strong, decisive personalities whom he called "Uebermenschen" ("Overmen" or Supermen). See F. Nietzsche, BEYOND GOOD AND EVIL 56 (H. Zimmern, tr., 1907).

18. *Id.* at 227–28. (Emphasis in the original.)

19. *Id.* at 229–30. (Emphasis in the original.)

20. *Id.* at 28.

21. F. Nietzsche, THE DAWN OF DAY 170 (J. Volz, tr., 1903).

22. F. Nietzsche, DIE FROHLICHE WISSENSCHAFT 214–215 (1900). Translated in R. Beck, PERSPECTIVES IN PHILOSOPHY 371–72 (1961). (Emphasis in the original).

23. See R. Unger, *The Critical Legal Studies Movement*, 96 HARV. L. REV. 563 (1983).

24. See J. Schlegel, *Introduction*, 28 BUFF. L. REV. 203 (1979), introducing D. Kennedy, *The Structure of Blackstone's Commentaries*, 28 BUFF. L. REV. 205 (1979), and other "critical legal studies" essays.

25. R. Unger, KNOWLEDGE AND POLITICS 52 (1975).

26. See, *inter alia*, D. Caplan, *A Scholarly War of Words over Academic*

Freedom, 7 THE NAT'L. L. J. 1 (February 11, 1985). See also P. Carrington, *Of Law and the River*, 34 J. LEG. ED. 222 (June 1984).

27. See R. Schacht, HEGEL AND AFTER 175–76 (1975).

28. Jaspers, Lowith, Morgan, and Kaufman have argued against Nietzsche's being a nihilist. *Id*. at 177.

29. Danto has argued that nihilism is "the central concept of his philosophy." A. Danto, NIETZSCHE AS PHILOSOPHER 22 (1965).

30. *Supra*, note 26. Carrington has insisted: "One cannot believe in the worth of one's professional skill and judgment as a lawyer unless one also has some minimal belief in the idea of law and the institutions that enforce it. What cannot abide is the embrace of nihilism and its lesson that who decides is everything, and the principle nothing but cosmetic." P. Carrington, *Of Law and the River*, 34, J. LEG. ED. 222, 227 (June 1984).

31. *Supra*, note 25.

32. R. Unger, LAW IN MODERN SOCIETY 1–46 (1976).

33. *Supra*, note 25.

34. *Id*. at 51–55, 52.

35. *Id*. at 52.

36. *Id*.

37. *Id*.

38. *Id*. at 52–53.

39. *Id*. at 53.

40. *Id*.

41. *Id*.

42. *Id*. at 54.

43. *Supra*, note 32 at 134. Unger noted that the "development to which I have referred did not occur everywhere at the same pace or with the same emphasis. There were countries in which the centralizing impetus of the monarch prevailed over the autonomy of the estates and the defense of their law. . . . In other societies, . . . a renewed aristocracy, often in alliance with enriched merchants groups and with the professional people, captured a major part of the state machine." *Id*. at 164.

44. *Id*. at 49–52.

45. *Id*. at 53.

46. *Id*. at 54–55.

47. *Supra*, notes 26 and 30.

48. *Supra*, note 23 at 563, n. 1. Unger has offered, as examples of the first "tendency," D. Kennedy, *The Structure of Blackstone's Commentaries*, 28 BUFF. L. REV. 205 (1979), and M. Kelman, *Interpretive Construction in the Substantive Criminal Law*, 33 STAN. L. REV. 591 (1981); and as examples of the second "tendency," D. Trubek, *Complexity and Contradiction in the Law*, 11 LAW & SOC'Y. REV. 527 (1977), plus D. Kairys, ed., THE POLITICS OF LAW: A PROGRESSIVE CRITIQUE (1982).

49. *Id*. Unger conceded that many writings fall within neither "tendency," such as Gordon, *Historicism in Legal Scholarship*, 90 YALE L. J. 1017 (1981);

Parker, *The Past of Constitutional Theory—And Its Future*, 42 OHIO ST. L. J. 223 (1981); Simon, *The Ideology of Advocacy: Procedural Justice and Professional Ethics*, 1978, WIS. L. REV. 29 (1978); and Stone, *The Post-War Paradigm in American Labor Law*, 90 YALE L. J. 1509 (1981). *Id*. at 564, n. 1.

50.   One difference between critical legal studies and marxian "critical criminology" is that, in the former, unlike the latter, "there is no claim that other structures besides the economic are irrelevant to legal discourse," but only "that the economic structure is dominant and mediates others." See P. Gabel, *Intention and Structure in Contractual Conditions: Outline of a Method of Critical Legal Theory*, 61 MINN. L. REV. 601, 619, n. 27 (1977). See also D. Kennedy, *Form and Substance in Private Law Adjudication*, 80 HARV. L. REV. 1685, 1728 (1976), and L. Althusser, *Structure in Dominance: Contradiction and Overdetermination*, in FOR MARX 200–218 (1970).

51.   D. Kennedy, *Form and Substance in Private Law Adjudication*, 89 HARV. L. REV. 1685, 1725–37 (1976). The periods are 1800–1870, 1850–1940, and 1900–present.

52.   NORRINGTON V. WRIGHT, 115 U.S. 188 (1885).

53.   HELGAR CORP. V. WARNER'S FEATURES, INC., 222 N. Y. 449, 119 N. E. 113 (1918).

54.   P. Gabel, *Intention and Structure in Contractual Conditions: Outline of a Method for Critical Legal Theory*, 61 MINN. L. REV. 601, 612 (1977). In other words, the older case accepted no "degrees of default" on a contract, which the newer case did accept.

55.   In the *Helgar* case, 1918, unlike the *Norrington* case, 1885, the court left various factual judgments such as purpose, intent, and willfullness to the jury. *Id*.

56.   *Id*.

57.   *Id*.

58.   *Id*. at 613.

59.   232 U.S. 383 (1914).

60.   See D. Jones, THE LAW OF CRIMINAL PROCEDURE—AN ANALYSIS AND CRITIQUE 588 (1981).

61.   M. Kelman, *Interpretive Construction in the Substantive Criminal Law*, 33 STAN. L. REV. 591, 672 (1981).

62.   *Id*. at 596, 600–615, 620, 627–28, 633, 637, 641, 664–65, 667–68.

63.   *Id*. at 606.

64.   *Id*. at 612.

65.   *Id*. at 633.

66.   *Id*. at 636. (Emphasis in the original.)

67.   *Id*.

68.   *Id*. at 616.

69.   *Id*. at 620–22.

Bibliography

Adams, S. "The Jukes Myth." 2 *Saturday Review* 48, 1955.

Akers, R. *Deviant Behavior: A Social Learning Approach*. Belmont, 1977.

Akers, R. et al. "Social Learning and Deviant Behavior: A Specific Test of a General Theory." 44 *American Sociological Review* 636, 1979.

Alder, H. and M. Worthington. "The Scope of the Problem of Delinquency and Crime as Related to Mental Deficiency." 30 *Journal of Psycho-Aesthetics* 47, 1925.

Alexander, F. and W. Healy. *Roots of Crime*. New York, 1935.

Alexander, F. and H. Straub. *The Criminal, the Judge, and the Public*. Glencoe, 1956.

Alinsky, S. *Reveille for Radicals*. Chicago, 1946.

Allen, G. *Legal Duties*. Oxford, 1931.

Ancel, M. *The Indeterminate Sentence*. New York, 1954.

Annan, N. *The Curious Strength of Positivism in English Political Thought*. London, 1959.

St. Anselm. *Prologion*. S. Deane, tr. Chicago, 1903.

St. Thomas Aquinas. *Summa Theologica*. New York, 1911.

Aristotle. *Nicomachean Ethics*. F. Peters, tr. London, 1898.

Aschaffenburg, G. *Crime and Its Repression*. A. Albrecht, (tr.) Munich, 1903; reprinted Montclair, 1968.

St. Augustine. *City of God*. J. Healey, tr. London, 1893.

Baer, A. *Der Verbrecher in Anthropologischer-Beziehung*. Leipsig, 1893.

Bandura, A. *Aggression: A Social Learning Analysis*. Englewood Cliffs, 1973.

———. "The Social Learning Perspective: Mechanisms of Aggression," in H. Toch, ed., *Psychology of Crime and Criminal Justice*, 1979.

———. *Social Learning Theory*. Englewood Cliffs, 1977.

Bar, K. *A History of Continental Criminal Law*. South Hackensack, 1968.

Barnes, H. "The Historical Origin of the Prison System in America." 12 *Journal of Criminal Law and Criminology* 58, 1921.

———. *The Evolution of Penology in Pennsylvania: A Study in American Social History*. 1927; reprinted Montclair, 1968.

———. *The Repression of Crime: Studies in Historical Penology*. 1926; reprinted Montclair, 1969.

———, and N. Teeters. *New Horizons for Criminology*. Englewood Cliffs, 1951.

Barry, J. *Alexander Maconochie of Norfolk Island: A Study of a Pioneer in Penal Reform*. Melbourne and London, 1958.

Beccaria, C. *Essay on Crimes and Punishment*. H. Paolucci, tr. Indianapolis, 1963.

von Bemmelen, J. "The Constancy of Crime." 2 *British Journal of Criminology* 208, 1952.

————. "Willem Adriaan Bonger," in H. Mannheim, ed., *Pioneers in Criminology*. Chicago, 1960; reprinted Montclair, 1972.

Bentham, J. *A Fragment on Government and an Introduction to the Principles of Morals and Legislation*. J. Barns and H. Hart, eds. London, 1982.

————. *The Constitutional Code*. 17; reprinted New York, 1983.

————. *Panopticon or Inspection House*. London, 1791.

————. *The Rationale of Punishment*. R. Smith, tr. London, 1830.

————. *Theory of Legislation*. R. Hildreth, tr. London, 1905.

Bernaldo de Quirós, C. *Modern Theories of Criminality*. A de Salvio, tr. Boston, 1911.

Bianchi, H. *Position and Subject-Matter of Criminology*. Amsterdam, 1956.

Blackham, H. *Six Existentialist Thinkers*. London, 1952.

Blackstone, W. *Commentaries on the Laws of England*. London: 1952.

Bogen, D. "Juvenile Delinquency and Economic Trends." 9 *American Sociological Review* 178, 1944.

Bonger, H. *Introduction to Criminology*. Haarlem, 1932 and London, 1936.

————. *Race and Crime*. Haarlem, 1939, and London, 1943; reprinted Montclair, 1969.

Bonger, W. *Criminality and Economic Conditions*. H. Horton,tr. Boston, 1916.

Bowring, J. ed. *The Works of Jeremy Bentham*. London, 1843.

Burgess, E. "The Growth of the City," in R. Parks, E. Burgess and R. McKenzie, eds., *The City: The Ecological Approach to the Study of the Human Community*. Chicago, 1928.

Burgess, E. et al. "The Chicago Area Project." *National Probation Association Yearbook* 8, 1937.

Burgess, R. and R. Akers. "A Differential Association—Reinforcement Theory of Criminal Behavior." 14 *Social Problems* 128, 1966.

Caldwell, C. *Elements of Phrenology*. New York, 1824.

Cantor, N. *Crime and Society*. New York, 1939.

Carpenter, M. *Our Convicts*. London, 1864; reprinted Montclair, 1969.

Carr-Saunders, A. et al. *Young Offenders: An Enquiry into Juvenile Delinquency*. Cambridge, England, 1942.

Carus, C. *Principles of a New Scientific Craniology*. Berlin, 1840.

Chilton, R. "Continuity in Delinquency Area Research: A Comparison of Studies for Baltimore, Detroit and Indianapolis." 29 *American Sociological Review* 71, 1946.

Chinard, G. ed. *The Commonplace Book of Thomas Jefferson: A Repertory of His Ideas on Government. Boston, 1939*.

Chirics, T. and G. Waldo. "Socioeconomic Status and Criminal Sentencing: An Empirical Assessment of a Conflict Proposition." 40 *American Sociological Review* 768 , 1975.

Christiansen, K. *Kriminologie*. 000; reprinted Rutherford, 1983.

Clark, J. and E. Wenninger "Socio-Economic Class and Area Correlates of Illegal Behavior Among Juveniles," in M. Wolfgang, et al., eds., *The Sociology of Crime and Delinquency*. New York, 1970.

Clay, J. "On the Effect of Good and Bad Times on Commitals to Prison." 18 *Journal of the Statistical Society of London* 74, 1855.

Clay, W. *The Prison Chaplain*. London, 1861; reprinted Montclair, 1969.

Clinard, M. *Anomie and Deviant Behavior*. Glencoe, 1964.

Clinard, M. and R. Quinney. *Criminal Behavior System: A Typology*. New York, 1973.

Cloward, R. and L. Ohlin. *Delinquency and Opportunity*. Glencoe, 1960.

Cohen, A. et al., eds. *The Sutherland Papers*. Bloomington, 1956.

Colinvaux, P. *Introduction to Ecology*. New York, 1973.

Colquhoun, P. "A Treatise on the Police of the Metropolis," in A. Cohen, et al., eds. *The Sutherland Papers*. Bloomington, 1956.

Cortés, J. with F. Gatti. *Delinquency and Crime: A Biopsychosocial Approach*. New York, 1972.

Coser, L. *The Functions of Social Conflict*. Glencoe, 1956.

Crawford, W. *Report on the Penitentiaries of the United States*. 1835: reprinted Montclair, 1969.

Critchley, T. *A History of Police in England and Wales*. New York, 1967.

Currie, E. "A Dialogue with Anthony Platt." 8 *Issues in Criminology* 28, 1973.

Dahrendorf, R. *Class and Conflict in Industrial Society*. Palo Alto, 1958.

———. "Out of Utopia: Toward a Reorientation of Sociological Analysis." 64 *American Journal of Sociology* 45, 1958.

———. "Toward a Theory of Social Conflict." 2 *Journal of Conflict Resolution*. 170, 1958.

Darwin, C. *The Descent of Man*. New York, 1902.

———. *The Expression of the Emotions in Man and Animals*. Chicago, 1965.

Davenport, C. "Heredity and Crime." 13 *American Journal of Sociology* 402, 1907.

———. *Heredity and Crime*. New York, 1911.

de Fleur, L. "Ecological Variables in Cross-Cultural Study of Delinquency." 45 *Social Forces* 556, 1967.

de Vries, H. *The Mutation Theory*. J. Furmer and A. Darbishire, trs. Chicago, 1909–10.

Dewey, J. *The Public and Its Problems*. New York, 1927.

Doleschal, E. and N. Klapmuts. "Toward a New Criminology." 5 *Crime and Delinquency* 607, 1973.

Dostoevsky, F. *Crime and Punishment*. C. Garnett, tr. New York, 1965.

Douglas, J. "Deviance and Order in a Pluralistic Society," in J. McKinney and E. Tiryakian, eds., *Theoretical Sociology: Perspectives and Development*. Chicago, 1970. "Draft of a Prison System." *Transactions of the Fourth National Prison Congress*, New York, 1876.

Drahms, A. *The Criminal: His Personnel and Environment*. 1900; reprinted Montclair, 1971.

Driver, E. "Charles Buckman Goring," in H. Mannheim, ed., *Pioneers in Criminology*. Chicago, 1960; reprinted Montclair, 1972.

Dugdale, R. *The Jukes: A Study in Crime, Pauperism, Disease, and Heredity*. New York, 1877.

Durkheim, E. *De la division du Travail Social*. Paris, 1927.

———. *The Rules of Sociological Method*. S. Solovay and J. Mueller, trs. Glencoe, 1965.

———. *Suicide*. J. Spaulding, tr. New York, 1951 and Glencoe, 1966.

East, N. *The Adolescent Criminal*. London, 1942.
————. *Society and the Criminal*. London, 1949.
Eells, K. *Intelligence and Cultural Differences*. Chicago, 1951.
Elliot, D. and H. Voss *Delinquency and Dropout*. Lexington, 1974.
Ellis, H. *The Criminal*. London and New York, 1913; reprinted Montclair, 1973.
Elmes, J. *Hints for the Improvement of Prisons*. London, 1817.
Elton, C. *The Ecology of Invasions by Animals and Plants*. New York, 1958.
Empey, L. *American Delinquency*. New York, 1978.
————. *Juvenile Justice*. New York, 1979.
Engels, F. *The Condition of the Working Class in England in 1844*. London, 1892.
Esmein, A. *Histoire de la Procedure Criminelle en France*. Paris, 1973.
Estabrook, A. *The Jukes in 1915*. New York, 1916.
Exner, F. *Kriminalbiologie*. Munich, 1939.

Faulds, "On the Skin Furrows of the Hand." *Nature*, 1880.
Ferrero, G. *Criminal Man According to the Classification of Caesare Lombroso*. 1911;
    reprinted Montclair, 1972.
Ferri, E. "Dei limiti fra diritto penale ed antropologia criminale." 1 *Archivio di psi-
    chiatria*, 1880.
————. *Principiis di diritto penale*. Torino, 1928.
————. *Criminal Sociology*. J. Kelley and J. Lisle, trs. Boston, 1917.
————. "The Delinquent in Art and Literature." 60 *Atlantic* 233, 1897.
————. *The Positive School of Criminology*. Chicago, 1913.
Fink, A. *The Causes of Crime: Biological Theories in the United States, 1800–1915*.
    Philadelphia, 1938.
Fletcher, J. "Moral and Educational Statistics of England and Wales." 12 *Journal of
    the Statistical Society of London* 51, 1849.
Fletcher, R. "The New School of Criminal Anthropology." 4 *American Anthropologist*
    201, 1891.
Forsyth, W. *History of Trial by Jury*. London, 1852.
Fox, R. "The XYY Offender: A Modern Myth." 62 *Journal of Criminal Law* 199,
    1970.
Freud, S. *The Complete Works of Sigmund Freud*. London and Frankfurt, 1940.
Friedlander, K. *The Psycho-Analytical Approach to Juvenile Delinquency*. London, 1947.

Gallie, W. "Liberal Morality and Socialist Morality." *Philosophy* 24, 1949.
Galton, F. Fingerprints. London and New York, 1893.
Garofalo, R. *Criminology*. R. Millar, tr. Boston, 1914; reprinted Montclair, 1968.
Gillin, J. *Criminology and Penology*. New York, 3rd ed. 1945.
Glaser, D. and K. Rice. "Crime, Age and Employment." 24 *American Sociological
    Review* 679, 1959.
————. *Crime in Our Changing Society*. New York, 1978.
Glover, E. *The Roots of Crime*. London, 1960.
Glueck, S. *Mental Disorder and the Criminal Law*. Boston, 1925.
————. "Theory and Fact in Criminology: A Criticism of Differential Association." 7
    British Journal of Criminology 92, 1956.
Glueck, S. and E. Glueck. *Physique and Delinquency*. New York, 1956.
————. *Unraveling Juvenile Delinquency*. New York, 1950.

Goddard, H. *Feeblemindedness*. New York, 1914.

———. *The Kallikak Family: A Study in Heredity of Feeblemindedness*. New York, 1925.

Goffman, E. *Stigma: Notes on the Management of Spoiled Identity*. New York, 1963.

Gordon, D. "Capitalism, Class and Crime in America." 19 *Crime and Delinquency* 163, 1973.

———. "Class and the Economics of Crime." 3 *Review of Radical Politics and Economics* 51, 1971.

Gordon, R. "Prevalence: The Rare Data in Delinquency Measurement and Its Implications for the Theory of Delinquency," in M. Klein, ed., *The Juvenile Justice System*. New York, 1976.

Goring, C. *The English Convict: A Statistical Study*. London, 1913; reprinted Montclair, 1972 with the *Schedule of Measurements and General Anthropological Data*.

Gross, H. *Criminal Psychology*. H. Kallen, tr. Vienna, 1897 and Boston, 1912.

———. *Encyclopaedia of Criminalistics*. Leipzig, 1901.

———. *Handbuch fr̈ Untersuchungsrichter*. Munich, 1893.

Grünhut, M. *Penal Reform*. 1948; reprinted Montclair, 1972.

Guttentag, M. "The Relationship of Unemployment to Crime and Delinquency." 24 *Journal of Social Issues* 105, 1968.

Hagemann, M. *Handwörterbuch der Kriminologie*. Berlin-Leipzig, 1939.

Hayner, N. "Delinquent Areas in the Puget Sound Region." 38 *American Journal of Sociology* 314, 1933.

Healy, W. and A. Bronner. *Delinquency and Criminals: Their Making and Unmaking*. New Haven, 1926; reprinted Montclair, 1969.

———. *New Light on Delinquency and Its Treatment*. New Haven, 1936.

Hirschi, T. *Causes of Delinquency*. Berkeley, 1969.

Hirschi, T. and M. Hindelang. "Intelligence and Delinquency: A Revisionist Review." 42 *American Sociological Review* 572, 1977.

Hodges, D. "Marxism as Social Science." *Marxism*, 1970.

Holland, G. *Vital Statistics of Sheffield*. London, 1843.

Holmes, O. "The Path of the Law." 10 *Harvard Law Review*, 1897.

Home, H. (Lord Kames). *Historical Law-Tracts: Criminal Law*. Edinburgh, 1792.

Hooton, E. *The American Criminal: An Anthropological Study*. Cambridge, 1939; reprinted Montclair, 1969.

———. *Crime and the Man*. Cambridge, 1939.

Hopkins, A. *Prisons and Prison Building*. New York, 1930.

Horton, J. "The Dehumanization of Anomie and Alienation: A Problem of the Ideology of Sociology." 5 *British Journal of Sociology*, 1964.

Howard, J. *The State of the Prisons in England and Wales*. London, 1792; reprinted Montclair, 1972.

Hunt, C. *Life of Edward Livingston*. New York, 1864.

Hunter, H. "XYY Chromosomes and Klinefelter's Syndrome." 1 *Lancet* 984, 1966.

Hurwitz, S. *Criminology*. Copenhagen, 1935.

Jacobs, P. et al. "Aggressive Behavior, Mental Subnormality, and the XYY Male." 208 *Nature* 1351, 1965.

Jeffery, C. "The Historical Development of Criminology," in H. Mannheim, ed., *Pioneers in Criminology*. Chicago, 1960; reprinted Montclair, 1972.

Jensen, A. *Bias in Mental Testing*. New York, 1980.

———. "How Much Can We Boost IQ and Scholastic Achievement?" 39 *Harvard Education Review* 1, 1969.

Johnson, W. *The T'ang Code*. Princeton, 1979.

Jonassen, C. "A Reevaluation and Critique of the Logic and Some Methods of Shaw and McKay," in H. Vonn and D. Petersen, eds., *Ecology, Crime and Delinquency*. New York, 1971.

Jones, D. *Crime Without Punishment*. Lexington, 1979.

———. *The Health Risks of Imprisonment*. Lexington, 1976.

———. *The Law of Criminal Procedure: An Analysis and Critique*. Boston, 1981.

Jones, D. and C. Jones. *The Sociology of Correctional Management*. New York, 1976.

Kamin, L. "Burt's IQ Data." *Science*, 1977.

Kant, I. *Critique of Pure Reason*. Leipzig, 1781; reprinted New York, 1929 and 1965.

———. *Critique of Practical Research*. Leipzig, 1788; reprinted New York, 1956.

———. *Critique of Judgment*. Leipzig, 1790; reprinted Oxford, 1928.

Keeton, G. and G. Schwarzenberger, eds. *Jeremy Bentham and the Law*. 1948.

Kemp, J. *The Philosophy of Kant*. London and New York, 1968.

Kenison, F. "Charles Doe," in H. Mannheim. ed., *Pioneers in Criminology*. Chicago, 1960; reprinted Montclair, 1972.

Kinberg, O. *Basic Problems of Criminology*. Copenhagen, 1935.

Kobrin, S. "The Chicago Area Project: A 25-Year Assessment." *Annals of the American Society of Political and Social Science* 19, 1959.

———. "The Formal Logical Properties of the Shaw-McKay Delinquency Theory," in H. Voss and D. Petersen, eds., *Ecology, Crime and Delinquency*. New York, 1971.

Kobrin, S. et al. "Criteria of Status Among Street Groups." 4 *Journal of Research in Crime and Delinquency* 98, 1967.

Korner, S. *Kant*. New Haven, 1955 and 1982.

Kretschmer, E. *Körperbau und Charakter*. Munich, 1921.

Krisberg, B. *Crime and Privilege: Toward a New Criminology*. Englewood Cliffs, 1975.

Lacassagne, J. "Marche de la criminalité en France de 1825 à 1880." *Revue scientifique* 674, 1881.

Landers, B. *Towards and Understanding of Juvenile Delinquency*. New York, 1954.

Lane, R. *Policing the City: Boston 1822–1855*. Cambridge, 1967.

Lasswell, H. and A. Kaplan. *Power and Society*. New Haven, 1950.

Latham, E. *The Group Basis for Politics*. Ithaca, 1952.

Leek, S. *Phrenology*. New York, 1970.

Lemert, E. *Human Deviance, Social Problems, and Social Control*. New York, 1967.

———. *Social Pathology*. New York, 1951.

Lewis, N. *A Short History of Psychiatric Achievement*. New York, 1941.

Lewis, O. *The Development of American Prisons and Prison Customs, 1776–1845*. 1922; reprinted Montclair, 1967.

Lewis, W. *From Newgate to Dannemora*. Ithaca, 1965.

Lindesmith, A. and Y. Levin. "The Lombrosian Myth in Criminology." 42 *American Journal of Sociology* 653, 1937.

von List, F. *Strafrechtliche Aufsätze und Vorträge*. Berlin, 1905.

Lombroso, C. "Atavism and Evolution." *Contemporary Review, July, 1895*.

———. *Crime: Its Causes and Remedies*. Boston, 1912; reprinted Montclair, 1968.

———. *L'Uomo delinquente*. Milan, 1876 and Torin, 1878.

Lombroso, C. and G. Ferrero. *The Female Offender*. London and New York, 1895.

Lottier, S. "Distribution of Criminal Offenses in Metropolitan Regions." 29 *Journal of Criminal Law, Criminology and Police Science*, 1939.

Maclean, N. et al. "A Survey of Sex Chromosome Anomalies Among 4, 515 Mental Defectives." 1 *Lancet* 293, 1962.

Maestro, M. *Ceasare Beccaria and the Origins of Penal Reform*. Philadelphia, 1973.

Maine, H. *Ancient Law*. New York, 1864.

Maitland, F. *Justice and Police*. London, 1885.

Mann, E. *Manual of Psychological Medicine and Allied Nervous Disorders*. New York, 1883.

Mannheim, H. *Group Problems in Crime and Punishments*. Montclair, 1971.

———. ed. *Pioneers in Criminology*. Chicago, 1960; reprinted Montclair, 1972.

Mark, V. and F. Ervin. *Violence and the Brain*. New York, 1970.

Martineau, H., tr. *The Positive Philosophy of Auguste Comte*. New York, 1858.

Marx, K. *Theories of Surplus Value*. R. Simpson, tr. London, 1969.

Mayhew, H. and J. Binney. *The Criminal Prisons of London*. London, 1862.

von Mayr, G. *Moral Statistik mit Einscluss der Kriminal Statistik*. 1917.

McElwee, T. *A Concise History of Eastern Penitentiary of Pennsylvania*. Philadelphia, 1835.

McKelvey, B. *American Prisons* Chicago, 1936; reprinted Montclair, 1968.

McRae, I. "The Ying Concubine." *District Lawyer*, Vol. 8, No. 5, pp. 39–47, 1984.

Merton, R. "Social Structure and Anomie." *American Sociological Review*, 1938.

———. *Social Theory and Social Structure*. Glencoe, 1957.

Merton, R. and A. Ashley-Montagu, "Crime and the Anthropologist." 42 *American Anthropologist* 384, 1940.

Miller, W. "The Impact of a 'Total-Community' Delinquency Control Project." 10 *Social Problems* 168, 1962.

———. "Lower Class Culture as a Generating Milieu of Gang Delinquency." 14 *Journal of Social Issues* 5, 1958.

Mohr, G. and R. Gundlach. "The Relation Between Physique and Performance." 10 *Journal of Experimental Psychology* 117, 1927.

Morris, T. *The Criminal Area*, London, 1957.

Morrison, W. "Are Our Prisons a Failure?" 61 *Fortnightly Review* 459, 1894.

———. *Crime and Its Causes*. London and New York, 1891.

———. *Juvenile Offenders*. London, 1896 and New York, 1897.

———. "Excessive Sentences." *The Times* (London), February 2, 1892.

———. "The Increase of Crime." 31 *Nineteenth Century* 950, 1892.

———. "The Interpretation of Criminal Statistics." 60 *Journal of the Royal Statistical Society 1, 1897*.

———. *"Prison Reform: Prisons and Prisoners."* 63 *Fortnightly Review* 781, 1898.

———. "The Problem of Crime." 1 *Mind: Quarterly Review of Psychology and Philosophy* 489, 1892.

———. "Reflections on Theories of Criminality." 35 *Journal of Mental Science* 14, 1889.

Murchison, C. *Criminal Intelligence*. Worcester, 1926.

Nagel, E. *Logic without Metaphysics*. Glencoe, 1957.

Neild, J. *State of the Prisons in England, Scotland and Wales*. London, 1812.

Nietzsche, F. *Also sprach Zarathustra*. Leipzig, 1892 and 1922.

———. *Beyond Good and Evil*. W. Kaufmann, tr. New York, 1966.

———. *The Dawn of Day*. J. Volz, tr. New York, 1903.

———. *Die Fröhliche Wissenschaft*. 1901; trans. in R. Beck, *Principles of Philosophy*. New York, 1961.

———. *The Will to Power*. 1889; W. Kaufmann and R. Hollingdale, trs. New York, 1968.

Nordenshiölt, E. *The History of Biology*. New York, 1928.

Noyes, W. "The Criminal Type." 24 *Journal of Social Science* 31, 1888.

von Oettingen, A. *Die Moralistatistik in ihrer Bedeutung für eine Sozialethik*. Erlangen, 1874.

"On the Prisons of France." Twenty-third Annual Report of the Prison Association of New York. Albany, 1868.

Overholser, W. "An Historical Sketch of Psychiatry." 10 *Journal of Clinical Psychopathology*. 1949.

Padua, Marsilius of. *The Defender of Peace*. A. Gewirth, tr. New York, 1927.

Palmer, F. "The Effects of Minimal Early Intervention on Subsequent IQ Scores and Reading Achievement." Report to the Education Commission of the United States, 1976.

Phillipson, C. *Three Criminal Law Reformers: Beccaria, Bentham, Romilly*. New York, 1973.

Pike, L. *A History of Crime in England*. Montclair, 1968.

Pinatel, J. *Traité élémentaire de science pénitentiare et de défense sociale*. Paris, 1950.

Platt, A. "Prospects for a Radical Criminology in the United States." 1 *Journal of Crime and Social Justice* 2, 1974.

Platt, A. et al. "The Origins of the 'Right and Wrong' Test of Criminal Responsibility and Its Subsequent Development in the United States: An Historical Survey." 54 *California Law Review* 1227, 1966.

Polk, K. "Urban Social Areas and Delinquency." 14 *Social Problems* 320, 1967.

Poore, B. *The Federal and State Constitutions, Colonial Charters and Other Organic Laws of the United States*. Washington, D.C., 1878.

Pound, R. "A Survey of Social Interests." 57 *Harvard Law Review* 39, 1943.

———. *Social Control through Law*. New Haven, 1942.

Price, W. and P. Whatmore. "Behavior Disorders and Pattern of Crime in XYY Males Identified at a Maximum Security Hospital." 1 *British Medical Journal* 533, 1967.

Price, W. et al. "Criminal Behavior, Mental Subnormality, and the XYY Male." 213 *Nature* 815, 1965.

Prince, M. *The Dissociation of a Personality*. New York, 1906.

———. *The Unconscious*. New York, 1914.

Plucknett, T. *A Concise History of the Common Law*. London, 1948.

Pudover, S. ed. *The Complete Jefferson*. New York, 1943.

Quinney, R. *Class, State, and Crime*. New York, 1977.

———. *Criminology: Analysis and Critique of Crime in America*. Boston, 1975.

————. *Critique of Legal Order*. Boston, 1975.
————. *The Social Reality of Crime*. Boston, 1970.

Radzinowicz, L. *A History of English Criminal Law and Its Administration from 1740*. London, 1948.
————. *Ideology and Crime*. New York, 1966.
Ray, I. *A Treatise on the Medical Jurisprudence of Insanity*. Boston, 1838.
————. *Contributions to Medical Pathology*. Boston, 1873.
Reckless, W. "Containment Theory," in M. Wolfgang, et al., eds., *The Sociology of Crime and Delinquency*. New York, 1970.
————. *The Crime Problem*. New York, 1961.
Reddaway, W. *Documents of Catherine the Great—The Correspondence with Voltaire and the Instructions of 1767*. London, 1768.
Reik, L. "The Doe-Ray Correspondence, a Pioneer Collaboration in the Jurisprudence of Mental Disease." 63 *Yale Law Journal* 183, 1953.
Reinemann, J. "Juvenile Delinquency in Philadelphia and Economic Trends." 20 *Temple Law Quarterly* 576, 1947.
Rennie, Y. *The Search for Criminal Man*. Lexington, 1978.
Reports of the Prison Discipline Society of Boston. 1855; reprinted Montclair, 1972.
Riclefs, R. *Ecology*. Newton, 1973.
Rivera, R. and J. Short. "Significant Adults, Caretakers, and Structures of Opportunity: An Exploratory Study," in J. Short, ed., *Gang Delinquency*. New York, 1968.
Rodin, G. "William Douglas Morrison," in H. Manneheim, ed., *Pioneers in Criminology*. Chicago, 1960; reprinted Montclair, 1972.
Rothman, D. *The Discovery of the Asylum Social Order and Disorder in the New Republic*. New York, 1971.
Russell, W. "Abstracts of the Statistics of Crime in England and Wales from 1839–1843." 10 *Journal of the Statistical Society of London* 38, 1847.

Saleilles, R. *The Individualization of Punishment*. R. Jastrow, tr. Boston, 1912.
Salisbury, John of. *The Statesman's Book of John of Salisbury*. J. Dickinson, tr. New York, 1927.
Sandburg, A. et al. "XYY Genotype." 268 *New England Journal of Medicine* 585, 1963.
Sarbin, T. and J. Miller. "Demonism Revisited: The XYY Chromosomal Anomaly." 5 *Issues in Criminology* 199, 1970.
Sartre, J. "Existentialism Is a Humanism," in W. Kaufmann, ed., *Existentialism from Dostoevsky to Sartre*. New York, 1966.
Scarr, S. and R. Weinberg. "IQ Test Performance of Black Children Adopted by White Families." 31 *American Psychologist* 726, 1976.
Schlapp, M. and E. Smith. *The New Criminology* New York, 1928.
Schmid, C. *Social Saga of Two Cities: An Ecological and Statistical Study of the Trends in Minneapolis and St. Paul*. St. Paul, 1937.
Schwendinger, H. *Crime and Social Justice*. Berkeley, 1974.
Schwendinger, H. and J. Schwendinger. "Defenders of Order and Guardians of Human Rights," in I. Taylor, P. Walton, and J. Young, *Critical Criminology*. New York, 1975.
————. "Delinquency and Social Reform: A Radical Perspective," in L. Empey, ed., *Juvenile Justice*. New York, 1979.

————. "Rape Victims and the False Sense of Guilt." 13 *Crime and Social Justice* 4, 1980.

Scott, P. "Henry Maudsley," in H. Mannheim, ed., *Pioneers in Criminology*. Chicago, 1960; reprinted Montclair, 1972.

Sellin, T. "Enrico Ferri," in H. Mannheim, ed., *Pioneers in Criminology*. Chicago, 1960; reprinted Montclair, 1972.

————. "The Lombrosian Myth in Criminology." 42 *American Journal of Sociology* 898, 1937.

————. "The Negro and the Problem of Law Observance and Administration in the Light of Social Research," in C.Johnson, ed., *The Negro in American Civilization*. New York, 1939.

————. *Research Memorandum on Crime in the Depression*. New York, 1937.

Shafer, S. *Theories in Criminology*. New York, 1974.

Shaw, C. *Brothers in Crime*. Chicago, 1938.

————. *The Jackroller*. Chicago, 1930.

————. *The Natural History of a Delinquent Career*. Philadelphia, 1931.

Shaw, C. and J. Jacobs. "The Chicago Area Project." *Procedures of the American Prison Association* 40, 1939.

Shaw, C. and H. McKay. *Juvenile Delinquency and Urban Areas*. Chicago, 1969.

————. "Social Factors in Juvenile Delinquency," in *Report on the Causes of Crime*. Chicago, 1931.

Sheldon, W. *Varieties of Delinquent Youth: An Introduction to Constitutional Psychiatry*. New York, 1949.

Simon, R. *The Jury and the Defense of Insanity*. New York, 1967.

Singer, C. and E. Ashworth. *A Short History of Medicine*. New York, 1928.

Skinner, B. and H. Voss. *Delinquency and Dropout*. Lexington, 1974.

Slawson, J. *The Delinquent Boys*. Boston, 1926.

Snodgrasse, R. "Crime and the Constitution Human: A Survey," 42 *Journal of Criminal Law, Criminology and Police Science* 18, 1951.

Sorrentino, A. "The Chicago Area Project After 25 Years." *Federal Probation* 40, 1959.

Stephen, L. *A History of the Criminal Law of England*. London.

Stone, C. "A Comparative Study of the Intelligence of Three Hundred Fifty–three Men of the United States Army." 12 *Journal of Criminal Law and Criminology* 238, 1921.

Sutherland, E. "Critique of Sheldon's *Varieties of Delinquent Youth*." 16 *American Sociological Review* 10, 1951.

————. *White Collar Crime*. New York, 1949.

————. *Principles of Criminology*. Philadelphia, 1939.

————. *The Professional Thief*. New York, 1938.

Sykes, G. "The Rise of Critical Criminology." 65 *Journal of Criminal Law and Criminology* 206, 1974.

Taft, D. *Criminology*. New York, 1956.

Tannenbaum, F. *Crime and the Community*. New York, 1938.

Tarde, G. *La criminalité comparée*. Paris, 1886.

————. *Etudes pénales et sociales*. Paris, 1892.

————. *Penal Philosophy*. R. Howell, tr. Boston, 1912; reprinted Montclair, 1968.

Taylor, I., P. Walton, J. Young. *Critical Criminology*. New York, 1975.

————. *The New Criminology*. London, 1973.

Taylor, L. *Born to Crime*. Westport, 1984.

Teeters, N. *Penology from Panama to Cape Horn*. Philadelphia, 1946.

Teeters, N. and J. Shearer. *The Prison at Philadelphia: Cherry Hill*. New York, 1957.

Thrasher, F. *The Gang*. Chicago, 1927.

Tobias, J. *Urban Crime in Victorian England*. New York, 1964; reprinted Montclair, 1972.

Tsao, W. *Rational Approach to Crime and Punishment*. Taipei, 1955.

Turati, F. *Crime and Social Question*. Torin, 1883.

Turk, A. *Criminality and Legal Order*. Chicago, 1969.

Turnbull, R. *A Visit to the Philadelphia Prison*. New York, 1796.

Vaux, R. *Brief Sketch of the Origin and History of the State Penitentiary for the Eastern District of Pennsylvania at Philadelphia*. Philadelphia, 1872.

Vold, G. *Theoretical Criminology*. New York, 1958.

Vorse, M. *Labor's New Millions*. New York, 1969.

Walker, C. *American City: A Rank and File History*. New York and Toronto, 1937.

Walsh, R. "A Deduction from the Statistics of Crime for the Last Ten Years." 20 *Journal of the Statistical Society of London* 37, 1857.

Walsh, W. *An Introduction to Philosophy of History*. London, 1958.

Weihofen. *The Flowering of New Hampshire*. 22 *University of Chicago Law Review* 356, 1955.

Weihofen, H. *The Urge to Punish*. London, 1957.

Wells, H. *The Outline of History*. Garden City, 1961.

Wey, H. "Criminal Anthropology." *Proceedings of the National Prison Association* 274, 1890.

Whyte, W. *Street Corner Society*. Chicago, 1943.

Wiers, P. "Wartime Increase in Michigan Delinquency." 10 *American Sociological Review* 515, 1945.

Wilson, E. *On Human Nature*. Cambridge, 1978.

Wilson, J. and R. Herrnstein. *Crime and Human Nature*. New York, 1985.

Wilson, M. *The Crime of Punishment*. New York, 1931.

Wilson-Vine, M. "Gabriel Tarde," in H. Mannheim, ed., *Pioneers in Criminology*. Chicago, 1960; reprinted Montclair, 1972.

Wolfgang, M. "Developments in Criminology in the United States with Some Comments on the Future." Paper presented at the Fifth National Conference, Institute of Criminology, University of Cambridge, 1973.

Index

About the Author

DAVID A. JONES is Professor of Interdisciplinary Studies in Law and Justice and Professor of Sociology at the University of Pittsburgh, and he is serving in his third term as Governor Dick Thornburgh's appointee to the Pennsylvania Commission on Sentencing. Among his earlier publications are *The Law of Criminal Procedure, The Law of Marriage,* and *Crime Without Punishment.* He is a member of the Bars of the Supreme Court of the United States, Massachusetts, New York, Pennsylvania, the District of Columbia, and every Federal appeals court.

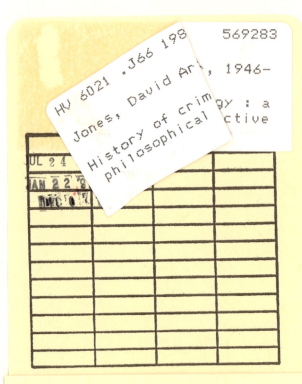